Library of
Exact Philosophy

LEP

Springer-Verlag Wien New York

Library of Exact Philosophy 10

Raimo Tuomela

Theoretical Concepts

Springer-Verlag Wien New York 1973

Printing type: Sabon Roman
Composed and printed by Herbert Hiessberger, Pottenstein
Binding work: Karl Scheibe, Wien
Design: Hans Joachim Böning, Wien

ISBN 3-211-81119-2 Springer-Verlag Wien - New York
ISBN 0-387-81119-2 Springer-Verlag New York - Wien

Library of Congress Card Number 73-80989
Printed in Austria

To the memory
of my parents

General Preface to the LEP

Exact philosophy can be described as the field of philosophy tilled with exact tools, i. e. logic and mathematics. Exactness concerns the methods or tools, not the subject. Regardless of its subject, a piece of philosophical investigation qualifies as exact as long as it involves a precise statement of the problems, a careful analysis of the key concepts and principles, and an attempt at systematization. If the outcome is a full fledged theory with a definite mathematical structure, and moreover a theory that solves some important philosophical problems, so much the better.

It is worth while, nay exciting and urgent, to try the exact method in every branch of philosophy — in semantics, epistemology, philosophy of science, value theory, ethics, legal philosophy, the history of philosophy, and perhaps even in aesthetics. The more exactly we proceed in handling genuine philosophical problems, the narrower should become the gap between the humanities on the one hand, and mathematics and science on the other. And the better we bridge this gap the lesser will be the chances that the anti-intellectualist trends will destroy contemporary culture.

Some great philosophers have worked in exact philosophy: not only Carnap and Russell but also Bolzano, Leibniz, and Aristotle. A whole school, the Vienna Circle, was devoted to the enterprise of reconstructing philosophy in an exact manner and in the light of the sciences. The Library of Exact Philosophy is a new link in this long thin chain. It was established in 1970 in order to stimulate the production and circulation of significant additions to *philosophia more geometrico*. The LEP has already made a contribution to that goal, and it is hoped that it will incorporate further works dealing in an exact way with interesting philosophical issues.

Zürich, April 1973

Mario Bunge

Preface

In this book I have investigated the logical and methodological role of the much debated theoretical concepts in scientific theories. The philosophical viewpoint underlying my argumentation is critical scientific realism.

My method of exposition has been to express ideas first in general terms and then to develop and elaborate them within a specific formal framework. It is assumed in the book that the reader has a relatively good knowledge of the basic techniques and results of modern symbolic logic, including model theory.

Examples from actual science are mostly from the social sciences. I have deliberately omitted a treatment of a number of characteristic features which are particular to theoretical concepts in the more developed sciences, such as modern physics.

This book owes very much to Professor Jaakko Hintikka, to whom I wish to express my deep gratitude. Especially at the beginning of this project in 1968/69 when I was doing research for my doctoral degree at Stanford University I worked with him closely.

Most of this book was written in 1971/72 while I was in Montreal on leave from the University of Helsinki and held a Killam post-doctoral fellowship from Canada Council. I want to thank warmly Professor Mario Bunge, director of the Foundations and Philosophy of Science Unit at McGill University, who helped me much both in scientific and unscientific matters in the writing of this book.

Mr. Ilkka Niiniluoto read the whole manuscript carefully. I am very grateful to him for many sharp critical remarks and good suggestions. I also wish to thank all the other people who commented on the manuscript. Mr. David Miller skillfully corrected the language of parts of this work.

I gratefully acknowledge the grant from the Emil Aaltonen Foundation in 1971 to support my research project.

D. Reidel Publishing Company has kindly permitted me to use passages from the following articles of mine: Towards a General Theory of Auxiliary Concepts and Definability in First-Order Theories (together with Jaakko Hintikka), in: Hintikka, J., and P. Suppes (eds.), Information and Inference, D. Reidel, Dordrecht, 1970, pp. 298—330; Deductive Explanation of Scientific Laws, Journal of Philosophical Logic, Nos. 3/4, Vol. 1, 1972, pp. 369—392, and Model Theory and Empirical Interpretation of Scientific Theories, Synthese, Nos. 1/2, Vol. 25, 1972, pp. 165—175.

Finally, I wish to thank my wife Sirkka for her patience and generous help while I was writing this book.

Helsinki, May 1973

Raimo Tuomela

Contents

Chapter I

Theoretical Concepts in Science

1. The Problem of Theoretical Concepts

1.1. It is often claimed that the progress of modern science is in great part due to the use of theories which go beyond purely empirical or observational laws, and thereby give us better understanding of the factual regularities and singular factual events (directly observable or not) studied. In addition to providing us with deeper understanding, insight, and explanation, theories are also supposed to help us to control the world, through technology; and this presupposes that with theories we can make successful predictions about the events studied.

It is obvious that how well and to what extent one succeeds in attaining these goals must depend on the theories one has constructed to give understanding of the world, to systematize, explain, and predict empirical laws and events, and on how these theories are put to use. Here we tacitly assume that empirical statements retain their structure to some reasonably great extent when different theoretical attempts are made to systematize and explain them — even if the semantical and ontological interpretation of these statements may change in the course of these attempts.

It is no longer a heresy among philosophers that the goals of science cannot really be achieved by purely empirical laws, but *only* by introducing and employing theories containing so called theoretical terms (such as 'electron', 'gene', 'refractory goal response') which are not explicitly definable on the basis of observational concepts[1]. It must, however, be admitted that relatively few really good and compelling arguments have been presented to support this view. Or, to make a weaker claim, most philosophers of science are willing to admit at least that the goals of science are *better* achieved by using theories than by using purely empirical laws. See, for example, FEIGL (1950), CARNAP (1956), HEMPEL (1958), KUHN (1962), and BUNGE (1967) as advocates of either of these claims.

On the other hand, we still have theoreticians who claim that theories (with theoretical concepts which are not explicitly defined in terms of observables) are unnecessary (or even undesirable) in science. Advocates of this view can be found especially in behavioristic psychology (for instance, such famous psychologists as SKINNER (1953) and (1969), HULL (1943); see also the discussion in HEMPEL (1965)). Among philosophers, BOHNERT (1967), (1968) and CORNMAN (1972), can be mentioned as recent and much more sophisticated advocates of this standpoint. To illustrate the above instrumentalistic view by two quotations from psychology, consider an ordinary prediction situation in psychology when some response is predicted, given a stimulus and a law connecting the stimulus to the response. The argument has been put as follows: "If you have a secure equational linkage extending from the antecedent observable conditions through to the consequent observable condition, why, even though to do so might not be positively pernicious, use several equations where one would do?" (HULL (1943), p. 284). Skinner argues: "Unless there is a weak spot in our causal chain so that the second link is not lawfully determined by the first, or the third by the second, then the first and third links must be lawfully related. If we must always go back beyond the second link for prediction and control, we may avoid many tiresome and exhausting digressions by examining the third link as a function of the first." (SKINNER (1953), p. 35).

---

1 We shall later in this chapter discuss different possibilities to dichotomize scientific concepts into theoretical and observational, as much depends on the precise nature of this dichotomy.

Note that we use the word 'concept' both for linguistic and extralinguistic entities. Each time the word occurs the context should make it clear what is meant. When the word 'term' is used it refers, of course, only to a linguistic entity. Symbols will be used autonymously whenever this cannot be expected to cause confusion. Otherwise single quotes are employed.

We now seem to have arrived at a *paradox of theorizing*. This paradox is that "if the terms and the general principles of a scientific theory serve their purpose, i. e., if they establish definite connections among observable phenomena, then they can be dispensed with since any chain of laws and interpretative statements establishing such a connection should then be replaceable by a law which directly links observational antecedents to observational consequents." (HEMPEL (1958), p. 186).

If we add two obvious premises to the above paradox we get a general version of the well-known *theoretician's dilemma* (see e. g. HEMPEL (1958), p. 186 and CORNMAN (1972), p. 83 ff.). Below we state and discuss it only as far as theoretical terms (and not theoretical principles) are concerned. The dilemma can thus be given in the following form:

(1) Theoretical terms either serve their purpose or they do not serve it.

(2) If they do not serve it, they are dispensable.

(3) If they serve their purpose, they establish relationships among observable phenomena.

(4) If they establish such relationships, the same relationships can be established without theoretical terms.

(5) If these same relationships are so established, theoretical terms are dispensable.

Hence:

(6) Theoretical terms are dispensable.

A satisfactory solution to the theoretician's dilemma requires, of course, a detailed analysis of the goals of science as well as of the different ways by which these can be reached. More specifically, we obviously need to know what the purpose or purposes of theoretical terms are and what is meant by the dispensability of theoretical terms. In addition, we have to know what the relationships that the theses (3)—(5) speak about are and what is involved in establishing them. An analysis of the problems will obviously lead to several qualifications of the above premises.

CORNMAN (1972) has recently presented an interesting and detailed account and defense of the premises of the theoretician's dilemma. We shall later discuss his elaborations of the premises and criticize his conclusions. In other words, we shall adopt the role of a philosophical realist contra an instrumentalist and empiricist. Not only shall we try to solve the theoretician's dilemma in a negative way by criticizing the arguments of an instrumentalist but we shall also try to say something positive concerning the various gains due to the use of theoretical concepts in science. This naturally presupposes at least a discussion of the problem of theoretical terms.

1.2. *The problem of theoretical terms,* that is, the general philosophical and methodological problem about the nature and use of theoretical terms in scientific theories, can in our opinion be divided into the problem of the semantical and philosophical *interpretation* of theoretical terms and the problem of their methodological *function.*

In the problem of interpretation we include questions like *ontological commitment,* and the *meaning* and (cognitive) *significance* of theoretical terms. Apart from a few digressions, we shall not discuss the problems of ontological commitment and significance systematically. To questions of meaning we shall devote one chapter. Our main concern in this book is, however, the problem of the methodological function of theoretical terms. That is, we shall primarily discuss their role within adequate deductive and inductive systematization. These notions — which have unfortunate instrumentalistic overtones — are to be understood in a very comprehensive sense so as to capture what is essential in scientific understanding, explanation, prediction, and so on.

More specifically, we are concerned with (1) what, if anything, can philosophically and methodologically be "gained" from the use of the so called theoretical (or auxiliary) concepts (this presupposes a detailed analysis of the theoretician's dilemma), and (2) what kinds of definability relations can hold between theoretical and observational concepts in a scientific theory. We are also interested in (3) how different aspects of definability (for example, openness of auxiliary concepts) are related to the gains resulting from the use of such concepts; that is, in the connections between (1) and (2).

There is a fairly extensive philosophical and methodological literature, mostly in the empiricist tradition, dealing with the role of theoretical terms in scientific theories. Logical and foundational concepts and results, however, play a surprisingly small role in these discussions, despite the wealth of results concerning definability and related concepts established by logicians. Virtually the only central results cited are Craig's (general) elimination theorem and Ramsey's elimination result, and the purpose of bringing them up is all too often to deny that they have any relevance at all. For instance, the possible consequences of Craig's (less general but in certain respects more informative) interpolation theorem have not caught the fancy of philosophers of science.

We shall in this book apply logical tools and results rather extensively. However, many of the modern logical techniques are often either too sophisticated for the methodological problems in question or they are philosophically insufficient. Therefore we shall try to define a number of simpler logical concepts, and to establish a few results that hold for these concepts. When needed, these extensional logical tools are supplemented with intensional and less exact methods.

Most of our logical results are elementary. Moreover, that many of them are established only for theories reconstructable within first-order predicate logic might be considered a restriction on their applicability to interesting methodological situations. However, it seems to us that some of these new results put into clearer perspective several features of the role that theoretical concepts play or may play in scientific theories. Not unexpectedly, some of these new ideas and results are closely related to the logical theory of definition (Chapter IV). It will turn out that different aspects of definability can really be related to various problems of deductive and inductive systematization, too.

One methodologically fruitful way of studying the role of theoretical concepts in science is to investigate detailed attempts and programmes for eliminating them — even if one does not in the last analysis want to eliminate them oneself. (By elimination here we mean the replacement of a theory containing theoretical concepts by a theory consisting of exactly those of its theorems in which only observational or empirical concepts occur.) For one thing, in trying to establish step (4) in the theoretician's dilemma it is usually assumed that it can be done by relying on either Craig's general replacement result or Ramsey's elimination technique (cf. CORNMAN (1972)). Secondly, if an elimination attempt fails (or turns out to be open to serious criticism), the reasons for this failure may produce helpful clues to why theoretical concepts are needed, and what desiderata should therefore be imposed on a good scientific theory. But this is still not all. We shall, in fact, see that the logical results involved in

Craigian and (semantical) Ramseyan elimination programme can in a sense be used to argue for the inclusion of theoretical concepts in first-order scientific theories rather than for their elimination.

Some of the main reasons for employing theoretical concepts in science are the following. Theoretical concepts give us deeper understanding, information, and an explanation of the world. They afford economy, simplicity, and coherence in describing the world. Furthermore, they make scientific theories capable of (observational) growth, heuristically fruitful, and manageable. They may also help to make theories better testable and corroborable. We shall in this book undertake an attempt to clarify and discuss in various contexts most of these alleged advantages of theoretical concepts. The two main methodological contexts within which we shall discuss these questions are, on the one hand, theory construction ("theoretical generalization") and, on the other hand, the application of established theories to explain and predict empirical statements (especially empirical laws and generalizations).

Most, though not all, of our examples and illustrations are from the social sciences. More specifically, we usually have in mind those parts of the social sciences where the methods of natural science seem to be applicable without doubt (e. g. economics, social demography, behavioristic psychology). Consequently we shall not explicitly deal with problems of intentionality and other related problems.

1.3. This book is mainly about methodological problems but we shall occasionally discuss various epistemological, semantical, and ontological issues as well. Even when discussing methodological questions it is often necessary — explicitly or implicitly — to rely on a more or less definitely specified philosophical standpoint. In general, we accept a version of *scientific realism* in the case of ontological, epistemological, and semantical issues. This realistic viewpoint is coupled with an *empiricist methodology* (in questions of testing, explaining, etc.): Every scientific theory, possibly conjoined with some auxiliary scientific statements, should have some nontautological empirical (deductive or inductive) consequences not derivable from the auxiliary statements alone. This is a requirement of (indirect) *empirical testability*.

Let us now briefly describe the kinds of realism we in general adopt. From the various forms of realism we subscribe to *critical scientific realism* in ontological and epistemological questions. It can be characterized by the following theses (cf. BUNGE (1969), pp. 98—99; also cf. the radical critical realism of MANDELBAUM (1964), p. 221):

(CR 1) There are things in themselves, that is, objects whose existence does not depend on any mind. (Notice that there are also artifacts which depend on minds for their design and operation.)

(CR 2) Things in themselves are knowable, though partially and by successive approximations only.

(CR 3) Any knowledge of a thing in itself is attained jointly by experience (in particular by scientific experiment) and by reason (in particular by theorizing).

(CR 4) Factual knowledge is hypothetical rather than apodictic. Hence it is corrigible and not final.

(CR 5) Any knowledge of a thing in itself is distorted and symbolic (and hence indirect).

The first of these theses is ontological while the other ones are epistemological. (CR 1) can be coupled with and refined by various (e. g. materialistic) assumptions concerning the nature of things in themselves. But here we shall not pursue our discussion in that direction.

Theses (CR 1) and (CR 2) say that there are things "out there" and that they are knowable. Hence they are presuppositions of scientific research. On the other hand, any scientific hypothesis about the existence of a special kind of object, or its properties, is corrigible.

This kind of critical realism — contrary to empiricism — makes the traditional distinction between the thing in itself (as it exists) and the thing for us (as known to us). However, in distinction to e. g. Kant, critical realism maintains that 1) the thing in itself can be known in a gradual fashion and that 2) the thing for us is not the one presented to the senses but — in opposition to empiricism — rather the one characterized by scientific theory (cf. BUNGE (1969), p. 99). We can thus have factual knowledge which is not empirical (i. e. sensible *stricto* or *lato sensu*)[2].

Because of remark 2) above, within critical scientific realism there is not as close a connection between observability and knowledge as there is in a Kantian type of epistemology. Notice that in our account

2 In this book the word 'factual', as applied to conceptual or linguistic items, is used in two basic senses to mean 1) about the world or 2) synthetic (contingent). Context will make it clear which sense is meant.

it is central that observations become laden with *scientific theory*. Notice furthermore that it is perfectly compatible with our (CR 1)—(CR 5) to hold the view of *radical* critical realism: *No* qualities of objects as they are experienced by us are *identical* with the properties of objects as they exist in the physical world independently of us.

A feature that distinguishes critical realism from other kinds of realism is expressed by (CR 5): Knowledge about the thing itself is primarily obtained by means of scientific theories, but the thing itself is not knowable without distortion (that is, without removing or adding aspects). Scientists form concepts and ideas to represent things in themselves and theorize by means of the resulting conceptual structures. Concepts and ideas are made up by people. They can be and often are changed in many ways and even given up altogether.

We shall in this book often make the assumption that certain aspects of our world can be represented by means of the framework of either first-order or second-order logic (and model theory). This involves a "*modelling*" of these aspects of our world in a certain way. Such modelling always brings about some distortion, which is important to keep in mind. Better means of representation can and should always be sought after.

These remarks may suffice for our realistic ontology and epistemology in this context. Next we will say something about questions of meaning. An empiricist semantics is usually built in parallel with an empiricist epistemology, so that the meanings of theoretical concepts and statements are derived by some kind of semantical osmosis from the observational language, which is assumed to be semantically fully understood. This empiricist account of meaning is called the *partial interpretation view*, as the meanings do not thus become fully specified. We shall later discuss it in detail. In accordance with our realist background philosophy we do not accept the empiricist account of meaning but instead *semantical realism*. The (mild) version of semantical realism we accept in this book can be summarized by the following thesis, as far as the purely theoretical predicates of a scientific theory are concerned:

(SR) (a) The theoretical predicates of all scientific theories generally refer to factual external objects and represent aspects of these objects. (b) The meanings of theoretical concepts are in general determined by the (interpreted) scientific theory (or theories) in which they occur (see Chapter V).

The denial of what (SRa) asserts gives a version of (*semantical*) *instrumentalism*. For a semantical (and methodological) instrumentalist, in distinction to a realist, theories are mere tools without meaning and they are neither true nor false. An empiricist semantics is often instrumentalist, although it need not be so.

We shall not here go into the problem of classifying instrumentalists (and empiricists). It suffices to say that below in speaking about *instrumentalism* we mean any methodological doctrine which considers theories as mere tools for organizing observational data so that the theoretician's dilemma is acceptable. Such a methodology is usually coupled with a rejection of semantical, epistemological and ontological critical realism in our sense.

2. Theoretical and Observational Concepts

2.1. In the previous section we dichotomized scientific concepts into *theoretical* and *observational* concepts. (A corresponding division of scientific statements into theoretical and observational statements is made in the usual and obvious way.) The precise nature of such a dichotomy is not of very great importance in *all* methodological and especially not in most technical contexts. Then we simply neutrally divide the extralogical terms of a theory into a set λ and a set μ such that $\lambda \cap \mu = \phi$. In some cases we call the members of μ "auxiliary" and the members of λ "non-auxiliary". But in many contexts, e. g. in evaluating the problem of the indispensability or desirability of theoretical concepts, it is important to be rather clear about the *content* of the dichotomy.

In this book we shall be mainly interested in the following interpretations of the μ-predicates versus the λ-predicates ("terms"):

(1) theoretical — observational;

(2) explanatory — descriptive;

(3) new — old.

(1) will be our primary interpretation. Traditionally it refers to a distinction between empirical or perceptual (phenomenal) objects and properties in distinction to nonempirical or nonperceptual ones. There are, however, great difficulties connected with this interpretation, as has frequently been pointed out in the literature. We shall below discuss them briefly and make a proposal for a theoretical-observational dichotomy (in a technical sense) to be employed in this book.

In general terms, by the *explanatory-descriptive* interpretation we shall below primarily refer to the following methodological situation: Assume that scientific investigation starts with describing some (observable) phenomena. The vocabulary in which the resulting induced scientific laws and other statements are expressed is called (merely) descriptive. Next assume that these descriptive laws are explained by theories introducing concepts of a new kind. These concepts will be called explanatory.

The *new-old* dichotomy either plainly refers to the growth of scientific theories and knowledge or marks a semantic distinction. In the latter case old terms are semantically well understood concepts occurring in our previous or contemporary theories. New concepts are usually less well understood concepts, which are introduced into contemporary theories or which enter completely new theories.

Let us now turn to the main topic of this section: the theoretical-observational dichotomy of concepts. A natural point to start with is the "partial interpretation" view of the problem (cf. BRAITHWAITE (1953), CARNAP (1956), HEMPEL (1958), ROZEBOOM (1963), (1970)). For representatives of this view theoretical terms — in distinction to observational ones — are terms which refer to unobservable objects and properties and which are semantically totally unintelligible unless they are given (partial) interpretation through their relationships to the semantically unproblematic observational terms. Let us express this in the form of the following two theses:

(1) Scientific terms can be uniformly dichotomized into theoretical and observational terms so that theoretical terms refer (only) to unobservables whereas observational terms refer (only) to observables.

(2) It is impossible to give intelligible semantical rules for theoretical terms whereas observational terms are semantically relatively unproblematic.

As examples of (intended) theoretical terms we have 'electric field', 'electron', 'virus', 'gene', 'latent aggression', 'meaning response'. Observational terms are in the partial interpretation account assumed to be either perceptual or empirical terms *stricto sensu*, such as 'red', 'hot', or they are empirical terms *lato sensu*, such as 'water', 'iron', 'volume', 'choice', 'aggression'. Among empirical terms *lato sensu* we distinguish between *idealized* and *experimental* ones (see Chapter

V). Idealized empirical terms can have any kind of mathematical structure (e. g. continuous real-valued functions) whereas experimental terms are finite and concrete. (In general a scientific theory proper does not contain such experimental terms.)

By a semantical rule for a term '*P*' we mean statements in the metalanguage usually of the form "'*P*' means latent aggression' (or the like, cf. Chapter V). Claim (2) thus amounts to saying that in the case of theoretical terms no intelligible phrases (of the natural or scientific language used for scientific communication) can be found to make up a semantic rule, whereas in the case of observational terms such phrases can be found. (Probably one would have to qualify the last statement by saying that if one does not succeed in finding such a phrase, the meaning of the observational term can then be given by ostension.) Theoretical terms can thus get only partial interpretation through correspondence rules or interpretative systems stated in the object language (cf. Chapter V). (Correspondence rules in the form of explicit definition would give full interpretation, though, but they are usually considered methodologically inappropriate by the partial interpretation theorists.)

The task facing an advocate of the partial interpretation view is then to give a clear-cut *semantical* criterion for dichotomizing scientific concepts into theoretical and observational so that statements (1) and (2) above are satisfied. Have the partial interpretation theorists succeeded in this? The answer is fairly clearly negative. This has been demonstrated e. g. in the recent investigations by PUTNAM, ACHINSTEIN, and SPECTOR (see PUTNAM (1962), MAXWELL (1963), ACHINSTEIN (1965) and (1968), SPECTOR (1966)).

Let us briefly consider observational terms. According to the partial interpretation theorists' analysis, observational terms are terms whose referents are observable. However, none of the partial interpretation theorists have given or even attempted to give a thorough analysis of observability. They have at most given examples of observable entities and properties. What critics have tried to show is that there is no uniform context-independent criterion for observability which conforms to the above conditions (1) and (2). To establish this result critics have proceeded to show by examples that the intended classification always depends on particular contexts and some intended contrasts. For instance, it can be claimed that trained scientists are able to observe even electrons, genes, viruses, latent aggressions in some — but maybe not in all — contexts and in some senses of 'observe', while e. g. laymen would not be able to do this. The contexts upon which observability depends involve many factors, like, for instance, observability by bare senses versus by instruments, or by "low-power" instruments (e. g. eye-glasses) versus "high-power" instruments (e. g. strong telescopes). Perhaps the most important fact about observability is that it is determined by the conceptual framework and related beliefs ("background knowledge" and "internalized" theories) of the observer (cf. our condition (CR1) of critical scientific realism in Section I. 1.).

It is precisely this last fact that makes all scientific terms "theory-laden", at least to some extent. This also shows that there is no clear-cut nonpragmatic criterion for distinguishing direct from indirect observability (cf. HEMPEL (1958)). In addition, there is thus no absolutely stable observation language, as the scientist's background assumptions and beliefs can and do change with his theories. There may, however, be more and less stable language usages. On this basis it is conceivable that some uniform pragmatic criteria for observationality could be given, even if the previous attempts to do this seem to have failed (cf. SPECTOR's (1966) criticisms of MAXWELL's (1963) and CARNAP's (1937) attempts). But, as we just indicated, this would not of course lead to the kind of semantical criterion required by conditions (1) and (2).

As all attempts to find a semantical theoretical/observational dichotomy starting from observability seem to fail, one might try to begin with theoretical instead. (Notice that we cannot define theoretical terms as unobservational as long as we do not have a criterion of observationality.) There are a number of properties suggested as sufficient and/or necessary for characterizing theoreticity. Thus it has been argued that theoretical terms establish conceptual organization (e. g. HANSON (1957), RYLE (1956)) and that theoretical terms are theory-dependent (e. g. RYLE (1956), HANSON (1957), FEYERABEND (1965)). Furthermore, theoretical terms are more abstract and more precise than observational terms (e. g. CARNAP (1937), HEMPEL (1952) and (1958)). Theoretical terms have been considered more hypothetical (as to the evidence for the existence of their referents) than observational terms (e. g. HEMPEL (1958)). Still another criterion, mentioned surprisingly seldom, is that theoretical concepts have explanatory power (e. g. SELLARS (1963), CORNMAN (1968) and (1971)).

Here again the critics of the partial interpretation view have argued convincingly by examples that the above properties of theoretical terms do not create a semantical theoretical/observational dichotomy of the required kind. More specifically, Spector and Achinstein have claimed that the above properties may give rise to *several context-dependent criteria,* which cannot be combined into a *single general criterion* satisfying conditions (1) and (2) (cf. SPECTOR (1966), p. 104 and ACHINSTEIN (1965), p. 198). On the other hand, as e. g. Achinstein admits, the above criteria create many different useful classifications of concepts, although not of the kind compatible with the partial interpretation view (cf. ACHINSTEIN (1965), p. 202). Even if Achinstein claims that the emerging classifications are context-dependent there are no convincing arguments to show that some of these criteria cannot be combined to generate a general (but possibly context-dependent) criterion. In other words, each or at least some of the above properties of theoretical terms may conceivably create a general context-dependent criterion for theoreticity (and maybe for observationality, too) such that different properties in different contexts determine this.

Why should conditions (1) and (2) for a theoretical/observational dichotomy be accepted? We briefly mentioned the partial interpretation theorists' grounds for this in the previous section. However, we believe, in accordance with the critics of that view, that there are no good reasons whatever for adopting conditions (1) and (2) and, indeed, the empiricist view upon which they rest. As to criterion (1), one can give many examples showing that unobservable objects may have observational properties and that observable objects may have non-observational properties (almost independently of what can plausibly be intended by observationality). For instance, it is semantically understandable what Newton meant by *red* corpuscles and what is meant by saying that water contains *hydrogen molecules* (cf. PUTNAM (1962), p. 243).

It is much more difficult to give conclusive arguments for rejecting condition (2). However, we shall in this book accept the view that in most actual cases of scientific theories it is plausible to accept a realist viewpoint, which implies that theoretical terms (whatever is meant by them in a finer analysis) are or can be meaningful and intelligible and that the meanings of observational terms may be unstable and problematic in a number of ways. Theoretical terms primarily get their meaning — however vague it may be — through their various relationships to previously understood (theoretical) terms in a theoretical discourse (cf. our discussion in Chapter V).

Theoretical terms usually stand only in *contingent* deductive, inductive, or analogical relationships to observational terms. Such observational terms serve as *indicators* giving empirical (or even perceptual) import to the theoretical terms, or rather to the theoretical discourse containing these theoretical terms (cf. TUOMELA (1968a)). We shall in Chapter V discuss the semantical problems connected with theoretical terms in more detail.

Our above remarks are also valid for the meanings of observational terms. (Observationality is not a semantical property.) From our account follows that the meanings of theoretical terms are problematic but not in the sense the partial interpretation theorists assumed. It also follows, as we saw, that the meanings of observational terms are problematic and that they need not be stable.

2.2. Let us now proceed to discuss somewhat more concretely how a theoretical/observational dichotomy of scientific terms could be created so that it would not be subject to the above critical remarks. To appreciate better the difficulties involved, we shall start by considering a recent attempt by Cornman to create such a dichotomy and then proceed to a somewhat related suggestion of our own.

CORNMAN (1968 and 1971) tries to give a separate account for observationality and for theoreticity. Let us first consider his most recent definition of observational (qualitative or quantitative) terms given in CORNMAN (1971), p. 69:

"'O' is an observational (qualitative, quantitative) term $=_{df}$ (1) the following is true: 'Some (O, instance of O) is observable by any standard observer under standard conditions' *and* (2) for any nonlogical (qualitative, quantitative) term '*P*', if 'Something is an O (has O)' entails 'Something is a *P* (has *P*)', then '*P*' meets condition (1) and 'Any *P* (the property *P*) is physical' is true."

According to Cornman, condition (1) can be interpreted as

(1′) Under standard conditions, some O-thing (instance of an O-property) would be a proper observation stimulus for any standard observer *S*, such that as a result the O-thing (the property O) would appear in some way to *S*.

Here 'proper observation stimulus' and 'appear in some way' are technical terms of CHISHOLM (1957). A proper observation stimulus is, roughly speaking, a stimulus which directly stimulates a receptor so that nothing affects the stimulation transmitted from it before the stimulation affects the receptors. The phrase 'appear in some way' is equal to "sensing" (e. g. being visible).

Let us first consider condition (1'). It seems to us that even alone it is too restrictive to give a scientifically interesting explicate of 'observational term' (*lato sensu*). For instance, observation by means of instruments or some medium (e. g. mirror) are excluded by (1'). It follows that almost no scientific theories can contain observational terms.

As to condition (2), it was included to exclude so-called theory-laden observational terms, and as it is to be taken in conjunction with (1'), the class of observational terms becomes very small indeed as far as scientific purposes are concerned. It is not difficult to invent examples of terms ordinarily labelled observational which do not qualify as such by (2). Consider first the complex predicate 'is a closed non-transparent box'. Now, if x is a closed non-transparent box it follows that x must have an inside. However, 'is the inside of a closed non-transparent box' is not a predicate qualifying as observational by (1'), nor by (1) *simpliciter*. Hence 'is a closed non-transparent box' is not an observational predicate. Secondly, consider the action statement '*S* signs a check'. Normally it would be classified as an observational statement. But this statement entails that '*S* performs an (intentional) action'. However, something being an intentional action is not physical, even if it has a physical "movement" component. Hence the original statement becomes non-observational in virtue of Cornman's condition (2).

Let us next proceed to Cornman's definition of theoreticity, which is the following (CORNMAN (1971), p. 77):

"'*T*' is a (scientific) theoretical term $=_{df}$ (1) '*T*' is a nonlogical constant in a (scientific) explanatory vocabulary which is not an empirical term, i. e. neither an observation term nor an observationally defined term nor a pure disposition term, *or* (2) '*T*' is a nonlogical constant introduced into a language as part of the vocabulary of a (scientific) theory in order to explain the behavior of observable entities by generalizations, whether empirical or requiring nonempirical terms, sufficient to establish inferential relationships among empirical statements."

Condition (1) of this definition is supposed to incorporate as a sufficient condition of theoreticity Carnap's "high probability-criterion", according to which theoretical terms are terms occurring in sentences which can at best be inferred with high probability from observational statements (cf. CARNAP (1956), p. 69).

What is interesting and important in both of Cornman's sufficient conditions of theoreticity is that they emphasize the explanatory role of theoretical concepts, even though no further clarification of this is given in the definition. However, it becomes clear from Cornman's comments that theoretical concepts are or can be essential for explaining the behavior of observable events.

Condition (2) clearly allows for observational theoretical terms. Cornman gives 'temperature' as an example of such a term. Condition (1) again excludes observational terms. But there do not seem to be any other differences between conditions (1) and (2), as Cornman seems to mean by explanatory vocabulary in condition (1) exactly what condition (2) says about it. Thus one of these conditions is superfluous after it has been decided whether or not to allow for observational theoretical terms.

2.3. It may now seem that it is not possible to give a flawless characterization of theoretical and observational terms. Perhaps one could simply resort to a classification on an intuitive basis without an explicitly formulated general criterion. We shall not go that far but we admit that presently at least it is extremely difficult to find a sharply formulated and acceptable criterion — even if the partial interpretation theorists' conditions of adequacy are abandoned.

However, we think that one should be satisfied with a somewhat vague analysis, provided it gives some important information. For instance, Cornman's definition of theoreticity clearly gives some philosophical and methodological clarification by connecting theoreticity with explanatory power, in spite of the notorious vagueness of the latter notion. In our proposal below we shall emphasize this connection. But our definition of observational terms will be given entirely in pragmatic (or methodological) terms, as this seems to be best in accordance with scientific practice while it seems to avoid the above criticism.

We propose the following characterization for observational/theoretical division of the primitive predicates of a scientific theory (here we can use symbols autonymously):

A nonlogical concept P occurring in a theory T belonging to a paradigm K is called *observational* with respect to theory T if and only if every representative scientist within K can (validly and reliably) "measure" P in the typical applications of T without relying on the truth of the theory T.

A nonlogical concept *P* occuring in a theory *T* belonging to a paradigm *K* is called *theoretical* with respect to *T* if and only if (a) *P* is not observational (with respect to *T*) in the strong sense that of every representative scientist within *K* it is true to say that he cannot "measure" *P* in *all* typical applications of *T* without relying on the truth of *T*, and (b) *P* has been introduced into *T* in order to explain the behavior (i. e. those aspects of it *T* accounts for) of the objects *T* is about.

Instead of (b) we might, in the spirit of Cornman, alternatively consider:

(b*) *P* has been introduced into *T* in order to explain the behavior (i. e. those aspects of it *T* accounts for) of the *observable* objects *T* is about.

Notice that in (b*) (and of course in (b)) the behavior to be explained by means of *T* (and *P*) may not be describable without theoretical terms. But even so (b*) seems too strong. For *T* may not be about any observable objects at all. (We assume here that 'observable object' is an intuitively understandable phrase.)

To be sure, our empiricist methodology and the requirement of (indirect) empirical testability entail that every scientific theory must have at least indirect (potential) contact with the empirical world (see Section I. 1.). Thus, if a scientific theory *T* does not itself have observational content, it must have a scientific extension *T** which has observational (empirical) content. Then, presumably, *T** will at least partly be about observable objects, too. But still we can keep our characterization of the theoreticity of predicates and the requirement of empirical testability analytically separated.

Let us next comment on some of the key notions occurring in the above definitions.

First, by 'paradigm' we mean Kuhn's paradigm in the sense of a constellation of group commitments (see e. g. Postscript to Kuhn (1969), 2nd ed.). We shall not here attempt to explicate further this admittedly vague notion. We assume that the members of a scientific community sharing the same paradigm have accepted at least some scientific theories as true or as worthy of rational belief. *T* is assumed to be one of them.

By "measuring" a concept (predicate) *P* we mean correctly assigning the predicate to those entities to which it belongs (i. e. to objects with *P*-quality). This shall of course be the case also when *P* is a relation-term or a quantitative term, even if our definition has, for simplicity, been formulated only for a monadic predicate. Many auxiliary assumptions may of course be needed when establishing such a measurement procedure, which may thus be quite complex[3]. In the case of a monadic predicate P, the measurement results with respect to a set of objects are given by atomic sentences $\pm P(a_i)$ for all objects a_i in the domain. Let us call them evidence reports or statements. If P is observational we speak of observational evidence statements. By extension, we shall call all statements containing only observational terms (including quantified ones) observational statements even if no finitary measurement procedure of the above kind may exist for some of them. Similarly by extension, we also call observational those statements that are obtained from concrete experimental reports by idealizing experimental notions (cf. "temperature" as a real function versus temperature as "pointer readings").

It is *compatible* with our characterization of theoreticity to assume that theoretical predicates can at least on some occasions be *used evidentially,* either "indirectly" (i. e. with the help of the axioms of the theory T) or "directly". However, our characterization of theoreticity gives no guarantee of evidential use. Still, we shall in the sequel assume that good theoretical concepts do have some evidential uses.

Our characterization of the observationality of a term P does not explicitly say anything about the observability or nonobservability of the P-objects or the P-quality. We shall assume in our applications, however, that what a typical scientist can validly and reliably measure is something which is *prima facie* observable, i. e. observable by means of unaided senses or ("low-power") instruments. Thus our experimental observational terms are *prima facie* empirical *lato sensu.* We shall not try to give a more precise definition of observability here. However, e. g. Cornman's definition of observability is certainly too narrow (see above) and hence unacceptable. (See ACHINSTEIN (1968) for good discussion on observability.)

When we said that observation terms *prima facie* refer to observable things or qualities we meant that this is their typical or usual referring task. But by extension of language usage, an observational

3 Notice that in the special case when some of these auxiliary assumptions contain new concepts and are deducible from theory T our criterion for a theoretical/observational dichotomy obviously needs some elaboration to avoid circularity. (This was pointed out to me by Mrs. Marja-Liisa Kakkuri-Ketonen.) But here we cannot go deeper into this problem.

predicate can be applied to nonobservable objects, too, at least in some cases. (After all, observability of objects and qualities, at least as far as "pure" perception is concerned, is a gradual matter.) By the same token, theoretical terms may sometimes be used to refer to observables, too.

We still have some notions to be explained. We use the adjective 'representative' in our characterization of observational terms. It is a notoriously difficult word which can be considered synonymous with 'typical', 'standard', and 'normal', at least in the present context. The notion is an idealized one and hard to describe in operational terms. For instance, a statistical interpretation (=most) would not do as such. We shall here rely on the reader's intuitive understanding and hope that the notion carries some information.

Similarly, 'can' is idealized, too. It is not purely descriptive, but carries with it an "under normal conditions"-clause. It also refers to any possible (past, present, future) measurement-occasions which are "normal".

The phrase 'typical applications' refers somewhat vaguely to possible typical experiments etc. in which T is tested or used to explain data. We shall later in Chapter V discuss what can be meant by the intended or typical domains of objects in T.

The notions of reliability and (concept) validity of measurement are to be understood in their normal sense, that is, in the way they are employed e. g. in the social sciences. (Cf. TUOMELA (1970a) for an explicate of concept validity and for psychological examples of our theoretical/observational division.)

The notion of theoreticity of terms has been explicated by referring to the notion of explanation (clause (b)). We shall discuss the notion of explanation in some detail in Chapter VII; here we just rely on the reader's intuitive understanding of the notion.

Let this suffice as the clarification of the phrases occurring in our methodological characterization of a theoretical/observational classification of concepts. A critic may now argue that our division is not exhaustive. That is, in our classification there may be extralogical scientific terms which are neither observational nor theoretical. For one may possibly conceive of nonobservational primitive terms which are not explanatory. (Among terms that are defined, but only *partially* (observationally) defined, there may quite well be nonobservational *and* nonexplanatory terms.) We shall here adopt the convention that in those rare clear cases, if any, where a nonobservational primitive term can be said to be nonexplanatory, it is still classified as a μ-term so that the set $\lambda \cup \mu$ of the extralogical scientific predicates of a theory T is an exhaustive dichotomy.

As a result of our technical explicates of 'observational' and 'theoretical' we see that they fairly closely match the dichotomy 'descriptive' versus 'explanatory'. It is, however, still possible that some terms which are observational according to our characterization of observationality are also explanatory terms, even if no theoretical terms in the sense of our definition can be merely descriptive.

Our methodological characterization of theoreticity explicates the notion of 'T-ladenness' or 'laden-with-theory T'. Concepts which are theoretical with respect to T are thus T-laden whereas concepts observational with respect to T are not T-laden, although they are normally laden with the conceptual burden of other theories. It should be emphasized again that as our definitions are paradigm-dependent they are relative to some background knowledge (or assumptions), that is, to a certain way of conceptualizing and "seeing" the world. Therefore changes in the accepted hypotheses and assumptions may result in reclassifying theoretical and observational terms.

We have on purpose given our definitions of observability and theoreticity of concepts in general, somewhat vague and sometimes philosophically difficult terms. However, our characterizations seem to be adequate for the purposes of this book. But it is well conceivable that our dichotomy can be made precise to meet more demanding standards; and even in its present form it does not seem to be refutable by the arguments of the previous critics of the traditional theoretical/observational dichotomy (cf. PUTNAM (1962), ACHINSTEIN (1965), and SPECTOR (1966)).

Chapter II

Elimination of Theoretical Concepts

1. Craig's General Replacement Programme

1.1. It is generally agreed that explanation and prediction are central functions of scientific theories. It can be argued that explanation and prediction are subactivities of scientific systematization, broadly understood (cf. HEMPEL (1958), p. 174). Scientific systematization consists of deductive and inductive systematization. These notions will be defined below. Later we shall be concerned with the role of theoretical concepts in scientific explanation (and, to some extent, in prediction as well). It will indeed then be seen that at least some interesting aspects of explanation and prediction are special cases of our broad notion of scientific systematization.

As is usual in contemporary analytic philosophy of science, we shall mainly consider scientific theories and scientific systematization from a logico-linguistic point of view. Hence the tools and results of modern logic may help us when investigating the role of theoretical concepts in scientific systematization. We argued in the last chapter that a logical elimination programme, like that of Craig or Ramsey, should be of interest to all philosophers and methodologists of science who want to understand the function of theoretical concepts; for this is one question to which a replacement programme gives or should give some kind of answer.

A satisfactory formal elimination programme will obviously play a central part for all kinds of philosophical reduction attempts since such a programme can be given various interpretations. Physicalism, phenomenalism, behaviorism, and nominalism may be stated as examples of historically important schools of reduction. In each case of reduction, a dichotomy between two kinds of statements (let us call them instrumentalistically auxiliary and nonauxiliary) on the subject matter is established, and an attempt is made to reduce the set of auxiliary (e. g. theoretical) statements to the set of nonauxiliary (e. g. observational) statements. A satisfactory elimination programme shows how this can be done.

It is no wonder that in trying to establish the premises of the theoretician's dilemma instrumentalists commonly refer either to Craig's or to Ramsey's elimination technique. It is condition (4) of the theoretician's dilemma that concerns us in the first place (see Chapter I). We shall here consider the following modification of it (cf. also CORNMAN (1972), p. 85):

(4′) If the theoretical terms of a theory T establish observational scientific systematization, then the Craigian transcription of T preserves its observational scientific systematization.

Notice that while (4) speaks generally about relationships between observable phenomena, (4′) asumes that all these relationships can be subsumed under the general notion of scientific systematization. While this transition may seem dubious to some, we shall accept it here, even if it may make the instrumentalist's position stronger. The present transition forces us to change the formulation of theses (3) and (5) to:

(3′) If theoretical terms serve their purpose, they establish scientific systematization among observational statements.

(5′) If the Craigian transcription of a theory T preserves the observational scientific systematization established by T, theoretical terms are dispensable.

In accordance with our *methodological* empiricism and to give the instrumentalist some more playground we shall below accept (3′) as valid. It is clearly valid at least for theories having observational content, which we are here mostly interested in. If a theory T does not have observational content, it must have, according to our requirement of (indirect) empirical testability (Chapter I), a scientific extension T^* with observational content, and (3′) can be regarded as valid with respect to T^*. (Notice that (3′) specifies only *one* of the purposes theoretical terms have; see Section II.2.) The fate of (5′) will be discussed below.

We shall in this chapter assume that the primitive concepts of the science under consideration have been effectively divided into *auxiliary* and *nonauxiliary* concepts[1]. Then we define statements containing auxiliary concepts to be auxiliary, while the rest are nonauxiliary. We may still make a further distinction between *preferred* and *nonpreferred* nonauxiliary (e. g. observational) statements. For instance, strictly (finitely) observational statements might be called preferred statements in distinction to other observational statements.

It is customary and useful to distinguish replacement programmes which (1) in the first instance replace (a) individual auxiliary terms or (b) single sentences, from those which (2) are primarily concerned with the replacement of theories (sets of statements, frameworks). Often quoted in connection with the first kind (especially (1) (a)) is Russell's well-known 'supreme maxim' of philosophizing: 'Wherever possible, logical constructions are to be substituted for inferred entities' (RUSSELL (1917), p. 150). But there are equally well-known objections to this sort of programme (cf. e. g. HEMPEL (1958)).

In this chapter we will consider only the second kind of replacement programme and, more specifically, the general and first-order versions of Craig's solution to it. In Chapter III the method of Ramseyan eliminability will also be discussed.

Before we go into the details of Craig's replacement programme we shall define some notions which we shall need later. Let us consider some theory T which axiomatizes in some formal scientific language the content of a given science[2]. In technical contexts we generally mean by a theory a (recursive) set of statements — some of which have to be essentially general — closed under deduction[3]. Sometimes we simply mean by theory the statement, if any, axiomatizing a theory in the former wider sense. When confusion can arise, we shall clearly distinguish these two notions. (Of course a theory is *philosophically* much more than a deductively closed set of

1 One might here start criticizing again the whole replacement attempt by saying it is not possible to make a nonarbitrary auxiliary/nonauxiliary dichotomy. However, we think that at least in the case of the theoretical/observational interpretation a dichotomy can be created on methodological grounds in the sense of Section 2 of Chapter I.

2 By calling a formal language *scientific* we mean that its extralogical concepts have a factual scientific interpretation in the sense of Chapter V.

3 In this book the words 'formula', 'sentence', and 'statement' can in general be regarded as synonyms.

statements, but for our present technical purposes the above clarification will suffice.) We denote the set of nonauxiliary (observational) extralogical constants of T by λ while the set of its auxiliary (theoretical) extralogical constants is denoted by μ. We denote by $\mathscr{L}(T)$, briefly $\mathscr{L}$, the underlying logic (a set of well-formed formulas, logical axioms, and rules of inference) of the theory T. When we want to display the set of extralogical symbols of a language $\mathscr{L}$ or a theory T we simply write, respectively, $\mathscr{L}(\lambda \cup \mu)$ and $T(\lambda \cup \mu)$. We shall accordingly denote by $\mathscr{L}(\lambda)$ the sublanguage of $\mathscr{L}(\lambda \cup \mu)$ obtained from the latter by omitting the set μ (and the corresponding formulas, axioms, and rules of inference).

We shall assume that all the essential "background" notions and assumptions assumed by the theory have been axiomatized along with the proper scientific content of the theory. Thus the extralogical axioms of T will include axioms for the mathematical notions presupposed by our theory T. In addition, all the other scientific theories and background assumptions directly presupposed by T are below assumed to have been axiomatized and incorporated within the set of extralogical axioms of T.

Now we can define what can be meant by deductive systematization. We say that a (deterministic or probabilistic) theory T in $\mathscr{L}(\lambda \cup \mu)$ establishes *deductive systematization* with respect to $\mathscr{L}(\lambda)$ if and only if

(a) $T \cup \{F\} \vdash G$

(b) not $F \vdash G$

for some formulas F and G in $\mathscr{L}(\lambda)$. We notice that by the deduction theorem conditions (a) and (b) are equivalent to

(a′) $T \vdash F \supset G$

(b′) not $\vdash F \supset G$.

The notion of *inductive systematization* can be defined analogously, the only essential difference being that instead of the relation of deducibility or provability '$\vdash$' we now use a relation of inducibility 'I' and that (a) will have several explicates. We shall defer the discussion of the properties of 'I' till Chapter VIII.

We shall be concerned only with *nomological* scientific systematization, viz. systematizations involving theories or laws. If the premises include only deterministic laws we are dealing with *deterministic* scientific systematization. If probabilistic laws or theories occur among the premises we speak about *probabilistic* systematization, independently of whether the systematization is deductive or inductive. Furthermore, we may distinguish between *actual* and *potential* scientific systematizations depending on whether the premises are accepted as true or their truth values are unknown.

Next we define that two sets of statements T_1 $(\lambda \cup \mu)$ and $T_2(\lambda \cup \eta)$ are *functionally equivalent for deductive systematization* with respect to $\mathscr{L}$ (λ) if and only if for all statements F and G in $\mathscr{L}$ (λ)

$$T_1 \cup \{F\} \vdash G \text{ if and only if } T_2 \cup \{F\} \vdash G.$$

Now consider the set

$$O_T = \{F \text{ in } \mathscr{L}\ (\lambda) \mid T \vdash F\}$$

of the observational or nonauxiliary consequences of a theory T $(\lambda \cup \mu)$. We can now prove

Theorem II. 1. The theory T and the set O_T of its observational consequences are functionally equivalent for deductive systematization with respect to the observational language $\mathscr{L}$ (λ).

The simple proof can be given concisely in two parts as follows:

A.	(1) $T \cup \{F\} \vdash G$	(premise)
	(2) $T \vdash F \supset G$	((1), deduction theorem)
	(3) '$F \supset G$' belongs to O_T	((2), definition)
	(4) $\{F \supset G, F\} \vdash G$	(modus ponens)
	(5) $O_T \cup \{F\} \vdash G$	((3), (4))
B.	(1) $O_T \cup \{F\} \vdash G$	(premise)
	(2) $O_T \vdash F \supset G$	((1), deduction theorem)
	(3) $T \vdash O_T$	(definition)
	(4) $T \vdash F \supset G$	((2), (3), transitivity of deduction)
	(5) $T \cup \{F\} \vdash G$	((4), converse of deduction theorem)

(In the usual logical terminology we might as well have said here that T is a conservative extension of O_T with respect to $\mathscr{L}$ (λ).)

It is important to notice that O_T is not a recursive but only a recursively enumerable set of statements. (Hence it is not a theory in the proper sense of the word.) The aim of a replacement programme (of the second kind) is to provide an *effective (recursive)* method for replacing the auxiliary expressions of a theory axiomatizing a science by nonauxiliary ones, so that the nonauxiliary content of the science is left unchanged. Thus in a replacement programme we are looking for a recursively axiomatized theory T' which axiomatizes O_T. It is important, too, that not only should the statements of T' replace those of T, but the derivations of the nonauxiliary statements of T from its axioms should also be replaced by derivations of the statements of T' from its axioms.

We can thus better understand why we have to transform thesis (4) of the theoretician's dilemma argument into something like (4′) (rather than to accept the noneffective replacement established by O_T). The notion of dispensability essential to the theoretician's dilemma can now be qualified in one direction. Let us say that the theoretical terms (members of μ) of a theory $T(\lambda \cup \mu)$ are *logically indispensable for deductive systematization* if and only if

1) $T(\lambda \cup \mu)$ achieves deductive systematization between some F and G in $\mathscr{L}(\lambda)$;
2) there is no (recursively axiomatizable) subtheory $T'(\lambda)$ of $T(\lambda \cup \mu)$ which achieves at least the same deductive systematization.

A theoretical term is called logically dispensable (for deductive systematization) if and only if it is not logically indispensable. The replacement of 'deductive' by 'inductive' in the above definition gives us a definition for the *logical indispensability for inductive systematization* of theoretical terms. If a theoretical term is found to be logically dispensable for the purposes of both deductive and inductive systematization we say that it is *logically dispensable for scientific systematization*[4].

We shall from here on denote by (2′), (5″), and (6′) the theses of the theoretician's dilemma argument obtained from (2), (5′), and (6), respectively, by writing 'logically dispensable for observational scientific systematization' instead of the unqualified 'dispensable'. Our notion of logical dispensability is naturally a most favorable explicatum of dispensability for an instrumentalist. But even if theoretical terms were logically dispensable within both deductive and inductive systematization they might still be indispensable (or at least desirable)

4 It is important to notice that in this book we discuss questions of indispensability relative to some theory and its subtheories in $\mathscr{L}(\lambda)$. Hence we do not *explicitly* take into account the possible "heuristic power", etc. that the original theory may have concerning some other conceptual frameworks.

in some other respects. Therefore, to get to (6) from (6′) we need the following additional instrumentalistic premise:

If theoretical terms are logically dispensable for the scientific systematization of observational statements, they are dispensable.

1.2. Let us now go on to describe Craig's general replacement programme in detail (cf. Craig (1953) and (1956)). We still have to sharpen our tools somewhat. Let us first list some conditions that all our theories (deductive systems) have to satisfy (cf. Craig (1956)):

(i) The set of applications of a rule of inference is effectively defined.
(ii) The set of logical axioms is effectively defined.
(iii) The set of extralogical axioms is effectively defined.
(iv) The set of formulas is effectively defined.
(v) Every axiom is either logical or extralogical.
(vi) No axiom is both logical and extralogical.
(vii) Every theorem of T is a formula of $\mathscr{L}(T)$.

Conditions (ii), (iii), and (v), imposed on T, together imply that the set of axioms of T is recursively defined. Together with (i) this implies that the set of proofs in T also is effectively defined. Conditions (i) and (ii) imply that the set of proofs in $\mathscr{L}(T)$ (which includes the logical axioms and rules of inference of T) also is recursively defined.

Now we assume that T satisfies the following conditions:

(a) (i) – (vii)
(b) An effective dichotomy is given which distinguishes the auxiliary expressions (members of μ) of T from the nonauxiliary (members of λ).
(c) If a formula contains an auxiliary expression, then the formula itself is auxiliary.

Notice that the following kinds of formulas occur in our theory T (we now use the theoretical/observational dichotomy):

(A) formulas containing exclusively theoretical concepts;
(B) formulas where both theoretical and observational concepts occur ("correspondence rules");
(C) preferred formulas (containing only observational concepts);

(D) nontheoretical formulas where only observational concepts occur; but these are not-preferred or not strictly observational formulas (for example, formulas whose truth values cannot be determined by a finite number of observations might sometimes be included in this class; cf. Section 1.2.).

Our replacing theory T' must contain formulas only of kinds (C) and (D).

For Craigian elimination the following further restrictions must be imposed upon T:

(d) If no expression in a formula A is auxiliary, then no expression in the conjunction A & A &...& A is auxiliary.

(e) The rule 'From A, derive A & A &...& A' is valid in $\mathscr{L}$ (T).

(f) The rule 'From A & A &...& A, derive A' is valid in $\mathscr{L}$ (T).

Of these (d) can be regarded as entirely obvious, and conditions (e) and (f) are usually considered acceptable (they are valid in a wide variety of systems of logic), although in principle we can replace them by other rules of inference (see CRAIG (1953), p. 30). In the sequel (f) will be referred to as the rule of simplification.

The replacing theory T' consisting of only nonauxiliary formulas is subjected to the following conditions:

(1) No formula of T' contains auxiliary expressions.

(2) T' and T are functionally equivalent for deductive systematization with respect to $\mathscr{L}$ (λ).

(3) (a) Any rule of inference of $\mathscr{L}$ (T') is valid in $\mathscr{L}$ (T). In addition, any theorem of $\mathscr{L}$ (T') is a theorem of $\mathscr{L}$ (T).

(b) Any rule of inference of $\mathscr{L}$ (T), restricted in its application and yield to nonauxiliary formulas, is valid in $\mathscr{L}$ (T'). Moreover, any theorem of $\mathscr{L}$ (T) which contains no expressions regarded as auxiliary is a theorem of $\mathscr{L}$ (T').

After all this, a solution to our problem can be given. Abstractly stated, it says:

Theorem II. 2. If a theory can be given a recursively enumerable set of axioms it can also be given a recursive set of axioms (see CRAIG (1953)).

In other words, the recursively enumerable set of observational consequences of T can be recursively axiomatized. Stated in terms of the above discussion we can give Theorem II. 2. the following specialized form:

*Theorem II. 2**. For any theory T satisfying conditions (i)—(vii) and (a)—(f) above one can effectively construct a theory T' satisfying conditions (i)—(vii) for a formal system, and conditions (1)—(3) for replacing entire proofs.

Let us now assume that we have a Gödel numbering for all the sequences of symbols of T, and hence also for proofs in $\mathscr{L}(T)$, since proofs can be represented as sequences of sequences of symbols. Consider then any conjunctions A & A &...& A. On the basis of the assumptions made above we can determine effectively whether or not:

(α) the number of occurrences of A in A & A &...& A is a Gödel number of a proof in $\mathscr{L}(T)$;

(β) This proof is a proof of A; and

(γ) A contains no expressions regarded as auxiliary.

Similarly, given a conjunction A & A &...& A we can decide whether or not:

(α') the number of occurrences of A in A & A &...& A is a Gödel number of a proof in T which is not a proof in $\mathscr{L}(T)$.

Now we construct a system T' and its logic $\mathscr{L}(T')$ in the following manner. As the axioms of $\mathscr{L}(T')$, i. e., the logical axioms of T', we choose exactly those conjunctions A & A &...& A for which (α), (β), and (γ) hold. As rules of inference of $\mathscr{L}(T')$ we take the rule of simplification and the rules of inference of $\mathscr{L}(T)$, restricting their application and yield to nonauxiliary formulas. As extralogical axioms of T' we take exactly those conjunctions A & A &...& A for which (α'), (β), and (γ) hold. The formulas of T' will, of course, be the nonauxiliary formulas of T. Craig has given a proof to show that the above construction and the theory T' thus obtained really are appropriate (see CRAIG (1956), pp. 54f.; cf. also STEGMÜLLER (1970), pp. 384—392). However, we will not repeat it here.

Craig's above theorem proves that premise (4') of the theoretician's dilemma argument is indeed valid and thus acceptable.

2. The Significance of Craig's Replacement Programme

2.1. We are now ready to make an attempt to evaluate the philosophical significance, if any, of Craig's replacement programme. Like most authors who have written about this we will consider the question more generally: What does the above construction tell us about the role of auxiliary (especially theoretical) concepts in science? Craig's result may give us some clue to this more general question even if the elimination programme itself were considered to fail in some sense, or, more strongly, even if the whole attempt to perform any kind of elimination is regarded as misconceived. All kinds of views on Craig's general result are to be found in the literature; here we will survey some of the most important of its criticisms.

To begin with, and to get further motivation, let us take some extreme views. BARKER ((1957), p. 147) regards Craig's elimination result as philosophically important and, having described the results, says:

> "This fact is important because it shows that there cannot be any logical advantage to be gained by introducing theoretical expressions into a scientific system. By introducing theoretical expressions one cannot obtain a system which is richer than would otherwise be possible with regard to the observational statements derivable from it (richer in its "cash value") or more economical than would otherwise be possible with regard to its array of primitive terms. Whatever degree of richness and economy may be desired, these always can be secured at least as well through the adoption of a system containing no theoretical expressions whatever."

To go to the other extreme: "Although the method allows us to avoid the use of expressions regarded as auxiliary, nothing seems to be gained thereby." (CRAIG (1956)) "Thus due to its failure to give deductive coherence and integrity the importance of Craig's paper lies in the challenge to explain why the device he offers is unimportant; for this raises the whole question of the objectives of philosophical replacement programmes." (GOODMAN (1957))

Let us now discuss somewhat more systematically some critical remarks and problems raised by Craig's general result. Most of the remarks apply also to his treatment of the first-order case. However, for that case neater results can be obtained by using distributive normal forms (see Section II. 3.).

We divide the critical remarks into three groups. The first contains more or less direct criticism of some logical features of Craig's construction, which taken as such is of course formally faultless. The second group contains various philosophical remarks directed against Craig's construction (though they are not necessarily relevant to how well Craig succeeded in his task as defined above). These remarks contain various additional criteria for an elimination programme to be philosophically interesting. The bulk of philosophers' criticisms falls into this group. Thirdly, there are criticisms which are in principle against all kinds of reduction (especially the elimination of theoretical concepts). We think that something about the role of auxiliary or theoretical concepts in science can be learned from each of these types of criticism, and this in itself is one good reason for taking them up here. It should be noticed, however, that only the criticisms in the first group are relevant to the theses in our last version of the theoretician's dilemma argument constituted by (1), (2′), (3′), (4′), (5″), and (6′).

Let us begin with a logical question that has not been mentioned in the literature on Craig's result. This problem is the nature of the rules of inference and logical axioms of $\mathscr{L}$ (T') and $\mathscr{L}$ (T), as well as the extralogical axioms of T'. Usually, the notion of an axiom (in its widest sense) is identified with a recursive one-place predicate of the Gödel numbers of the formulas or sentences in question; and, similarly, the notion of a rule of inference is identified with a recursive two-place predicate of the same Gödel numbers (see CRAIG (1953), pp. 30—31, HINTIKKA (1966b), p. 238). However, as has been pointed out by HINTIKKA (1966b), p. 238f., this identification does not do full justice to what we intuitively mean by an axiom or a rule of inference, and here the adoption of some kind of unnatural axioms and rules of inference may make it possible to reproduce the effect of auxiliary concepts (cf. also HERMES (1950)). For an axiom and a rule of inference should depend only on what the formulas or sentences say — in some straightforward sense of saying. The Gödel number of a formula, however, depends on many other things besides this. For instance, it depends on the purely notational features of the formula in question. To give an example, the number of repetitions of a member of a conjunction does not in any interesting sense make a difference to what the formula or sentence in question says, but, of course, it will make a considerable difference to its Gödel number.

More generally, we require that our axioms and rules of inference should be extendable to such axioms and rules of inference which satisfy the requirement that provability relations between formulas should not be affected by purely sentential (truth-functional) transformations of the formulas (or their parts) or permutations of free singular terms (HINTIKKA (1966b), p. 238f.)[5].

---

5 By a purely sentential transformation we mean here the replacement of a truth-function of certain atomic or quantified formulas by a tautologously equivalent truth function of the same formulas.

From this kind of considerations it is possible to define precisely what is meant by a natural axiom and a natural rule of inference (see HINTIKKA

An interesting consequence of adopting such axioms and rules of inference is that not every logical truth, say F, of first-order predicate logic can be proved by using only formulas of no greater quantificational depth (see Section II. 3.) than F. (This observation is also relevant to our discussion of Craig's interpolation result in the first-order case.)

What consequences does all this have when applied to Craig's replacement method described above? Let us repeat what conditions (α), (β), and (γ) say: a conjunction A & A &... & A (n members) is a logical axiom of T' if and only if n is the Gödel number of a proof of A in $\mathscr{L}$ (T). Similarly (α'), (β), and (γ) tell us that a conjunction A & A &... & A (n members) is an extralogical axioms of T' if and only if n is the Gödel number of a proof of A in T which is not a proof in $\mathscr{L}$ (T). Thus there are many redundancies among both the logical and extralogical axioms of T'. First, corresponding to every nonauxiliary formula A of T (there are an infinite number of them by condition (vii) above) we have a conjunction of A's as an axiom (as guaranteed by our condition above). Secondly, owing to the unnaturalness (in the above sense) of Craig's underlying logic, we get for each A infinitely many conjunctions of A's in T', one corresponding to each notationally different proof of A in the original theory.

Relevant in this connection is Craig's self-criticism (CRAIG (1956), p. 50) that we may have in T' an extralogical axiom and a logical axiom which are both conjunctions, though with different numbers of conjuncts, of the same A (see condition (vi)). This is because we may have in T one proof of A which is also a proof in $\mathscr{L}$ (T), and another which is not. But a restriction to natural logical axioms and rules of inference (in the sense of Hintikka) will at least in the first-order case (cf. HINTIKKA (1966b)) solve Craig's puzzle: "this violation

---

(1966b), p. 238f.): A two-place general recursive relation R qualifies as a *natural rule of inference* if and only if there is a similar relation R' which has the following properties:

1) If xRy then $xR'y$ (for any Gödel numbers x and y);

2) the ancestral relation of R holds between two Gödel numbers if and only if the ancestral relation of R' holds between them;

3) if x and x' are the respective Gödel numbers of two sentences which can be transformed into each other by purely propositional transformations of themselves and of their subsentences as well as permutations of free singular terms in them, then $xR'y$ whenever $x'R'y$ and $zR'x$ whenever $zR'x'$.

An analogous definition can be given for a natural axiom.

of the intension of (vi) seems unavoidable in some cases, no matter how we may try to modify the construction of S [our T']."

There are two other interesting logical criticisms, put forward, for example, by Black, Smart, and Maxwell. They are directed specifically against the construction described above to illustrate Theorem II. 2. and II. 2.*. The first is that the rule of simplification makes the new theory T' very trivial as a deductive system (Black (1966)). (Recall, however, that the rule of simplification is not the only rule of inference of (T').) In stating this criticism Black apparently thinks that we do not usually need other rules of inference as we want only to derive the observational theorems of T from T', and for this task the rule of simplification suffices. Secondly, the rules for generating the axioms of T' involve direct of indirect reference to T (Black (1966), p. 250, Smart (1968), p. 150), as we have just seen above. In testing whether a nonauxiliary formula belongs to T' we refer to proofs in T, and hence at least to names of auxiliary expressions. A related third criticism is that Craig's replacement programme is of no help in inventing new theories ("the context of discovery") as the original theory T must already "be there". Furthermore, for the elimination of the auxiliary content of the science to be worth while, T must be a finished theory — allowing T to grow would spoil the construction. (Cf. Maxwell (1963), Scheffler (1963).)

An instrumentalist may answer these criticisms, which are directed against a specific construction to illustrate Theorem II. 2., by trying to find another kind of construction for which these criticisms fail to hold. For instance, as an answer to the second criticism, he may say that a purely numerical method can be used to bypass the actual construction of proofs in T'. This remark is also relevant to the third criticism in greatly weakening the sense of "being there". To the last critical remark our instrumentalist may briefly say that no more effort is needed in making the transcripted theory grow with respect to its observational content than in making the original theory grow observationally. The critics have not been able to point out which logical features essential for observational growth T has but T' does not have.

2.2. Let us next discuss our second group of criticisms, which for philosophical, rather than logical, reasons find Craig's replacement programme uninteresting or in some sense a failure. These criticisms admit the programme to eliminate all auxiliary expressions of a science in favor of nonauxiliary ones is plausible, even desirable, provided that the new system satisfies some further desiderata. Quite a few modern philosophers of science seem to take such a stand. We list here some of the additional desiderata proposed by philosophers who have discussed and criticized Craig's result. The resulting axiom system T' should be finite (HEMPEL (1963), NAGEL (1961), SCHEFFLER (1963)), perspicious (CRAIG (1956)), manageable (HEMPEL (1963)), heuristically fruitful and suggestive (Hempel, Scheffler). It should provide deductive coherence, integrity, and economy (GOODMAN (1957)). Each of these desiderata is in fact mentioned in a very lucid passage by Hempel quoted below. Having conceded that the replacing theory T' is functionally equivalent to the original theory T (in the sense that it establishes exactly the same deductive connections between the nonauxiliary formulas as T does) Hempel states his criticism.

"There are at least two reasons, however, which would make it distinctly inadvisable for science to avail itself of this possibility of avoiding theoretical terms. One of these was provided by Craig himself: He showed (1) that the "new" theoretical system constructed by his method always has an infinite set of postulates, irrespective of whether the postulate set of the original theory is finite or infinite, and (2) that his result cannot be essentially improved in this respect, for there is no general method which will yield, for any given system T, and for choice of V_B, a corresponding T_B [our T'] with a finite postulate set whenever a functionally equivalent theory with a finite postulate set exists. This means that the scientist would be able to avoid theoretical terms only at the price of forsaking the comparative simplicity of a theoretical system with a finite postulational basis, and of giving up a system of theoretical concepts and hypotheses which are heuristically fruitful and suggestive — in return for a practically unmanageable system based upon an infinite, though effectively specified, set of postulates in observational terms. Needless to say that this price is too high for the scientist, no matter how welcome the possibility of such replacement may be to the epistemologist." (HEMPEL (1963), p. 699).

Hempel then takes up another criticism — the impossibility of inductive systematization within T' — which he considers very central.

"The application of scientific theories in the prediction and explanation of empirical findings involves not only deductive inference, i. e., the exploitation of whatever deductive connections the theory establishes among statements representing potential empirical data, but it also requires procedures of an inductive character, and some of these would become impossible if the theoretical terms were avoided. Under this broader conception of the function of a scientific theory, then, T_B is *not* functionally equivalent to T." (HEMPEL (1963), p. 700).

Let us now comment on these desiderata that the Craigian transcription allegedly fails to preserve. The requirement of finite axiomatizability, insisted on by most of Craig's critics, seems to us unnecessary; it is hard to see why a recursive infinite set of axioms should be forbidden, especially if it can be made perspicuous (whatever is strictly speaking meant by that). Think of (first-order) Peano arithmetic as an example of a theory with an infinite number of axioms! (Maybe the critics would accept an infinity of axioms if they can be given by means of a finite number of schemata.) In fact, had Craig's general result (Thm. II. 2) rather been proved for systems containing only natural logical axioms and rules of inference (HINTIKKA (1966b)), the infinite axiom set would probably have been considerably more perspicuous. The use of distributive normal forms in the first-order case will in fact supply an infinite set of axioms that is a simple and, in a clear sense, perspicuous monotonically increasing chain. Even Craig's own treatment of the first-order case can be made to yield a somewhat more perspicuous axiom system than that given by the above method (see the next section).

We do not here intend to give any explication of the philosophically difficult and scientifically important notions of perspicuity, simplicity, heuristic fruitfulness, and suggestiveness. The analysis of these notions does not belong only to psychology; they have a quasi-psychological or rational component of meaning, the explication of which belongs to philosophical pragmatics. But however explicated, these properties are not likely to apply to the axiom system of Craig's general replacing theory T'; on this point we agree with the critics of Craig's 1956 construction.

We can agree with Hempel that inductive systematization is an important function of science. Hempel has tried to argue by means of a couple of examples (HEMPEL (1958), p. 214f. and (1963), p. 700) that theoretical concepts play an essential role in it. But without a systematic account of this matter, his case is hardly established. Hempel's examples involve an inductive leap from the instantiation of some of the observational (factually) necessary conditions of a theoretical property to the instantiation of this property. Thereafter new observational statements from statements concerning this theoretical property are inferred deductively. What Hempel has not shown is why we cannot simply use another inductive procedure, namely "direct inference", to pass from observable conditions to new observable instantiations, thereby avoiding the theoretical property altogether. Hence, some more penetrating account of the situation is needed to lend conviction to Hempel's argument.

We shall postpone our discussion of questions of inductive systematization till Chapter VIII. Therefore the issue of the possible logical indispensability of theoretical terms within inductive systematization will be left open in this chapter.

There is still one important standard argument against elimination programmes that has to be mentioned here. According to it, a transcribed theory does not preserve the explanatory power of the original theory. In other words, theoretical concepts are claimed to be indispensable for scientific explanation (cf. e. g. CAMPBELL (1921), SELLARS (1963)). As we will devote a whole chapter to problems of explanation, even this issue will have to remain undecided so far.

2.3. Let us now proceed to the third group of criticisms against Craig's construction. These criticisms are directed against any elimination whatever of auxiliary concepts. We restrict ourselves exclusively to the theoretical/observational dichotomy here. A necessary and perhaps a sufficient condition for not eliminating theoretical concepts seems to be their scientific significance. This is especially the case if the theoretical concepts are regarded as significant somehow in their own right or due to their nature (cf. our comment in Chapter V). An entirely different kind of notion of significance, viz. a methodological one, can be obtained from an instrumentalist because the common slogan is that for an instrumentalist a concept is scientifically significant if and only if it functions well in his theory. It may be that hardly anything more of interest can be said about the instrumentalist's position. But even if so, most if not all of our discussion in the sequel is relevant to an instrumentalist. For we will later in this book suggest some methodological (functional) reasons for using auxiliary concepts, and these arguments should be acceptable to an instrumentalist, too. Let us, however, now take up a type of reason an instrumentalist cannot use (due to the very idea of instrumentalism).

It is *ontological* reasons, more than any other, that incline philosophers to oppose the elimination of theoretical terms; and some form of realism is likely to be the ontological view embraced. For if a theoretical expression refers to some existing entity or property, then we gain nothing by eliminating its name from our theory; this is what a realist may say. Or he may hold that a theoretical term should not be considered immune from elimination merely because there are entities falling under it. In the limiting case he may say that theoretical entities and properties do exist and are interesting and significant in their own right. This is the view of Putnam, for example, when he writes:

"Describing the behavior of viruses, radio stars, etc., may not be the 'aim of science', but it is certainly an aim of scientists. And in terms of this aim one can give a very short answer to the question: Why theoretical terms? Why such terms as 'radio star', 'virus', and 'elementary particle'? *Because* without such terms we could not speak of radio stars, viruses, and elementary particles, for example — and we *wish* to speak of them, to learn more about them, to explain their behavior and properties better" (PUTNAM (1965), p. 257).

Putnam enlarges on this "short answer" by telling us that "(1) presupposes the existence of theoretical entities; and (2) presupposes the intelligibility of theoretical terms". And he goes on to defend his position by ordinary-language arguments, which we do not find very convincing, however.

Still we think (perhaps because of our realism) that it would be too far-going skepticism to doubt (1) and (2) in the case of established physical theories. (On the other hand, one could list many examples of theories or models in the social sciences where the situation is rather the opposite.)

One may still drive Putnam's arguments a little further and claim, as BUNGE (1967b) does, that at least physical theories do not contain any observational concepts and that therefore physical theories do not as such have any empirical content but only the factual content as specified by their theoretical statements. Thus the elimination of the theoretical content of a physical science would mean eliminating all of that science. What to say about Bunge's argument depends, of course, how the theoretical/observational dichotomy is established. (For instance, in our sense of Chapter I physical sciences contain or may contain also observational terms. Bunge calls *all* concepts occurring in a physical theory theoretical.) Furthermore, in this book we are mostly concerned with the social sciences, in most of which it is natural to reconstruct a theory so as to include contingent interpretative statements or correspondence rules connecting theoretical and observational terms, as we have all the time assumed above.

Smart, too, opposes elimination on realistic grounds:

"Craig's method can be applied only after we have first constructed the theory T, and that the success of T' is explained by the fact that the original theory T is true of the things that it is ostensibly about: in other words by the fact that there really are electrons or whatever is postulated by the theory T. If there were no such things, and if T were not true in a realist way, would not the success of T' be quite inexplicable? One would have to suppose that there were innumerable lucky accidents about the behavior of things mentioned in the observational vocabulary, so that they behaved miraculously *as if* they were brought about by the non-existent things ostensibly talked about in the theoretical vocabulary." (SMART (1968), p. 150f.)

On the basis of our discussion it is obvious that the acceptance of critical or practically any version of realism implies that significant theoretical terms are at least *ontologically indispensable* (even if they might still be in some other sense dispensable for a realist). But suppose an instrumentalist now claims that theoretical terms designate just artifacts and not aspects of real objects. How can such a dispute between a realist and an instrumentalist be settled?

What we are after here is a set of common criteria for deciding "external" ontological questions. Hence it will not take us very far to refer to Quine's well-known "quantificational" criterion of existence or to leave the problem unsolved as a merely practical one (CARNAP (1950)), or even to accept the following criterion by Hempel. "To assert that the terms of a given theory have factual reference, that the entities they purport to refer to actually exist, is tantamount to asserting that what the theory tells us is true; and this in turn is tantamount to asserting the theory". (HEMPEL (1965), p. 219) Hempel's methodological criterion clearly will not help us much as long as the truth of the theory is decided merely on the basis of its observational consequences.

CORNMAN (1972) offers an instrumentalistic criterion for non-existence, which seemingly gives us one possible type of external ontological criterion. Cornman's criterion is a direct continuation to the thesis (6) of the theoretician's dilemma[6] (see CORNMAN (1972), p. 84):

(7) If the theoretical terms of science are dispensable, then there is no reason to postulate the existence of any referents of theoretical terms, i. e. any theoretical entities.

(8) If there is no reason to postulate the existence of any theoretical entities, then it is unreasonable to believe that there are any theoretical entities, i. e. it is reasonable to accept scientific instrumentalism.

---

6 We use 'dispensable' for Cornman's 'unnecessary'. Cornman later in his paper qualifies his notion to mean logical unnecessity (dispensability) for the purposes of theory development, explanation, and prediction.

It is interesting to notice that while Putnam tries to argue for the indispensability of theoretical terms on the basis of the (independently) assumed existence of theoretical entities, Cornman argues in the opposite direction (though in the negative). Cornman's instrumentalistic criterion, however, turns out to be just a case of Hempel's above methodological criterion, for the question of the dispensability of theoretical terms is in his analysis again decided on the basis of the observational consequences of a theory. Thus, while Hempel's and Cornman's criterion does not as such contradict ontological realism, it, being only methodological, gives a rather uninteresting and too weak a criterion of existence.

When looking for better criteria of existence one apparently has to go beyond the theory as such (i. e. as a deductively closed set of statements) to the various metaphysical presuppositions which concern the subject matter of the theory and which in a sense have given rise to the theory. To name an example of the type of analysis needed here let us only mention BERGMANN's study of 1961 where several criteria of or rather evidence for existence are distinguished. But it would take us somewhat out of the main direction of our present study to go deeper into ontological questions here.

This ends our comments on Craig's general replacement programme and its criticisms. It remains to be seen whether we can at the present stage of our investigation make any definite conclusions concerning the theoretician's dilemma argument.

As we have indicated earlier, the evaluation of the theoretician's dilemma presupposes that we have some ideas and knowledge about the goals of science and the means for achieving these goals. Actually both the complex question of the goals and the question of the means of science are value-questions (although they possibly depend on somewhat different sources of value), unless the whole problem is considered only from the descriptive point of view of the sociology of science.

It has to be agreed that science is a multigoal enterprise, and (partly) because of this it is very difficult to say anything definite and (at the same time) informative about it. First, consider the following general statement about the goals of science:

(GS) The central aim of science is to create an integrated description of the general features of the world and to explain why the world is what it is.

Then consider a claim about the means of science:

(MS) The central aim of science is likely to be achieved by means of scientific theories which are (heuristically) fertile and manageable and provide deductive and inductive systematization (as well as integrity and economy).

The general claim (GS) is supposed to account for "understanding the world" and also for predicting and changing the world. Therefore it should be acceptable to both realists and instrumentalists, rationalists and empiricists, and so on. It is only when the underlying conceptual framework and presuppositions needed for describing and explaining aspects of the world are revealed that differences between philosophers become apparent.

If, for instance, a theoretician believes in the existence of hidden nonobservable entities and wants to theorize about them, then he adopts his conceptual framework in accordance with this, and thus he naturally needs theoretical terms in his theories. (Notice that he may believe in the existence of, say, electrons but not in the existence of, say, subconscious wishes. It may be sensible to be a realist in one scientific context and an instrumentalist in another.) Thus we have found at least one sense in which theoretical terms may be indispensable (for a realist in any case), viz. in theorizing about theoretical entities. Still, as we have seen, an instrumentalist need not accept this, but he can adopt (GS) in a weaker sense in which scientific systematization (in a broad sense) of observational statements is all that is included in (GS). However, we shall argue in a later chapter that even when understood in this weaker sense (GS) cannot be fulfilled without the introduction of theoretical concepts into theories. More specifically we shall argue that at least for some kind of scientific systematization (viz. explanation) theoretical terms are indispensable.

Let us now comment on (MS). The vague and general notions of (heuristical) fertility and manageability as well as those of deductive and inductive systematization (integrity, economy) are supposed to incorporate all the desirable features of theories brought up by Craig's critics. (The important methodological feature of empirical testability is assumed to be included within inductive systematization.) The question we have to face now is: Are any of these desiderata *logically* necessary for the attainment of (GS) or are all of them just (or at best) *contingently* necessary (or even desirable) for it (or is this dichotomy applicable here at all)? We shall here without further argument assume that they are at best contingently necessary. If so, they cannot with full force be applied to qualify the notion of dispensability in the theoretician's dilemma. Rather they come into question only after the issue of dispensability of theoretical terms has been settled, and they serve as criteria for ranking theories as to their "empirical adequacy" (or the like).

Let us finally summarize our present results concerning the acceptability of the theses of the theoretician's dilemma argument. The original unqualified version ⟨(1), (2), (3), (4), (5), (6)⟩ (in I.1.) was dismissed as vague and incomplete. Furthermore, we noticed that for a realist theoretical terms cannot at least be ontologically dispensable, which gives one more reason for us to reject the original form of the dilemma. The more interesting, though restricted version, arrived at earlier in this chapter, is ⟨(1), (2′), (3′), (4′), (5″), (6′)⟩. Of these theses (1) and (2)′ are trivially acceptable. We shall here also accept (3′) as a methodological requirement (recall our reservations in II.1.). But, as we in effect noticed, its acceptance is not directly related to the realism-instrumentalism controversy. Notice that in (3′) the notion of serving purpose means that *part* of the purpose of theoretical terms is to establish observational scientific systematization. But as we argued, that is not all that we require of theoretical terms. Hence (3′) cannot be strengthened into an 'if and only if'-statement in this sense of 'purpose'. Therefore, in the theoretician's dilemma argument it seems better to understand 'purpose' as a synonym of 'methodological purpose'. Methodological purpose can be taken to mean establishing observational scientific systematization. Understood in this sense the converse of (3′) becomes acceptable. Thesis (4′) was found plausible for deductive systematization in general, but has not yet been examined in the case of such special types of deductive systematization as explanation, nor has the issue of inductive systematization been considered. Thesis (5″) is trivially acceptable, as it follows logically from our definition of logical dispensability. The fate of (6′) cannot, of course, be judged yet.

We want to emphasize here and in the next chapters that even if a weak form of the theoretician's dilemma (such as the one just considered) were acceptable it may well be that stronger arguments for the *desirability* of employing theoretical terms in scientific theories can be given than what is involved in the vague and general remarks of Craig's critics. We shall soon see, for instance, that a good deal more in just this direction can be obtained from a study of the logical role of theoretical concepts than most critics of Craig seem to believe.

3. Replacement of First-Order Theories

3.1. It is surprising to note that philosophers of science have paid no attention whatever to the eliminability of auxiliary concepts in first-order theories, where neat, detailed and clear-cut results are available (see CRAIG (1960) and HINTIKKA (1964)). Such results should appeal to a reductionist (cf. thesis (4′) of the theoretician's dilemma argument), since many of the criticisms leveled against Craig's general replacement result can be avoided in the first-order case. Furthermore, as will later be shown in this section and in Chapter III, the first-order results, rather than encouraging us to eliminate can, in fact, give us strong reasons for employing auxiliary concepts (see our discussion on distributive normal forms in II.3.2.). We shall first concentrate on the results of CRAIG (1960). His study is an application of linear Herbrand-type deduction to the study of the relationships between theories and their subtheories. The most important logical result used (and actually proved) in this study is Craig's interpolation theorem (CRAIG (1957)).

The reader should be reminded that the results obtained in the first-order case can, at least in principle, be applied over a wide range. For we can formalize some ordinary version (for example, Zermelo-Fraenkel) of set theory within this logic. Furthermore, all the mathematics needed for formalizing practically any existing scientific theory can be axiomatized within set theory[7]. One theoretical drawback to this approach is that nonstandard models have to be tolerated.

Our discussion on Craig's results in the first-order case will proceed rather informally, so as to make clear the main ideas and results we need. Craig's study may be taken as an abstract clarification of the role of auxiliary concepts in first-order theories rather than as a replacement programme.

---

7 Alternatively, one may formalize directly the needed portions of mathematics without first formalizing the full set theory. Cf. MONTAGUE's (1961) first-order axiomatization of classical particle mechanics, where he started by formalizing differential and integral calculus directly in first-order predicate logic.

In his paper of 1960 Craig investigates what degree of economy, or at least regularity, can be achieved for all recursively axiomatizable first-order theories by using different axiom systems for them. He concentrates especially on the study of bases for subtheories, where a subtheory of a given theory of course consists of those theorems from which certain predicate constants are absent. Craig shows, among other things, that the types of deductive operations involving such predicate constants will be reduced to a minimum, so that their syntactical role in deductions will emerge more clearly. Let us now discuss Craig's results in some detail.

Consider an ordinary version of first-order predicate calculus with identity ($\mathscr{L}$) whose nonlogical symbols are predicates, functors, and individual constants. A *theory* is here any set of formulas which is closed under deduction in $\mathscr{L}$. A *basis* in $\mathscr{L}$ for a theory T is any subset B of T such that the closure under deduction of B in $\mathscr{L}$ is T. In other words, B is a recursively enumerable set of axioms for T. However, a basis need not be a recursive set and does not therefore always give a proper axiomatization of a theory. A (proper) *subtheory* of T is any set T' such that for some set $\mu = \{P_1, P_2, \ldots, P_k\}$ of nonlogical predicate symbols T' consists of those formulas in T from which the members of μ are absent. (Conditions (i)—(vii), (a)—(c), and (1)—(3) of Section II.1. are assumed to be satisfied.)

Suppose we are given any basis B for a theory T, and any set $\mu = \{P_1, P_2, \ldots, P_k\}$ of predicates which determines a subtheory T' of T. We will not describe Craig's method here, since it is fairly complicated and by no means intuitively obvious. Briefly, it is based upon building certain "developments" out of prenex normal forms. Let us just add that Craig shows that the axioms of one of these bases for T' fall under a specified scheme (or actually two schemes which are shown to coincide); however, this axiomatization does not at least to us appear as a paradigm of intuitive clarity. (See CRAIG (1960), p. 107). The linear deduction from B of the formulas in T' requires a variety of operations, but Craig points out than a deduction from B of the formulas in his B' (a basis for T') requires only a certain subset of these (universal instantiation and universally vacuous introduction can be avoided; see CRAIG (1960), p. 115). Furthermore, even this subset can be subjected to certain regularities. The types of operations no longer required, and these regularities together constitute, in Craig's opinion, a measure of the degree of economy achieved by B'. This enables one to compare different theories and/or different methods of deduction of the same observation formula C.

As we stated above, Craig's main result for the first-order case is an application of his interpolation theorem. We state it nontechnically (compare, CRAIG (1960), p. 103):

Theorem II.3. Let T be any theory, and C any consequence of T', the largest subtheory of T in which members of $\mu = \{P_1, P_2, \ldots, P_k\}$ do not occur. Then there are a recursive basis B of T and a recursive basis B' of T', such that B' is obtained from B by eliminating the members of $\mu = \{P_1, P_2, \ldots, P_k\}$ and $B' \vdash C$.

Let us not elaborate here on what is meant by the elimination of symbols, since the end of this section is devoted to this problem — and especially to how it is solved in the theory of distributive normal forms.

In Craig's construction each constructed basis B' will in general be infinite. In addition, B' will be highly redundant in the sense that each formula in T' is implied by a single formula in B'. Hence B' of course shares these two properties with the subtheory constructed in the general case (see Section 1. of this chapter). Furthermore, every B' includes a subset which is also a basis for T' and which is monotonic in the sense that its formulas can be arranged in a sequence B_1, $B_2, \ldots$, such that each B_{i+1} implies B_i: that is, we obtain a strictly increasing chain, which is not finitely axiomatizable. Such monotonic bases also turn out to be the most economical for systematizing the nonauxiliary statements. If T' has a finite basis (as is the case, for example, when the members of $\mu = \{P_1, P_2, \ldots, P_k\}$ are explicitly definable in terms of observables), then for some j each B_{j+e} $(e > 0)$ can be taken as the formula axiomatizing this subtheory. However, Craig shows (CRAIG (1960), p. 140) that there is no effective procedure for deciding whether or not a finite basis exists.

If B is a basis in $\mathscr{L}$ for T and if B is finite then one of Craig's monotonic bases B' for T' can, as we already remarked above, be described without explicit reference to B by a kind of axiom scheme. Craig shows further that in $\mathscr{L}$ a subtheory T' can be axiomatized by a scheme of this kind if and only if T' can be finitely axiomatized by using additional predicates (briefly, *f. a.*+). This notion, *f. a.*+, used in CRAIG and VAUGHT (1958), will be briefly discussed in Chapter VI.

In the case of first-order predicate logic without identity somewhat similar results are obtained. However, we will not discuss them here as they do not seem to bring any new methodologically interesting features into the picture.

Some philosophers of science (for example, MACH (1893), pp. 481—494, CAMPBELL (1920), pp. 122ff., NAGEL (1957), p. 209ff.) seem to think that theoretical concepts, and formulas where only theoretical concepts occur, play a special role in scientific systematization, a role more significant than that of correspondence rules, where both theoretical and observational concepts occur. However, in an arbitrary deduction from a basis B for T of a formula C in T', the syntactical role of the theoretical concepts $P_1, P_2, \ldots, P_k$ is not at all clear in general. What Craig shows is that we can replace this total deduction by one consisting of two phases, as we saw above. In the first phase we deduce from B a formula B_j belonging to the basis B' of T'. In the second phase C is deduced from this B_j, and in this latter derivation no theoretical concepts are present. Craig shows how to arrange the first phase of the deduction so that the types of operations are reduced to a kind of minimum, and in addition subjected to certain regularities. By virtue of these regularities the first phase of the deduction depends in only one respect on the eventual conclusion C. There is no initial portion of the deduction which is completely unaffected by C, and which would thus be common to all statements C.

Thus this kind of rearrangement renders the syntactical role of the theoretical concepts rather clear: they occur only in the first phase of deduction. The types of operations used, and the role of the theoretical concepts, is, however, the same for all axioms in B. Thus there is no proof-theoretic basis for making a profound distinction between definite Campbellian (purely theoretical) formulas and correspondence rules. (Notice, however, that in saying this we are in effect assuming that all scientific theories or at least the interesting ones can be given a first-order formalization).

As our results in Section I.2. and elsewhere in this book shows many other arguments for making a distinction can be found. Let us here call attention to one more of them. We have assumed that we are dealing with a finished and fully grown theory T. It may well be argued that a scientific theory can never be fully grown, in the sense that its correspondence rules are never definitely specified. For this kind of argument, see MACH (1893), DUHEM (1914), CAMPBELL (1920), and others; see also Hempel's article, HEMPEL (1958). Many psychological theories of personality could also be cited, for they hardly contain any definite theoretical statements, let alone correspondence rules.

3.2. The rest of this section is devoted to a study of Craig's interpolation theorem within the theory of *distributive normal forms* of first-order logic which has been developed by Hintikka (see e. g. HINTIKKA (1964) and (1965 a)). We shall later rely on the tools and results of this section when discussing the role of theoretical concepts and their definability within first-order theories.

When dealing with distributive normal forms we shall mostly confine our discussion to a first-order scientific language where predicates are the only extralogical constants present; however, all the results to be given below and in Chapters IV and VI by means of distributive normal forms can also be proved when individual constants and identities are present, unless otherwise stated. It will be assumed that functors have been replaced by predicates throughout. As we shall here systematically employ the theory of distributive normal forms, we start by a concise semitechnical exposition of them (for a full detailed treatment the reader is referred to the above and other works by Hintikka).

Let us indicate briefly what these distributive normal forms look like when considered from the point of view of a graph-theoretical semantics, and what role they play in our first-order language. For simplicity, we restrict our attention to the set of closed sentences of a first-order language with a fixed finite set of extralogical predicates (not all of which are monadic). This set is representable by an (inverted) tree whose nodes are certain sentences called *constituents*. Each constituent belongs to a certain level in the tree, and this level is called its *depth*. If one constituent can be reached from another by going down some branch or noter, the former is said to be *subordinate* to the latter.

Each closed sentence S (and hence each finitely axiomatized theory) of our language is characterized by the number of layers of nested quantifiers it contains at its "thickest"; this parameter will be called the *depth* of S in our discussion[8]. The constituents which are

8 Formally, the depth $d(S)$ of S can now be defined recursively as follows:
$d(S)=0$, if S is an atomic statement or an identity,
$d(S_1 \,\&\, S_2)=d(S_1 \vee S_2)$ = the greater of the numbers $d(S_1)$ and $d(S_2)$,
$d((Ex)\,S(x))=d((x)\,S(x))=d(S)+1$ where in $S(x)$ x has been substituted for some constant in S.

located at depth d in our tree structure all turn out to have the very same depth d according to this new definition of depth. Our two concepts of depth are thus essentially equivalent. Furthermore, each sentence S of depth d, i. e. $S^{(d)}$, can be effectively transformed into a (finite) disjunction of constituents of depth d.

What has been said here can be illustrated by the following tree-like analysis of S.

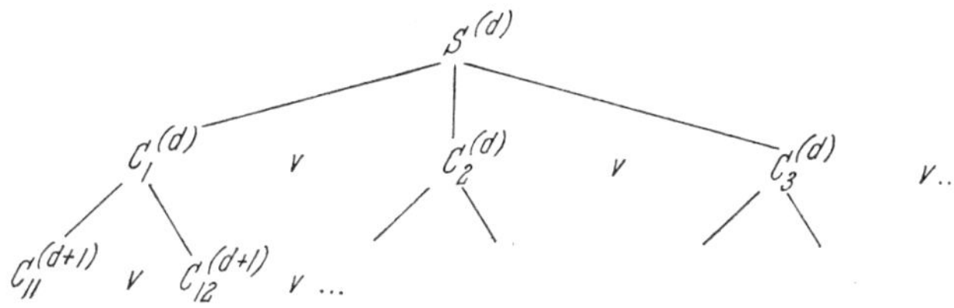

Diagram II.1

The representation of a sentence S of depth d as a disjunction of constituents of this depth d is called the complete disjunctive *distributive normal form* of S. Its representation as a disjunction of constituents of some greater depth $d+e$ is called its *expansion* at this depth. A constituent is equivalent to the disjunction of all its subordinate constituents of any fixed greater depth. Any two constituents of the same depth are mutually incompatible. Hence all the constituents compatible with a given one belong to branches passing through it. Each consistent *complete theory* compatible with S is given by the sentences of some branch of Diagram II.1. If all inconsistent constituents have been eliminated from the expansions of S the converse also holds.

This suffices to indicate the role of constituents and distributive normal forms in first-order languages. The structure of a constituent $C^{(d)}$ of depth d is given by a finite set of finite trees of length d. Each node of each of these trees is associated with an *attributive constituent*, describing what attributes an individual has and how it is related to all the individuals lower in the same branch. Each branch (from bottom to top) thus specifies a sequence of individuals having certain properties and related to each other in certain ways. These sequences are precisely those that exist in a world in which $C^{(d)}$ is true. The tree structure indicates the inter relations of the different kinds of sequences of individuals one may find in such a world.

Suppose we are given a first-order theory, axiomatized by $T(\lambda \cup \mu)$, or briefly T[9], whose concepts (predicates) have been dichotomized into observational (nonauxiliary) concepts and theoretical (auxiliary) concepts. Let the class of the former be λ and the class of the latter μ. (Thus $\lambda \cap \mu = \phi$.)

A natural question to ask is what our theory T says exclusively about the members of λ. This can be taken as a task to construct an observational basis for the theory axiomatized by T. The sense of "saying" is not immediately clear here, however. (Often it is assumed that the only sensible answer is the set of deductive consequences of T which contain no members of μ.) But this is not the only relevant question or the only relevant answer. We must also ask how efficiently and perspicuously the consequences exclusively about the members of λ would be formulated by rival theories. We must ask how much more clearly λ and μ together (connected by $T(\lambda \cup \mu)$) enable us to talk about λ than λ alone does. Speaking in methodological terms, a wide variety of questions falling under the notion of deductive systematization belongs here.

To discuss these questions, we must try to clarify what it is that T says explicitly about the members of λ. If this can be accomplished, questions of the sort just mentioned can be discussed by comparing the *unequal total* consequences concerning λ of different theories T which have the *same explicit* consequences concerning λ. We will now go on to describe the answer of HINTIKKA and TUOMELA (1970) to this problem.

A natural candidate for the explicit content of T about λ is obtained by taking T (assumed to be the only nonlogical axiom of the theory in question) and modifying it syntactically so as to put aside all the information that is not obviously about the members of λ. The result may be called *direct reduct* of T into the vocabulary λ.

How the direct reduct $r(S)$ of an arbitrary sentence S in the terminology $\lambda \cup \mu$ can be defined recursively is clearly seen if all the negation signs are driven as deeply into the sentences as they go — that is, so as to precede immediately an atomic sentence (or an identity when the symbol of identity is present). In this case, the recursive definition will be the following, assuming that $S, S_1, S_2, \ldots$ are arbitrary sentences, that U is an arbitrary sentence which contains no

9 T (or $T^{(d)}$) will normally denote a sentence axiomatizing a theory in contexts where the theory of distributive normal forms is employed. Frequently the theory itself is denoted by T, too.

occurrences of any member of μ, and that A is a negated or unnegated atomic sentence or identity which contains at least one occurrence of some member of μ or other:

$$r\,(S_1 \;\&\; S_2) = r\,(S_1) \;\&\; r\,(S_2)$$

$$r\,(S_1 \vee S_2) = r\,(S_1) \vee r\,(S_2)$$

$$r\,((Ex)\;S) = (Ex)\;r\,(S)$$

$$r\,(U) = U$$

$$r\,(A) = Ver.$$

These clauses are assumed to be applied starting from the outside. It is assumed that $-$, $\vee$, and & are the only sentential connectives present. *Ver* is the symbol for truth (a propositional constant, one of our logical constants). It is assumed that identically $(Ex)\;Ver = Ver = (x)\;Ver$, $S \;\&\; Ver = S$, $S \vee Ver = Ver$. It is easily seen that we can obtain the same result (after the preliminary dislocation of negation signs) simply by replacing each negated or unnegated atomic sentence (or an identity) which contains a member of μ by *Ver*. If we do not want to undertake the preliminary simplification, we can extend our recursive definition and put

$$r\,(-S) = -r\,(S),$$

provided that S is not atomic, and (instead of the last clause above)

$$r\,(A) = Ver \text{ or } -Ver$$

depending on whether A occurs within the scope of an even or odd number of negation signs.

All clauses of the recursive definition are quite trivial except the last, and this only instructs us to disregard all information that depends on the members of μ. It might thus seem that $r\,(S)$ is a workable explication of what S says explicitly about the members of λ; for note that $r\,(S)$ is always logically implied by S.

In the case of distributive normal forms, the direct reduction assumes an especially dramatic form. We simply omit from the normal form all atomic sentences containing members of μ together with the connectives which thereby become idle[10]. (For further details, see HINTIKKA (1965a), pp. 57—59.)

---

10 For a brief discussion of the problems due to the presence of identities and individual constants see HINTIKKA and TUOMELA (1970).

However, it turns out that the direct reduction just defined is not after all a very natural and explicit explication of the idea we are trying to get at. Not only does our direct reduction fail to be invariant with respect to logical equivalence. It turns out that the direct reduct $r(S)$ of a sentence S can even be altered by entirely trivial equivalence transformations — so trivial, indeed, that they can scarcely be said to make a difference to what S directly tells us concerning the members of λ. For instance, although

$$r(S \,\&\, (A \vee -A)) = r(S) \,\&\, ((r(A) \vee r(-A)) = r(S),$$

as might be hoped, we also have

$$r(S \vee (A \,\&\, -A)) = r(S) \vee (r(A) \,\&\, r(-A)) = Ver$$

which does not normally coincide with $r(S)$. Likewise we have

$$r((Ex)(S(x) \vee A(x)) \,\&\, (x)(-S(x) \,\&\, -A(x))) = (x)\, r(-S(x)),$$

which usually is not contradictory.

It seems to us that a natural way out of improving our notion is suggested by what has already been said. Suppose, for instance, that all the members of $\lambda \cup \mu$ are one-place (monadic) predicates. Then all that T can, in any case, say of the world is that the Carnapian Q-predicates (here called Ct-predicates) instantiated in it belong to a certain set of combinations of Ct-predicates (defined by reference to $\lambda \cup \mu$). What these admissible combinations are is spelled out by the several constituents in the distributive normal form of T. One of these constituents might, for example, say that the following attributive constituents or Ct-predicates (and only they) are instantiated:

$$Ct_1(x, \lambda, \mu),\ Ct_2(x, \lambda, \mu), \ldots,\ Ct_j(x, \lambda, \mu).$$

What this constituent says of the members of λ is obvious: it says that those and only those poorer Ct-predicates are instantiated that are obtained as direct reducts of the richer $Ct_1, \ldots Ct_j$ to the vocabulary of λ. In other words, $r(T^{(1)})$ (where $T^{(1)}$ is the distributive normal form of T) is in the monadic case an excellent explication of the idea the direct reduction r was supposed to define.

Somewhat surprisingly, for logical equivalents T' of T, $r(T')$ need not be equivalent to $r(T^{(1)})$. Thus it seems necessary to impose a certain amount of normalization on our idea of reduction. We define what will be called the *reduct proper* $pr(S)$ of an arbitrary formula $S(\lambda \cup \mu)$ of depth d as the direct reduct $r(S^{(d)})$ of the normal form $S^{(d)}$ of S at its own depth.

The naturalness of this definition can be argued for in the general (relational) case in the same way it was argued for above in the monadic case. A formula S of depth d says that combinations of certain ramified sequences of individuals can be found in the world in which S is true. (For an elaboration of this point, see HINTIKKA (1970).) As was pointed out above, each such combination of sequences is specified by a constituent $C^{(d)}$ of depth d (in the vocabulary $\lambda \cup \mu$). What $C^{(d)}$ says of the members of λ is, of course, that such interrelated sequences of individuals can be found as are obtained from those specified by $C^{(d)}$ by omitting all reference to the members of μ. That is to say, $r(S^{(d)}) = pr(S)$ spells out what S says of the members of λ, just as we suggested[11].

It is clear that $pr(S)$ is less sensitive to equivalence-preserving transformations than $r(S)$, is but it is not invariant under all such. For instance, $pr(S)$ is in general sensitive to tautological introduction of quantified subsentences, and thus to increase in depth. Hence normally we have, where d is the depth of S,

$$pr(S) = pr(S^{(d)}) \neq pr(S^{(d+e)}).$$

We can now see that when new extralogical constants, say the members of μ, are introduced into a statement S (over and above its old nonlogical constants, the set of which is λ), we can formulate statements T whose *direct import* for the members of λ is the same as that of S (that is, $pr(T)$ is equivalent to S) but whose total deductive consequences, even as far as λ only is concerned, are greater than those of S (that is, there are statements whose nonlogical constants all belong to λ which are logically implied by T but not by S). The methodological interests of this advantage depends on the method-

11 Here a certain intended ambiguity is present. We must assume that all trivially inconsistent constituents are eliminated from the normal form $S^{(d)}$ of S. However, sometimes it is useful to assume that all inconsistent (and not just all trivially inconsistent) constituents have been omitted. In fact, we shall in the sequel normally assume the latter, even if there is no effective method for doing that. This is the only main difference here. Otherwise our results remain valid, basically due to the completeness result established in HINTIKKA (1965a). (See HINTIKKA and TUOMELA (1970) for a more detailed discussion.)

ological status of our reduction proper. We shall discuss in more detail the present kind of theory construction and the gains accruing from the introduction of auxiliary concepts in Chapter VI.

From the theory of distributive normal forms it is known that the greater logical force of T as compared to S can be brought out by expanding T into deeper and deeper normal forms $T^{(d+e)}$. (See HINTIKKA (1965a and 1964).) The corresponding reducts (i. e. the sentences $r\,(T^{(d+e)})$) will then constitute a basis for the theory which consists of those consequences of T whose nonlogical vocabulary belongs to λ. The situation can therefore be illustrated by means of Diagram II.2. Here double arrows indicate logical equivalences and

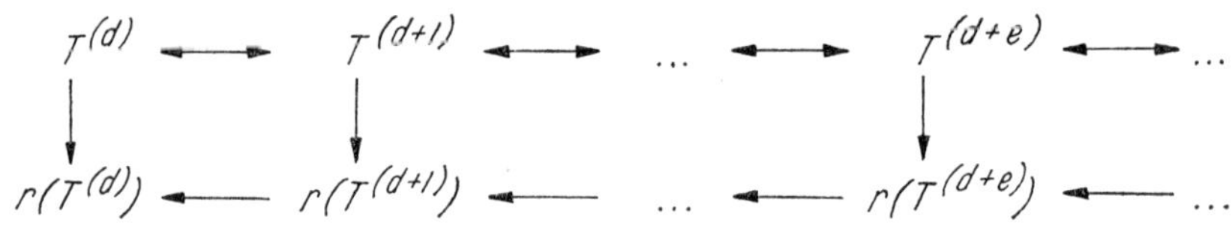

Diagram II.2

ordinary arrows (vertical and horizontal) indicate logical implications. Single arrows cannot, in general, be replaced by double ones. It is known that each logical consequence of T (that is, of $T^{(d)}$) whose extralogical vocabulary belongs to λ is implied by some member of the lower row in Diagram II.2.

In Diagram II.2. $r\,(T^{(d)})$ is, of course, assumed to be identical with $S^{(d)}\,(\lambda)$ and therefore equivalent with S, that statement we tried to "improve" by introducing the members of μ as auxiliary concepts. Notice also that T is not uniquely determined by S and μ; there usually are a great many statements (whose nonlogical vocabulary is $\lambda \cup \mu$) which can play the role of T with respect to a given S in Diagram II.2. Methodologically speaking this indicates that the construction of a richer theory is not a mechanical procedure but depends on the insight and the luck of the investigator. It also means that the theory axiomatized by $T^{(d)}\,(\lambda \cup \mu)$ is usually not a conservative (noncreative) extension of the theory axiomatized by $S^{(d)}\,(\lambda) = r\,(T^{(d)})$, although it is a conservative extension of the theory based upon the whole of the lower row.

Some further comments on our Diagram II.2. above are in order. The equivalences in the upper row are trivial. The reverse implications in the lower row of the diagram are also obvious. The implications between the two rows are due to the omission lemma of HINTIKKA (1965a). The fact that the members of the lower row axiomatize the set of all consequences of $T^{(d)}(\lambda \cup \mu)$ which contain members of λ only follows from the following *separation lemma* for first-order predicate logic with or without identity (HINTIKKA (1964), CRAIG (1960)):

Theorem II.4. Two first-order sentences $T = T^{(d_T)}(\lambda \cup \mu)$ and $S = S^{(d_S)}(\lambda \cup \eta)$ (with depths and extralogical constants as indicated and assuming that $\mu \cap \lambda = \mu \cap \eta = \lambda \cap \eta = \phi$) are incompatible if and only if for some d_0 their expansions at depth d_0 are separated with respect to λ.

We say that two sentences T and S are *separated* with respect to λ at depth d_0 if for each arbitrarily chosen pair $C_T(\lambda \cup \mu)$, $C_S(\lambda \cup \eta)$ of their constituents the reducts $r(C_T(\lambda \cup \mu))$ and $r(C_S(\lambda \cup \eta))$ are (not merely notationally) different at depth d_0. The monotonic basis of our subtheory which the lower row of Diagram II.2. gives us is one of the subbases investigated by CRAIG (1960) and discussed briefly earlier in this section.

Note that the deduction of a formula in the vocabulary λ depends in only one respect of the upper row — namely, the separation depth d_0. The expansion process in the upper row does not depend on the formula in the vocabulary λ to be deduced. This makes it more systematic than any other known method of building the subbasis (cf. CRAIG (1960)).

It may happen that the subtheory is finitely axiomatizable. Then (and only then) the implications of the lower row in Diagram II.2. will all turn into equivalences from some point on.

That the subtheory cannot be finitely axiomatized if the implications of the lower row do not eventually turn into equivalences follows from a familiar result (see for example ROBINSON (1953), p. 36) according to which the set of members of the lower row cannot then be equivalent to any single sentence. The members of the lower row form an axiom system for the subtheory; so this subtheory cannot be finitely axiomatized.

Chapter III

Model Theory and Ramsey-Elimination

1. Extendibility of Theories and Models

In this section we continue to discuss the role of auxiliary concepts in first-order languages, primarily from a semantical (model theoretic) point of view within the frame of theories which are extensions of some observational theories. In Section 2 of this chapter we will be especially interested in the relationships between Craigian and (proof theoretic and model theoretic) Ramseyan eliminability. Our emphasis will in this section be on logical rather than methodological and philosophical questions.

Let $\mathscr{L}'$ be a first-order language with identity. As extralogical symbols of $\mathscr{L}'$ $(=\mathscr{L}'(\lambda))$ we have predicates, and possibly functors, as well as individual constants. A language $\mathscr{L}$ $(=\mathscr{L}(\lambda \cup \mu))$ is called an *extension* of a language $\mathscr{L}'$ if the former includes the latter, and possibly contains some new extralogical constants. (The logical axioms and rules of inference are assumed to be the same in both $\mathscr{L}'$ and $\mathscr{L}$.) As in the previous sections we require of a *theory* T that it is a set of formulas of a language closed under deduction in that language. Denote by $\mathscr{L}(T)$ the language of T (i. e., a set of well-formed formulas plus logical axioms and rules of inference). In this section the logical axioms and rules of inference will be fixed, and we shall often use $\mathscr{L}(T)$ loosely to stand for the set of well-formed formulas of the language of T.

We now define a theory T to be an *extension* of a theory T' if and only if $T' \subseteq T$. T is a conservative extension of T' if and only if $T \cap \mathscr{L}(T') = T'$. We also see that if T is a non-conservative extension of T' then there may be formulas of $\mathscr{L}(T')$ which are theorems of T but not of T'. Thus by going from an observational theory T' to a theory T by introducing theoretical or μ-concepts we may have growth also with respect to observational or λ-consequences, which is not true for conservative extensions. (Notice that a theory T is always a conservative extension of its Craigian transcription T', since the latter is just the restriction of T to the language $\mathscr{L}(T')$.) We mean by growth in this connection merely an increase in the observational predictions of a theory, and thus a cumulation of scientific knowledge in the sense of evolution. Growth in the sense of revolution would mean abandonment of the old theory T in favor of a new theory. (However, in this book we shall mostly confine ourselves to the evolutionary aspects of growth, or intra-paradigm growth (Kuhn). Some of the cases treated below may, however, approximately fit some weak senses of revolutionary growth.)

Next we define the model theoretic notion of an expansion. Let $\mathscr{S}$ be a structure for $\mathscr{L}(T)$. By omitting from $\mathscr{S}$ the relations, functions, and distinguished individuals not having names in $\mathscr{L}(T')$ we obtain a structure $\mathscr{S}'$. The domains of $\mathscr{S}$ and $\mathscr{S}'$ are the same. $\mathscr{S}$ is now called an *expansion* of $\mathscr{S}'$, and $\mathscr{S}'$ a *restriction* of $\mathscr{S}$ (to $\mathscr{L}(T')$). We shall sometimes write $\mathscr{S}' = \mathscr{S}/\mathscr{L}(T')$.

We give below some simple theorems about the notions just defined. (For some further properties see for example SHOENFIELD (1967).)

Theorem III.1. Let $\mathscr{L}(T)$ be an extension of $\mathscr{L}(T')$. Then a theory T is an extension of a theory T' if and only if the restriction to $\mathscr{L}(T')$ of every model of T is a model of T'.

The proof goes as follows. Assume first that T is an extension of T'. Pick any model $\mathscr{M}$ of T. It is obvious that every closed formula of $\mathscr{L}(T')$ is true in $\mathscr{M}$ if it is true in its restriction $\mathscr{M}/\mathscr{L}(T')$, for the domains of these structures are the same. As a corollary to the closure theorem and the validity theorem (for these see SHOENFIELD (1967), pp. 32, 23, respectively) it follows that $\mathscr{M}/\mathscr{L}(T')$ must be a model of T'. Secondly, assume that for every model $\mathscr{M}$ of T, $\mathscr{M}/\mathscr{L}(T')$ is a model of T', and that F is some theorem of T'. Then F is true in every $\mathscr{M}/\mathscr{L}(T')$ and, hence, by what was said above, F must also be true in $\mathscr{M}$.

Theorem III.2. Let $\mathscr{L}(T)$ be an extension of $\mathscr{L}(T')$. Then, if T is an extension of T', and every model of T' has an expansion which is a model of T, then T is a conservative extension of T'.

The proof is very simple. We have to show that every theorem F of $T \cap \mathscr{L}(T')$ must be a theorem of T'. Assume the contrary. Then F is false in some model $\mathscr{M}'$ of T'. Hence $-F^c$ (the negation of the universal closure of F) is true in $\mathscr{M}'$. But then consider the corresponding expansion $\mathscr{M}$ of T. F^c is true in $\mathscr{M}$. But F is also true in $\mathscr{M}$ and hence F^c is true in $\mathscr{M}$. We have arrived at a contradiction.

But if T is a conservative extension of T' then it is not necessary for every model of T' to have an expansion which is a model of T. When finite models of T' are taken into consideration such an expansion can be found, but only if T contains no individual constant not in T'. We will return to a more detailed discussion of this in connection with Ramsey sentences.

But even if — given a model $\mathscr{M}'$ of T' — we cannot find an expansion of $\mathscr{M}'$ that satisfies T, there is nevertheless an elementary extension of $\mathscr{M}'$ which has an expansion satisfying T. (An elementary extension is defined as follows: A structure $\mathscr{S}$ for $\mathscr{L}$ is an *elementary extension* of a substructure $\mathscr{S}'$ of $\mathscr{S}$ if, whenever some elements of $\mathscr{S}'$ satisfy a formula of $\mathscr{L}$ in $\mathscr{S}'$ they also satisfy it in $\mathscr{S}$, and conversely.)

Theorem III.3. Let T be an extension of T'. Then T is a conservative extension of T' if and only if for every model $\mathscr{M}'$ of T', some expansion $\mathscr{N}$ of an elementary extension $\mathscr{N}'$ of $\mathscr{M}'$ is a model of T.

We start by proving the sufficiency. Suppose that T is a conservative extension of T'. Then $T' = T \cap \mathscr{L}(T')$. Let $\mathscr{M}'$ be an arbitrary model of T'. We have to show that there exists an elementary extension $\mathscr{N}'$ of $\mathscr{M}'$ such $\mathscr{N}'$ has an expansion $\mathscr{N}$ which is a model of T. Let $D(\mathscr{M}')$ be the diagram of $\mathscr{M}'$ with respect to $\mathscr{L}(T')$ (see SHOENFIELD (1967), p. 74). We claim that $T \cup D(\mathscr{M}')$ is consistent. For suppose the contrary. Then by the joint consistency theorem (SHOENFIELD (1967), p. 79), there is a closed formula F (in $\mathscr{L}(T) \cap \mathscr{L}(D(\mathscr{M}'))$) such that $T \vdash F$ and $D(\mathscr{M}') \vdash F$. Since $\mathscr{L}(D(\mathscr{M}')) \cap \mathscr{L}(T) = \mathscr{L}(T')$, and T is a conservative extension of T', we have $T' \vdash F$. But F is then true in $\mathscr{M}'$, and $D(\mathscr{M}') \vdash F$, which contradicts our assumption. Thus $T \cup D(\mathscr{M}')$ is consistent. Hence there is a model $\mathscr{N}^*$ for $T \cup D(\mathscr{M}')$. Let $\mathscr{N}$ be $\mathscr{N}^*$ restricted to $\mathscr{L}(T)$. Let $\mathscr{N}'$ be $\mathscr{N}$ restricted to the language $\mathscr{L}(T')$. Then T must be true in $\mathscr{N}$, and $\mathscr{N}$ is an expansion of $\mathscr{N}'$ by definition. It remains to show that $\mathscr{N}'$ is an elementary extension of $\mathscr{M}'$. Consider any F in $\mathscr{L}(T')$ such that F is true in $\mathscr{M}'$. Then $F \in D(\mathscr{M}')$ and F is true in $\mathscr{N}$ and in $\mathscr{N}'$. This concludes the proof of sufficiency.

Let us then prove necessity. Suppose that for every arbitrary model $\mathscr{M}'$ of T' there are structures $\mathscr{N}$ and $\mathscr{N}'$ such that $\mathscr{N}'$ is an elementary extension of $\mathscr{M}'$ and $\mathscr{N}$ is an expansion of $\mathscr{N}'$. Consider now any F in $\mathscr{L}(T')$ such that $T \vdash F$; we have to show that $T' \vdash F$. By the completeness theorem it suffices to show that F is true in every model $\mathscr{M}'$ of T'. Consider such a fixed $\mathscr{M}'$.

By assumption there are an elementary extension $\mathcal{N}'$ of $\mathcal{M}'$, and an expansion $\mathcal{N}$ of $\mathcal{N}'$ such that F is true in $\mathcal{N}$. Since F is in $\mathcal{L}$ (T'), F is true in $\mathcal{N}'$. We have to show that F is true in $\mathcal{M}'$. Suppose that on the contrary F is *not* true in $\mathcal{M}'$. Then $-F^c$ is true in $\mathcal{M}'$, and also in $\mathcal{N}'$, because $\mathcal{N}'$ is an elementary extension of $\mathcal{M}'$. But by our previous result F is true in $\mathcal{N}'$. Hence F^c is true in $\mathcal{N}'$. But this is a contradiction, and hence F^c must be true in $\mathcal{M}'$. Therefore F is true in $\mathcal{M}'$. Q. E. D.

Notice that since all theories are conservative extensions of their Craigian transcriptions, i. e. their maximal subtheories, this kind of model theoretic relationship obtains in all Craigian cases[1].

2. Ramsey-Eliminability of Theoretical Concepts

2.1. We turn now to a model theoretic investigation of Ramseyan eliminability. In an article published in 1931 Ramsey proposed a method by which theoretical concepts could in a certain sense be syntactically eliminated from a finitely axiomatized theory (see RAMSEY (1931)). For a theory axiomatized by a sentence $T(\lambda \cup \mu)$, containing the set of theoretical terms $\mu = \{P_1, \ldots, P_k\}$, consider the theory obtained from T by (second-order) existential generalization on all the theoretical terms, or, actually, variables corresponding to them: $(E\Pi_1)(E\Pi_2)\ldots(E\Pi_k)\,T(\Pi_1, \Pi_2, \ldots, \Pi_k)$. This is the so called *Ramsey sentence* T^R of the theory T; T^R has the important property that its observational consequences (consequences containing only members of λ as their extralogical constants) are exactly the same as those of T. Thus, using '$\vdash$' for provability in second-order logic, we have (cf. e. g. BOHNERT (1967)):

Theorem III.4. For every formula F solely in the vocabulary λ, $T \vdash F$ if and only if $T^R \vdash F$.

A proof is given below. For simplicity, we assume that $\mu = \{P\}$ and thus that $T^R = (E\Pi)\,T(\Pi)$.

A. If $T^R \vdash F$ then $T \vdash F$. This part is trivially true because T^R was obtained from T by existential generalization and because deduction is transitive.

B. The proof of the converse can be sketched as follows:

(1) $T \vdash F$	(premise)
(2) $\vdash T \supset F$	((1), deduction theorem)
(3) $\vdash (\Pi)(T(\Pi) \supset F)$	((2), universal generalization)

---

1 We say that T' is a *maximal subtheory* of T with respect to $\mathcal{L}$ (T') if and only if T is a conservative extension of T' with respect to $\mathcal{L}$ (T').

(4) $\vdash (\Pi)\,(T\,(\Pi) \supset F) \supset ((E\,\Pi)\;T\,(\Pi) \supset (E\,\Pi)\;F)$
(theorem of second-order logic)
(5) $\vdash (E\,\Pi)\;T\,(\Pi) \supset (E\,\Pi)\;F$ ((3), (4), *modus ponens*)
(6) $\vdash (E\,\Pi)\;T\,(\Pi) \supset F$ ((5), vacuous existential generalization)
(7) $(E\,\Pi)\;T\,(\Pi) \vdash F$ ((6), converse of deduction theorem)

Theorem III.4. can also be expressed by saying that the theory T and its Ramsey sentence T^R are *functionally equivalent* with respect to the observational language $\mathscr{L}\,(\lambda)$ (cf. Chapter II).

Another immediate consequence of Theorem III.4. is that if the Ramsey sentence of a theory has no nontautological observational or λ-consequences then the original theory does not have them either (and conversely). If one wants to equate having (deductive) λ-content with having (deductive) empirical import, then a theory has no empirical import if and only if its Ramsey sentence has no empirical import (cf. STEGMÜLLER (1970), p. 429, but also NIINILUOTO (1972a)).

A related methodologically interesting result basically relying on Theorem III.4. is the following, which we state as a theorem (cf. ROZEBOOM (1960), p. 372):

Theorem III.5. Two theories $T_1\,(\lambda \cup \mu_1)$ and $T_2\,(\lambda \cup \mu_2)$ with $\mu_1 \cap \mu_2 = \phi$ are logically incompatible if and only if they have logically incompatible consequences in $\mathscr{L}\,(\lambda)$.

The if-part of the proof is trivial. To prove the only if-part we first notice (relying on Theorem III.4.) that the two theories T_1 and T_2 have incompatible λ-consequences if and only if their Ramsey sentences are incompatible. Let us now show that the incompatibility (i. e. the inconsistency of the conjunction) of the theories T_1 and T_2 entails the incompatibility of their Ramsey sentences. For simplicity, assume that $\mu_1 = \{P_1\}$ and $\mu_2 = \{P_2\}$, and that Π_1 and Π_2 are the corresponding theoretical variables. Our initial assumption then becomes

$$\vdash -(T_1\,(\lambda \cup \{\Pi_1\})\;\&\;T_2\,(\lambda \cup \{\Pi_2\})).$$

Performing universal quantification over Π_1 and Π_2 and switching to existential quantifiers then gives

$$\vdash -(E\,\Pi_1)\,(E\,\Pi_2)\,(T_1\,(\lambda \cup \{\Pi_1\})\;\&\;T_2\,(\lambda \cup \{\Pi_2\})).$$

In general, as $\mu_1 \cap \mu_2 = \phi$, we can distribute the existential quantifiers corresponding to T_2 in front of T_2. Thus we get

$$\vdash -[(E\,\Pi_1)\;T_1\,(\lambda \cup \{\Pi_1\})\;\&\;(E\,\Pi_2)\;T_2\,(\lambda \cup \{\Pi_2\})],$$

from which the observational or λ-incompatibility of T_1 and T_2 follows immediately.

This theorem clearly shows the importance of observation in deciding between theoretically completely different but *observationally rivalling* theories. If, however, the theories have some common theoretical concepts, i. e. $\mu_1 \cap \mu_2 \neq \phi$, then the above theorem is no longer valid, but at least in principle the two theories can be compared on a theoretical level, too. In ROZEBOOM (1960) Theorem III.5. is proved also for the case $\mu_1 \cap \mu_2 \neq \phi$ by using a special semantic principle following from the Thesis of Semantic Empiricism (see Chapter V), which we do not accept.

One may of course also investigate the relationships between two theories which have different theoretical predicates but the *same observational consequences* (cf. GLYMOUR (1971)). Glymour gives a structural necessary condition of theory synonymy: the theories should have a *common intended model*. However, it seems to us that a sufficient condition of synonymy can be obtained by means of intensional semantic rules of the kind discussed in Chapter V, but not by model theoretic methods.

Before discussing Ramsey elimination in more detail let us define a related counterpart notion for further reference. This is the notion of the Carnap sentence of a theory originally introduced to explicate the analytic or conventional component of a theory T (cf. CARNAP (1966)). The *Carnap sentence* T^C of a theory is defined as

$$T^C =_{df} T^R \supset T.$$

We easily see that T^C has the following properties (see WINNIE (1971) for proof):

Theorem III.6. (a) $\vdash T^C \equiv (T^R \equiv T)$

(b) $\vdash T \equiv (T^R \,\&\, T^C)$

(c) $\vdash T \supset T^C$

(d) there is no nontautological formula F in $\mathscr{L}(\lambda)$ such that $T^C \vdash F$.

Property (a) then says that if and only if the truth of the Carnap sentence T^C can be assumed, the theory T and its Ramsey sentence T^R are equivalent. In other words, if, whenever it is the case that always when some kind of theoretical entities are assumed to exist in T^R then the theoretical entities spoken about in T are indeed such entities, then T and T^R are equal in their (extensional) content, and only then can they be said to have equal factual content. Property (b) says that the conjunction of the Ramsey sentence and the Carnap sentence of a theory amounts to the theory itself. Property (c) just reminds us of the fact that a theory entails its Carnap sentence (as well as it entails its Ramsey sentence). Finally, property (d) guarantees that the Carnap sentence has no observational content.

Let us now proceed to discuss Ramsey-eliminability. The set of observational models (i. e. models with respect to $\mathscr{L}$ (λ)) of a Ramsey sentence T^R is clearly the set of those models of the Craigian transcription of T that can be expanded to models of T. On the basis of this we can define the notion of the Ramsey-eliminability of a theoretical concept P of T. (We assume again the presence of only one theoretical concept. The generalization to a greater number is obvious.) We consider a theory T with $\lambda = \{O_1, O_2, \ldots, O_m\}$ as its set of observational concepts, and $\mu = \{P\}$ as its theoretical (or more generally, auxiliary) concept. We define a theoretical concept (extralogical constant) $P \in \mu$ of a theory T to be *semantically* (or *model theoretically*) *Ramsey-eliminable* if and only if there is a recursively axiomatizable subtheory T' (λ) of T ($\lambda \cup \mu$) such that all models $\mathscr{M}' = \langle \mathrm{D}, \mathrm{O}_1, \ldots, \mathrm{O}_m \rangle$ of T' (λ) have an expansion $\mathscr{M} = \langle \mathrm{D}, \mathrm{O}_1, \ldots \mathrm{O}_m, \mathrm{P} \rangle$ such that $\mathscr{M}$ is a model of T[2].

In other words, it is required in the above definiens that there is a subtheory T' (λ) of T ($\lambda \cup \mu$) which satisfies the following principle of *semantical noncreativity*:

T is *semantically noncreative* with respect to T' if and only if for every model $\mathscr{M}'$ of T' there is an expansion $\mathscr{M}$ of $\mathscr{M}'$ such that $\mathscr{M}$ is a model of T.

Other more restricted notions of semantical eliminability are obtained by requiring semantical noncreativity not with respect to the set of all models of T' but with respect to some special subclass of its models, for instance the set of models of T' with a specified domain D, or a set of standard or intended models of T' (and, possibly, of T).

Notice that if the theory T is semantically noncreative with respect to T' then by Theorem III.2. T is a conservative extension of T'. But does the converse of this hold? Can we always find such a subtheory T' of T which will guarantee semantical Ramsey-eliminability? The answer is no. Consider the following example of Scott, discussed in SNEED (1971), Chapter 3, p. 54. Let T ($\{O\} \cup \{P\}$) be a theory where P is a two-place theoretical (or auxiliary) predicate, and O a two-

2 We use Roman letters for model theoretic entities here and below.

place observational (or nonauxiliary) predicate. The axioms of $T(\{O\} \cup \{P\})$ are:

(i) $(x)(y)(Pxy \supset (Ez)(Oxz) \,\&\, (Ez)(Oyz))$
(ii) $(x)((Ez)(Oxz) \supset (Ey)(Pxy \,\&\, (w)(Pxw \supset w = y)))$
(iii) $(x)((Ez)(Oxz) \supset (Ey)(Pyx \,\&\, (w)(Pwx \supset w = y)))$
(iv) $(x)(y)(Oxy \,\&\, Oyz \supset Oxz)$.

The sentences of $T(\{P\} \cup \{O\})$ are true only in models $\langle D, P, O\rangle$ $(O, P \subseteq D \times D)$ in which there is one-one correspondence between individuals which stand in the first place in the O-relation and those which do not. It can be shown that there is no (finite or infinite) set T of sentences, containing only the predicate O and identity, which is true in exactly those models $\langle D, O\rangle$ where such a correspondence exists.

Thus P is not semantically Ramsey-eliminable in the theory $T(\{O\} \cup \{P\})$. It does some work in ruling out some observational states of affairs that are not eliminated by sentences of our observation language. This gives an explication to the vague notion of "observational richness" which the use of theoretical concepts in a theory may give us. (SNEED (1971) has in effect pointed out this.) This point is better appreciated if we recall Craig's elimination result in first-order logic. For, according to this result, a kind of syntactical Ramsey-eliminability is always possible. By this we mean the following. According to Theorem II.3. a recursively axiomatized maximal observational theory T' (Craigian transcription) can be found for every "richer" first-order theory T (such that T is syntactically noncreative with respect to T'). The conclusion of this theorem holds also when we replace the theory T in the antecedent by its Ramsey sentence T^R. Hence we can always eliminate our theoretical concepts syntactically but not necessarily semantically in a first-order language. In other words, there are theories whose maximal subtheories do not capture exactly the models of their Ramsey sentences. The class of observational models of T^R is in such a case a proper subclass of the class of models of a maximal observational subtheory of T.

However, in the case of finite models we always have semantical Ramsey-eliminability in a first-order language with identity (see CRAIG and VAUGHT (1958), p. 300f.):

Theorem III.7. Let T be a conservative extension of T', such that $\mathcal{L}(T')$ and $\mathcal{L}(T)$ differ only in their predicate symbols. Then every finite model of T' has an expansion which is a model of T.

In his famous paper 'Theories' Ramsey was concerned with finitary systems only and he seemed to believe that one "can easily eliminate the functions of the secondary system [our T] and so say in the primary system [our T'] all that the theory gives us" (RAMSEY (1931), p. 219). It seems to us that the model theoretic content of Ramsey's claim could be given exactly in the form of the above theorem (with the addition that T' has only finite models). It was unfortunate that Ramsey did not consider theories with infinite models as then he might have seen the possibility of nonexpandable models.

Let us now briefly consider what methodological interest the preceding theorems and the notion of semantical Ramsey-eliminability have in testing a theory T against a body of data or in employing T to explain these data. We assume that the (finitary) results of an experiment have been constituted so as to form a structure $\mathscr{S}_O$ such that $\mathscr{S}_O$ is a possible realization of the observational language (in the vocabulary λ). Now $\mathscr{S}_O$ may or may not be found to be a model of a (maximal) observational subtheory T' of T. Assume that it is (perhaps apart from some statistically nonsignificant deviations). Then, as $\mathscr{S}_O$ is a finite model it can (according to Theorem III.7.) be expanded into a model $\mathscr{S}$ of T without adding elements to the domain. From the present viewpoint it thus seems that theories with theoretical terms would not be indispensable in the case of finitary systems (finite models), which result would hardly be a great surprise to anybody.

Next suppose that our observational structure $\mathscr{S}_O$ is not a model of T' (this is the usual case). Then it may or may not have an extension which is a model of T'. Here we have a situation where, for logical reasons, new observations have to be made in order to test the theory T (and T') properly. (There may also be other, e. g. statistical reasons which demand the continuation of the experimentation, but we shall not discuss them here.) Now, if T' can have finite models, it may in some cases be possible to decide, by gathering (finitely many) new observations, whether or not $\mathscr{S}_O$ has an extension $\mathscr{S}'$ which is a model of T'. In the affirmative case we know on the basis of Theorem III.7. that $\mathscr{S}'$ has an expansion $\mathscr{S}$ which is a model of T. But in many scientific cases the observational theory T' has no finite models. (For instance, this is the case when T' presupposes the theory of real numbers and real valued functions in an essential way.) Then one has to make an inductive leap in order to infer whether $\mathscr{S}_O$

confirms T' (i. e. whether $\mathscr{S}_O$ has an extension $\mathscr{S}'$ which is — apart from experimental errors and the like — a model of T').

Now, consider such a model $\mathscr{S}'$ of T'. Theorem III.3. tells us that, provided T is a conservative extension of T', we can always find an elementary extension, say $\mathscr{S}''$, of $\mathscr{S}'$ such that $\mathscr{S}''$ can be expanded into a model of the richer theory T. On the one hand, an $\mathscr{S}'$ cannot always be expanded into a model of T (without adding new elements into the domain of $\mathscr{S}'$). Such cases are exactly the cases where the theoretical terms of T are not semantically Ramsey-eliminable. On the other hand, we know on the basis of Theorem III.3. and the fact that a theory implies its Ramsey sentence that even in such cases every model of T' is an elementary submodel of some first-order observational model of T^R.

The notion of semantical Ramsey-eliminability may be further clarified by the following interpretive remarks. Assume that we, according to Ramsey's suggestion, employ T^R to make the empirical claims of the theory T. (All the members of λ now have to be observational predicates.) On the basis of the above results one might now say that in the case of finite models theoretical concepts do not do any work that is directly related to the observable world. But they may do some real work in the case of infinite models. However, this is work that we cannot express in a first-order language. It is also hard to find out if this work is in some sense observable. That is, the theoretical concepts rule out some of the infinite models of the theory, but we do not know how this is reflected in our application which is a finite structure of observations. We do not have any general results which would tell what the finite parts (corresponding to our observations) of the infinite models ruled out by theoretical concepts would look like.

Nevertheless, it may be worth while to emphasize one philosophical point here. $\mathscr{L}(T)$ is here and elsewhere assumed to be an *interpreted* scientific language[3]. Thus we are dealing with intensional descriptions of objects and properties which determine the intended interpretations (models) of our theory T. The class of objects satisfying them is normally indefinitely large, usually of an infinite cardinality. Hence, infinite models can be considered more important than the applications (experiments) for the theory by which the theory is

---

3 We shall postpone our detailed comments on the interpretation of a scientific language till Chapter V.

tested but which are only finite restrictions of its intended interpretations. This can thus be regarded as an argument for the importance of using theoretical concepts which are not semantically Ramsey-eliminable[4].

It goes without saying that if a theoretical concept is explicitly definable then it is Ramsey-eliminable (in our semantical sense). But the converse, of course, is false. When a concept is Ramsey-eliminable it is perfectly possible that the interpretations of the observational concepts (members of λ) do not uniquely fix the interpretation of the theoretical concept and so, by Beth's theorem on definability, the latter is not explicitly definable in terms of the former. Moreover, the observational concepts may fix the interpretation of the theoretical concept uniquely in some models of T', while only restricting its values in a milder manner in some other models (see the next chapter for a study of these questions).

SNEED (1971) has criticized the Ramsey view sketched above by claiming that it does not do justice to e. g. scientific predictions. The procedure of "filling in" of values of theoretical terms in the expanded models — one set of values for each application — leaves out something important. Namely, individuals have many kinds of lasting properties which stay invariant from one application of the theory to another. Now, in so far as there occur some individuals in the domains of different applications, one can obviously make predictions over these applications concerning the durable properties of the individuals. One has to account for this kind of interconnection between the different applications (and hence models) of a theory. Sneed therefore introduces special constraints on models to take care of this (see SNEED (1971), Chapter IV).

But obviously there is another way out. For one can simply try to state in the language of the theory all that is needed concerning the preservation of properties, and there will automatically be the required interconnection between the different models of a theory. We will not here, however, investigate to what extent this programme can be carried out.

---

4 SIMON and GROEN (1972) argue that the theoretical concepts of (model theoretically) *finitely* and *irrevocably* testable (refutable) theories are always semantically Ramsey-eliminable. Even if some physical theories such as classical celestial mechanics may be reconstructed to satisfy these two operationalistic requirements of Simon and Groen, taken as general methodological maxims they seem to us definitely too strict.

Summing up some of the above remarks, we have been discussing the following two questions (assuming the truth of T): (1) how do theoretical concepts restrict what we can observe; and, conversely, (2) to what extent do the interpretations of the observational concepts fix the interpretations of the theoretical concepts? In answer to the first question we presented a few theorems (especially Theorem III.3.) together with some logical and methodological comments. Furthermore, it was noticed that theoretical concepts which are not Ramsey-eliminable may do some work in ruling out observable states of affairs permitted by the observational theory T. In the next chapter we will try to give a partial answer to question (2).

2.2. Recently a lively discussion has been going on about Ramsey sentences (see e. g. SCHEFFLER (1963) and (1968), HEMPEL (1965), BOHNERT (1967) and (1968), MAXWELL (1963) and (1970), STEGMÜLLER (1970)). We shall next make some comments on this discussion from the point of view of the eliminability of theoretical concepts.

The basic property of the Ramsey sentence T^R of a theory axiomatized by a sentence T is of course the one given by Theorem III.4. According to it, T^R preserves the deductive systematization of T concerning λ-statements. (We shall discuss the issue with respect to inductive systematization until Chapter VIII.) Therefore, and because T^R contains only members of λ among its extralogical constants, thesis (4) of the original version of the theoretician's dilemma can seemingly be established by means of the Ramsey sentence method at least in the case of deductive systematization. In fact, by employing the Ramsey method for theories whose theoretical terms are not semantically Ramsey-eliminable we even get some additional deductive systematization from a model theoretic point of view, as we just saw above. Thus, if we substitute 'Ramseyan' for 'Craigian' in the theses (4′) and (5″) to get (4″) and (5‴) we may accept the validity of the theoretician's dilemma in the fairly restricted form ⟨(1), (2′), (3′), (4″), (5‴), (6′)⟩ in the case of deductive systematization (cf. Chapter II).

As an elimination method the Ramsification technique has some advantages over Craig's general and first-order methods. First, it obviously preserves the structure of the original theory. (Thus all the structural relations — structural "meanings" — between theoretical variables and observable or λ-terms are the same as between the counterparts in the original theory.) Therefore, and in spite of being a second-order sentence, the Ramsey sentence also can be regarded as preserving the deductive coherence, integrity, perspicuity, and manageability of the original theory. We found earlier that in the general Craigian programme, and to a considerably less extent in the first-order Craigian replacement, the transcribing theory lacked these features of the original theory. It can also be argued that the Ramsey sentence preserves the heuristic fertility and suggestiveness of the original theory to a much greater extent than its Craigian counterpart.

Let us mention that it has recently been argued that Ramsey sentences provide a method of developing and creating theories and not only a method for the elimination of theoretical terms (BOHNERT (1967) and (1968) and MAXWELL (1970)). Instead of using thc full Ramsey sentences one should operate with the clauses occurring within the scope of the initial string of existential quantifiers. The principal reason for this proposal is of course that the two statements $(E\,\Pi)\,(T_1\,(\Pi)\ \&\ T_2\,(\Pi))$ and $(E\,\Pi)\ T_1\,(\Pi)\ \&\ (E\,\Pi)\ T_2\,(\Pi)$ are not logically equivalent; hence all additions to the original Ramsey sentence have to be made in the form of clauses falling under the scope of the initial existential quantifiers (cf. RAMSEY (1931), p. 237). The variables of the clauses are then used in fixed roles throughout the theorizing (as the mathematician's variables ε and δ of differential and integral calculus). Now one can systematize observational statements by employing these theoretical variables. Or, to put it in another and stronger way, one can thus even create a theory of *indirect* and *indefinite* descriptions. For one speaks about the theoreticals indirectly by means of observational statements and there is no commitment to the identity or number, etc., of the entities accounting for observational states of affairs. At least for explorative and newly born sciences this may seem a plausible programme of theorizing to begin with.

Still there are well-known difficulties with this kind of theorizing, at least when considered from the point of view of eliminating theoretical terms. These difficulties can be divided into two groups.

First, Ramsification swells the ontology of the original theory. For the existential quantifiers running over predicates commit the Ramsificationist at least to the existence of (new) classes, if not properties, under any ordinary account of semantics (such as ours above). The important consequence of this for elimination is that there is no guarantee that the new ontological entities are observable (cf. HEMPEL (1965), MAXWELL (1963)). Thus, even if the Ramsey sentence does not contain any theoretical (or nonobservational) expressions (predicates) and even if observational properties might be predicated to nonobservable entities, there will most likely be a growth of ontology to include (more) theoretical entities. Thus we may say that Ramsification is a method of theorizing for a realist rather than for an instrumentalist.

Another criticism related to the substitution-values of the predicate variables is this. It has frequently been remarked (see e. g. ACHINSTEIN (1968), p. 84, SCHEFFLER (1963), p. 218 ff.) that the Ramsey sentence of a theory may be tautological, even if the original theory is not and even if the substitution of empty predicates as values of variables is excluded. However, as has been pointed out by HINTIKKA and NIINILUOTO (1973), it has been tacitly assumed in these remarks that second-order variables can take all possible values (the standard interpretation of second-order logic), whereas within the (logically) more satisfactory nonstandard interpretation only a subset of all possible interpretations are allowed. Therefore, the charge of the triviality of the Ramsey sentence cannot really be evaluated before the critics specify what exactly they (model theoretically) mean by their notion of (second-order) tautology.

Next, several authors have pointed out the difficulties involved in adjoining new statements (such as new singular theoretical statements or new correspondence rules) to the original Ramsey sentence of a theory. As we noticed above, the way to solve these difficulties is to resort to communication by Ramsey clause (BOHNERT (1967)). But as was indicated, and as Bohnert has admitted, this presupposes, for instance, that the theoretical variables are immune to substitution by other variables. Thus they are treated as *quasi-constants* [5]. We can therefore conclude that the better Ramsification can be adjusted to serve as a method of theorizing, the worse it fares as a method of elimination. It thus seems justified to accept Hempel's conclusion, according to which Ramsey sentence qualifies as a method of elimination only, or at most, in letter but not in spirit.

Let us still emphasize that Ramsification nevertheless seems to give an interesting method of theorizing, at least for some descriptive

5 Perhaps this could be put as strongly as that we in effect assume the truth of the Carnap sentence of the theory, which is known to make the Ramsey sentence of the theory equivalent with the theory (see Theorem III.6. above).

sciences, as was indicated. Furthermore, contrary to Craigian elimination, it can be employed to throw light on the questions of the empirical "meaning" and significance of theoretical statements, even if the theoretical terms must in this approach be assumed to have no meaning *per se*. These topics will not, however, be discussed in this book (see STEGMÜLLER (1970), MAXWELL (1970), and CARNAP (1966)).

Chapter IV

Definitions and Theoretical Concepts

1. Determinate and Partially Determinate Definitions

1.1. In the methodology and philosophy of science questions of definability of concepts have traditionally occupied a central place. Furthermore, the strict positivist dogma for defining (or reducing) one's theoretical concepts in terms of observational terms and the recent advances in modern logic have given strong additional emphasis to the theory of definability.

Until recently there were few textbooks in logic and hardly any in the philosophy of science where recent results in the logical theory of definitions were discussed. As to the methodology and philosophy of science, the books by PRZELECKI (1969) and ESSLER (1970) have partly filled this gap. In this chapter we shall discuss the logic of definition, partly by relying on the theory of distributive normal forms. Our main purpose is to introduce some notions and results most of which are well-known to logicians but which seem to be almost unknown to philosophers and methodologists of science.

Let us specify our setup in some detail before going into technicalities. In most works on the logic of definition the focus has been on the study of sentences introducing (semantically) new concepts into one's theory. (Sometimes these sentences have been called meaning postulates.) Such sentences are required to satisfy certain criteria before qualifying as (completely or partially) defining sentences. For instance, the well-known criteria of eliminability and noncreativity are such proposed criteria.

In this chapter, however, our starting point is slightly different. We assume that we are given a theory axiomatized by a (first-order) statement $T(\lambda \cup \mu)$. Thus all the predicates of $\lambda \cup \mu$ are our primitive extralogical concepts[1]. What we want to do is to investigate how and to what degree the primitive concepts are (extensionally) interwoven or interconnected due to the logical form of the statements of the theory $T(\lambda \cup \mu)$. Accordingly, we should really speak of a *theory of logical interwovenness* rather than a logical theory of definability. Our main interest will be how the predicates of μ are connected to the set λ within $T(\lambda \cup \mu)$. Thus the definitions we shall be concerned with primarily link linguistic expressions (definienda) with other linguistic expressions (definientia). As these linguistic expressions normally stand for some concepts (constructs) we also have a connection between concepts. (We shall not in this chapter discuss nonverbal definitions such as so called ostensive definitions which link linguistic expressions with factual items.)

Traditionally definitions have mostly been considered statements of *cointensitivity* or *synonymity* which are true by convention or true due to the meanings of words. Within our theory of interwovenness no such assumption is made. We shall be concerned only with the structural extensional connections between concepts as determined by a scientific theory $T(\lambda \cup \mu)$. (Thus no assumptions concerning the analyticity or syntheticity of the theorems of $T(\lambda \cup \mu)$ are needed here.)

We shall start by discussing strong forms definition such as explicit, piecewise, relative, conditional, and partial definitions. These types of definitions may be called *determinate* (explicit and piecewise definitions) or *partially determinate* (relative, conditional, and partial definitions) in the sense that the definientia either always or under some specified conditions fix the interpretation of the definienda. In Section 2. we shall consider cases of *indeterminate* definability in which there is no such guarantee of fixing the interpretations of the members of μ in terms of those of λ. We shall below consider the definability (in first-order predicate logic) of monadic predicates only, but our results are immediately generalizable to any kind of predicates. Among the members of λ all kinds of predicates are allowed.

Not unexpectedly the basic logical result upon which a great deal of our logical discussion hinges is Craig's interpolation theorem and its application to the theory of distributive normal forms. We shall

1 As functors and individual constants can be defined in terms of predicates we do not explicitly consider their definability here (cf. SUPPES (1957) and ESSLER (1970)).

usually sketch proofs of our theorems only when they are not available in the literature.

We start by studying how *explicit definability* becomes manifested within distributive normal forms (i. e., within the general framework described in Section II.3.). (Cf. HINTIKKA and TUOMELA (1970).) For simplicity, we deal with the case of just one new concept, which is assumed to be a monadic predicate P. Consider a constituent $C_i^{(d+e)}$ occurring somewhere in the upper row of Diagram II.2. of Section II.3., that is in one of the normal forms $T^{(d+e)}(\lambda \cup \mu) = T^{(d+e)}(\lambda \cup \{P\})$. If all the occurrences of P at depths greater than 1 are omitted, the result (implied, of course, by $C_i^{(d+e)}$) will be of the following form:

$$(4.1)\quad \bigwedge_{m \in I_i} (Ex)(P(x) \,\&\, Ct_m^{(d+e-1)}(x)) \,\&\, \bigwedge_{n \in I_i'} (Ex)(-P(x) \,\&\, Ct_n^{(d+e-1)}(x)) \,\&\, (x)\Big(\bigvee_{m \in I_i} (P(x) \,\&\, Ct_m^{(d+e-1)}(x)) \vee \bigvee_{n \in I_i'} (-P(x) \,\&\, Ct_n^{(d+e-1)}(x))\Big).$$

Here all the attributive constituents contain only members of λ among their extralogical constants. $\bigwedge$ and $\bigvee$ are used for conjunction and disjunction, respectively. I_i is the index set of those attributive constituents which are solely in λ but which are connected with P in (4.1), and I_i' is the index set of attributive constituents connected with $-P$. We shall call the former kind of attributive constituents P-positive and those of the latter kind P-negative. Let us define

$$\alpha_i = \{Ct_{m1}, Ct_{m2}, \ldots\}, \quad m \in I_i;$$
$$\beta_i = \{Ct_{n1}, Ct_{n2}, \ldots\}, \quad n \in I_i'.$$

The crucial uncertainty factor is then the intersection

$$(4.2)\quad \alpha_i \cap \beta_i = \{Ct_{m1}, Ct_{m2}, \ldots\} \cap \{Ct_{n1}, Ct_{n2}, \ldots\} = \gamma_i.$$

The sets α_i and β_i are said to be *separated* if $\gamma_i = \phi$. In that case $C_i^{(d+e)}$ implies an *explicit definition* of P in terms of λ. In other words, $C_i^{(d+e)}$ implies a sentence of the form

$$(4.3)\quad (x)(P(x) \equiv \bigvee_j Ct_j^{(d+e-1)}(x)).$$

Here j may run over I_i and, in fact, it may go over any attributive constituents not in β_i. (Below we shall in general be concerned with the case $j \in I_i$ only.)

Now $C_i^{(d+e)}$ is normally much stronger than our richer theory $T^{(d)}(\lambda \cup \mu) = T^{(d)}(\lambda \cup \{P\})$ and hence the definability of P on the basis of the former does not imply definability on the basis of the latter. But assuming that $T^{(d)}$ does imply an explicit definition of P in terms of the members of λ, we can see that a situation of the kind we just considered will occur in *all* the constituents of some sufficiently deep $T^{(d+e)}$.

In order to see this, suppose that there is an explicit definition v of P of depth $d+e$. (If a definition of a depth lower than d exists, then so does one of depth d, and we can hence assume that $e \geq 0$). Then we can form the conjunction v & $T^{(d+e)}$ which is equivalent to a disjunction of conjunctions of the form

$$(4.4) \quad C_i^{(d+e)} \;\&\; (x)\,(P(x) \equiv \bigvee_j Ct_j^{(d+e-1)}(x)),$$

where $C_i^{(d+e)}$ is as before. Notice that $v = (x)\,(Px \equiv \bigvee_j Ct_j^{(d+e-1)}(x))$ is, of course, independent of i. By way of abbreviation, let us denote by δ_i the set of attributive constituents occurring in the definiens of v.

Since $C_i^{(d+e)}$ implies (4.1), it is easily seen that (4.4) is inconsistent unless, for each i,

$$(4.5) \quad \text{(a)}\ \delta_i \supseteq \alpha_i \text{ and}$$
$$\text{(b)}\ \delta_i \cap \beta_i = \phi.$$

But this implies that γ_i is empty for each i, as we required. (In other words, δ_i separates α_i and β_i.) For were this not the case with a disjunct, it would be eliminated when (4.4) is converted into its distributive normal forms, and hence this normal form will consist solely of constituents which do make γ_i empty. But since v (= the second conjunct of (4.4)) is implied by $T^{(d)}$ at depth $d+e$, the distributive normal form of their conjunction must be identical with $T^{(d+e)}$, assuming that all inconsistent constituents are eliminated.

Moreover, for explicit definition in $T^{(d+e)}$ we must have not only $\alpha_i \cap \beta_i = \phi$ for each i, but a *uniform* separation of α_i and β_i for all i in the sense that (4.5) holds for any i and a *constant* set δ ($\delta = \delta_i$ for each i).

Thus the definability of P will eventually be betrayed by the fact that all the consistent constituents of $T^{(d+e)}$ satisfy (4.5), and thereby explicitly show the definability of P. If only trivially inconsistent constituents are assumed to be eliminated in the disjunctions $T^{(d+e)}$, the same statement will hold, although the definability will usually manifest itself in this way much later.

Thus the standard procedure of converting a sentence into its normal form, increasing its depth and eliminating trivially inconsistent constituents is seen to have one more important systematic use (in principle). All relations of explicit definability are eventually brought into the open by this procedure. (We have proved this only for monadic predicates so far, but the generalization to other kinds of concepts is straightforward.)

One of the basic properties of explicit definability is given by the well-known Beth's theorem on definability, according to which model theoretic and proof theoretic (explicit) definability coincide. Beth's theorem in effect states that Padoa's criterion for proving the logical independence of concepts is not only sufficient but also necessary.

We use here the following formulation of model theoretic definability. Consider again a theory $T = T(\lambda \cup \mu)$ (with $\mu = \{P\}$) in a first-order language, and a structure $\mathscr{M}$ with domain D for $\mathscr{L}(\lambda)$. Then we define the set

$$K_T(\mathscr{M}) = \{\mathrm{P} \subseteq \mathrm{D} \mid \langle \mathscr{M}, \mathrm{P} \rangle \models T\}.$$

For convenience, we write here $\langle \mathscr{M}, \mathrm{P} \rangle$ for a possible model of $\mathscr{L}(\lambda \cup \{P\})$. In other words, the set $K_T(\mathscr{M})$ is the set of all $\mathrm{P} \subseteq \mathrm{D}$ which make the structure $\langle \mathscr{M}, \mathrm{P} \rangle$ a model for the theory $T(\lambda \cup \{P\})$. (We use Roman letters for model theoretic entities (e. g. sets).) We say that P is model theoretically definable in terms of λ in $T(\lambda \cup \{P\})$ exactly when the cardinality of this set of P's is at most one for every such $\mathscr{M}$, viz. if and only if $|K_T(\mathscr{M})| \leqq 1$ for all such $\mathscr{M}$. Now we can state Beth's theorem as follows (cf. KUEKER (1970), p. 428):

Theorem IV.1. For every $T(\lambda \cup \mu)$ the following conditions are equivalent:

(i) For every $\mathscr{M}$, $|K_T(\mathscr{M})| \leqq 1$;

(ii) there is a formula $G(x)$ of $\mathscr{L}(\lambda)$ such that

$$T \vdash (x)\,(P(x) \equiv G(x)).$$

Coming back to distributive normal forms, it may happen that each consistent $C_i^{(d+e)}$ of $T^{(d+e)}(\lambda \cup \mu) = T^{(d+e)}(\lambda \cup \{P\})$ satisfies only a part of the requirement (4.5) which guarantees explicit definability, in that we have $\alpha_i \cap \beta_i = \phi$ for each i, but no uniform separation which would satisfy (4.5) for some constant set δ of relevant attributive constituents. If this happens for some e, we shall say that P is *piecewise definable* in terms of λ at depth $d+e$ on the basis of $T^{(d)}(\lambda \cup \{P\})$. (Explicit definability can thus be considered a special case of piecewise definability.) If P is piecewise definable at some depth (on the basis of $T^{(d+e)}$) we shall simply say that it is piecewise definable (on this basis). Then each constituent $C_i^{(d+e)}$ of $T^{(d+e)}$ implies an explicit definition of form (4.3) of P in terms of λ. The definiens is here, of course, of depth $d+e-1$. However, unless (4.5) is satisfied for a constant δ, P is not explicitly definable in terms of λ.

Since $T^{(d+e)}$ is equivalent to the disjunction of the constituents $C_i^{(d+e)}$, it implies in these circumstances a disjunction of different explicit definitions. However, unless we have (4.5), there is no way of "reconciling" or "putting together" these definitions.

By an obvious extension of the argument we used above concerning explicit definability, it can conversely be shown that whenever $T^{(d)}$ implies a finite disjunction of different definitions of form (4.3), P is piecewise definable in terms of the members of λ on the basis of $T^{(d)}$. Here, then, we have a criterion of piecewise definability which is independent of distributive normal forms. Let us state it as a theorem:

Theorem IV.2. A predicate $P \in \mu$ is piecewise definable in terms of λ and on the basis of $T(\lambda \cup \mu)$ if and only if $T(\lambda \cup \mu)$ implies a finite disjunction of explicit definitions of P.

If this disjunction essentially contains only one disjunct, we then have a case of explicit definability on the basis of T. Other criteria are not hard to come by. If P is piecewise definable in terms of λ on the basis of $T^{(d)}$ at depth $d+e$, each model $\mathcal{N}$ of $T^{(d)}$ satisfies exactly one of the $C_i^{(d+e)}$. Hence, the corresponding explicit definition (4.3) is true in $\mathcal{N}$, which means that P is in the usual sense of the word *definable in* $\mathcal{N}$ in terms of the members of λ.

Conversely, assume that P is definable in terms of λ in each model $\mathcal{N}$ of $T^{(d)}$. Let the complete theory compatible with $T^{(d)}$ which holds in $\mathcal{N}$ be defined by the sequence of increasingly stronger constituents

$$C_i^{(d+f)}(\lambda \cup \{P\}), \qquad (f=0,1,2,\ldots).$$

(Cf. our Diagram II.1.)

If the explicit definition which holds in $\mathcal{N}$ is of depth $d+e$, $C_i^{(d+e)}(\lambda \cup \{P\})$ must satisfy $\alpha_i \cap \beta_i = \phi$. By letting the model vary (to go through all the models of $T^{(d)}$), and considering at one time each such complete theory determined by each such model $\mathcal{N}$, we find that this situation arises for every compatible sequence of constituents (of the above kind) also compatible with $T^{(d)}$. By the tree theorem (König's lemma), *all* of them will do this at some depth $d+e$. At this depth, P is thus piecewise definable in terms of λ in the theory $T^{(d)}(\lambda \cup \{P\})$[2]. Stated as a theorem this becomes:

Theorem IV.3. A predicate $P \in \mu$ is piecewise definable in terms of λ on the basis of a theory $T(\lambda \cup \mu)$ if and only if P is explicitly definable in every model of $T(\lambda \cup \mu)$.

Thus we have obtained a clear-cut syntactical criterion for a nonlogical predicate to be definable in each model of a first-order theory T in terms of (say) λ. A necessary and sufficient condition for this is that it be piecewise definable in terms of λ, given T.

Theorem IV.3. can also be stated in another and perhaps more illuminating way used in SVENONIUS (1959) and KUEKER (1970). Analogously with our notion of model theoretic definability, we define the set

$$K(\mathcal{M}, P) = \{\mathrm{P}' \subseteq \mathrm{D} \mid \langle \mathcal{M}, \mathrm{P} \rangle \cong \langle \mathcal{M}, \mathrm{P}' \rangle\},$$

where $\cong$ means isomorphism. Thus $\mathrm{P}' \in K(\mathcal{M}, P)$ exactly when there is an automorphism of $\mathcal{M}$ mapping P onto P′. It is important to notice that P is always an element of $K(\mathcal{M}, P)$ but that $K_T(\mathcal{M})$ may be empty. When $\langle \mathcal{M}, \mathrm{P} \rangle$ is a model of $T(\lambda \cup \mu)$ then $K(\mathcal{M}, P) \subseteq K_T(\mathcal{M})$. Now we have the following equivalent version for IV.3. (cf. KUEKER (1970), p. 430):

*Theorem IV.3.** For any $T(\lambda \cup \mu)$ the following conditions are equivalent:

(i) For every model $\langle \mathcal{M}, \mathrm{P} \rangle$ of $T(\lambda \cup \mu)$, $|K(\mathcal{M}, P)| = 1$;

(ii) there are formulas $G_i(x)$ of $\mathcal{L}(\lambda)$ such that

$$T \vdash \bigvee_{1 \leq i \leq n} (x)\,(P(x) \equiv G_i(x)).$$

Notice that what is here called piecewise definability is a kind of conditional definition. But it is a more general notion than what is sometimes referred to by this term. When the members of μ are piecewise definable in terms of λ on the basis of $T(\lambda \cup \mu)$, the following is

2 The latter part of this result amounts to the theorem on permutations in models due to SVENONIUS (1959).

logically true for some suitable conditions $C_1, C_2, \ldots, C_n$ which are mutually exclusive and collectively equivalent to $T(\lambda \cup \mu)$ (that is, their disjunction is logically equivalent to $T(\lambda \cup \mu)$):

$$\begin{array}{ll} T \supset (C_1 \supset Df_1) & \& \\ T \supset (C_2 \supset Df_2) & \& \\ \ldots\ldots & \& \\ T \supset (C_n \supset Df_n) & \end{array}$$

where each Df_i is a conjunction of explicit definitions of the members of μ in terms of the members of λ. In the special case in which the C_i contains no members of μ, we can turn this bunch of 'conditional definitions' into an explicit one. Piecewise definability here allows for the possibility, however, that the C_i contain theoretical or μ-predicates in addition to observational or λ-predicates. When this is irreducibly the case — as it often is — piecewise definability does not reduce to explicit definability.

Does a piecewise definition satisfy the traditional criteria of eliminability and noncreativity? Before answering this let us formulate these criteria for our present framework (see e. g. PRZELECKI (1969) for the more usual formulation).

Consider the definability of P in a deductively closed theory $T(\lambda \cup \{P\})$ in terms of the members of λ. We say that $T(\lambda \cup \{P\})$ defines P in terms of λ so as to meet the criterion of *eliminability* if and only if for every sentence F containing P there is a sentence G in $\mathscr{L}(\lambda)$ such that

$$T(\lambda \cup \{P\}) \vdash F \equiv G.$$

An explicit definition clearly meets this requirement, but a proper piecewise definition does not. However, piecewise definitions clearly meet the weaker criterion of eliminability which requires that whenever $T(\lambda \cup \{P\})$ is satisfied there is an eliminating sentence G for every F containing P. In other words, there is in general no single G that does the elimination but a finite number of such sentences G depending on which constituent of $T(\lambda \cup \{P\})$ is satisfied.

We say that a (deductively closed) theory $T(\lambda \cup \{P\})$ defines P *noncreatively* with respect to λ if and only if

$$T(\lambda \cup \{P\}) \cap \mathscr{L}(\lambda) \subseteq T'(\lambda).$$

where $T'(\lambda)$ is a maximal subtheory of $T(\lambda \cup \{P\})$ in $\mathscr{L}(\lambda)$. This is a syntactic criterion of noncreativity known to be logically weaker than its semantic counterpart discussed in Chapter III. All piecewise definitions (including explicit definitions) clearly satisfy this desideratum.

The concept of piecewise definability seems to have a considerable general theoretical interest. As examples of additional results that can be established for it, we mention here the following simple theorems:

Theorem IV.4. If the members of μ of a first-order theory $T^{(d)}(\lambda \cup \mu)$ (with or without identity) are piecewise definable in terms of λ, then they are semantically Ramsey-eliminable.

Theorem IV.5. If the members of μ of a first-order theory $T^{(d)}(\lambda \cup \mu)$ (with or without identity) are piecewise definable in terms of λ, then the maximal subtheory (reduct) of $T^{(d)}(\lambda \cup \mu)$ in $\mathscr{L}(\lambda)$ becomes finitely axiomatizable with $r(T^{(d+e)}(\lambda \cup \mu))$ as its axiom (for some $e \geq 0$).

Theorem IV.6. If $T(\lambda \cup \mu)$ is a theory in a monadic language with identity then all the members of μ in $T(\lambda \cup \mu)$ are semantically Ramsey-eliminable.

Theorem IV.7. In a monadic first-order theory $T(\lambda \cup \mu)$ without identity, the members of μ are semantically Ramsey-eliminable if and only if they are piecewise definable in terms of λ.

To recall from Section III.2., a concept of μ is semantically Ramsey-eliminable from a given theory $T(\lambda \cup \mu)$ if and only if $T(\lambda \cup \mu)$ has an axiomatizable subtheory $T'(\lambda)$ in $\mathscr{L}(\lambda)$ such that all the models of $T'(\lambda)$ have an expansion which is a model of the original theory. Let us briefly sketch how the proofs of these theorems go. To start with, Theorem IV.4. (and thus its consequence, the if-part of IV.7.) are quite obvious. In the case of any theory $T(\lambda \cup \{P\}) = C_1 \vee C_2 \vee \ldots \vee C_n$, each model of T is a model of exactly one of its constituents. Now pick a model $\mathscr{N}$ satisfying some $C_i^{(d+e)}$. We know that the explicit definition (4.3) must be true in $\mathscr{N}$. But then the members of λ fix the interpretation of P in $\mathscr{N}$ and we have an expansion (which is even unique) of the $\mathscr{L}(\lambda)$-restrict of $\mathscr{N}$.

As for Theorem IV.5., we see that for some depth $d+e$ we have explicit definitions for P in all the constituents of $T^{(d+e)}(\lambda \cup \mu)$. Thus we can eliminate P through its definientia in all the constituents and we see that from depth $d+e$ onwards the single arrows between the upper and lower rows in our Diagram II.2. turn equivalences; and hence the single arrows in the lower row also become equivalences after depth $d+e$. But then the subtheory can be finitely axiomatized by the sentence $r(T^{(d+e)})$.

As to the proof of Theorem IV.6., it is known that in this case each constituent $C_i(\lambda)$ in the poorer theory, i. e. in the reduct $r(T^{(d)})$, specifies how many individuals satisfy each of its $Ct(\lambda)$-predicates. More exactly, it has to specify for each attributive constituent whether it is exemplified by exactly $0, 1, \ldots, d-1$, or by at least d individuals. Ramsey-eliminability means here that one is able for each attributive constituent Ct_j to partition further the set of individuals (n_j in number) satisfying it into those which have the property P and those which have $-P$; this yields a model of the richer theory $T(\lambda \cup \{P\})$ with the same domain as the given poorer model. This can always be done. In the case of finite models we get a partition $n_j = n_j(P) + n_j(-P)$ (in the case of explicit definability, one of these numbers is zero for each attributive constituent of $C_i(\lambda)$). A partition to the same effect can also be made in the case of infinite models. (Compare HILPINEN (1966) and Theorem III.7.).

Now we can give a very simple monadic example illustrating piecewise and explicit definability. A sketch of the proof of Theorem IV.7. is then conveniently given in connection with the example.

We consider a monadic language without identy where $\lambda = \{O\}$ gives the observational vocabulary and $\mu = \{P\}$ the theoretical vocabulary. We have the following four possible Ct-predicates:

$$Ct_1 = O \;\&\; P$$

$$Ct_2 = O \;\&\; -P$$

$$Ct_3 = -O \;\&\; P$$

$$Ct_4 = -O \;\&\; -P$$

Out of the $2^4 = 16$ possible constituents pick the following:

$$C_1 = (Ex)\, Ct_1(x) \;\&\; (Ex)\, Ct_4(x) \;\&\; (x)\,(Ct_1(x) \vee Ct_4(x))$$

$$C_2 = (Ex)\, Ct_2(x) \;\&\; (Ex)\, Ct_3(x) \;\&\; (x)\,(Ct_2(x) \vee Ct_3(x))$$

$$C_3 = (Ex)\, Ct_1(x) \;\&\; (Ex)\, Ct_2(x) \;\&\; (x)\,(Ct_1(x) \vee Ct_2(x)).$$

Consider the definability of P on the basis of O in each of these constituents C_i ($i = 1,2,3$). We apply the criterion based on (4.2). In the expression $\alpha_i \cap \beta_i = \gamma_i$, is $\gamma_i = \phi$?

C_1: $\alpha_1 \cap \beta_1 = \{O\} \cap \{-O\} = \phi$; hence $\vdash C_1 \supset (x)\,(P(x) \equiv O(x))$;

C_2: $\alpha_2 \cap \beta_2 = \{-O\} \cap \{O\} = \phi$; hence $\vdash C_2 \supset (x)\,(P(x) \equiv -O(x))$;

C_3: $\alpha_3 \cap \beta_3 = \{O\} \cap \{O\} = \{O\}$; hence C_3 does not imply a definition of P.

(1) Consider a theory $T_1 = C_1$. We see that P is explicitly definable on the basis of O in T_1.

(2) If $T_2 = C_1 \vee C_2$, P is piecewise, but not explicitly, definable in terms of O in T_2 because both C_1 and C_2 imply a definition of P, though different ones. Thus we have

$$T_2 \vdash ((x)\,(P\,(x) \equiv O\,(x)) \vee (x)\,(P\,(x) \equiv -O\,(x))).$$

(3) Consider $T_3 = C_1 \vee C_2 \vee C_3$. P is not even piecewise, but only to a certain degree definable on the basis of O as C_3 does not imply an explicit definition of P.

It is now easy to see why Ramsey-eliminability implies piecewise definability in the monadic case without identity (Theorem IV.7.). We cannot have an expansion unless $\gamma_i = \phi$ in every C_i of the poorer theory $r\,(T)$. For $\gamma_i \neq \phi$ requires more than a one-element domain for satisfaction in the richer theory whereas the poorer theory may have a model with a one-element domain; consider, for instance, C_3 and $r\,(C_3)$ $(= (Ex)\,O\,(x)\ \&\ (x)\,O\,(x))$. Hence we do not have Ramsey-eliminability if $\gamma_i \neq \phi$. However, we can also say something about the degree of definability in this kind of situation, and this is what in general terms we shall do in the next section.

1.2. Our results concerning piecewise definability clearly show that it represents a strong form of definability. We shall next consider a milder notion of definability starting from model theoretic considerations. Consider thus a model $\mathcal{M}$ in $\mathcal{L}\,(\lambda)$ in which the consequence of a theory $T\,(\lambda \cup \{P\})$ in $\mathcal{L}\,(\lambda)$ holds true. Then consider all the possible ways of expanding $\mathcal{M}$ into a model $\langle \mathcal{M}, \mathrm{P} \rangle$ of the full theory $T\,(\lambda \cup \{P\})$. Assume that there are at most n possible interpretations for the predicate P in this case. Can we find a syntactic counterpart to this situation? KUEKER (1970) has given an affirmative aswer to this question. Let us state his important result as follows. (See KUEKER (1970), pp. 448—450.)

Theorem IV.8. For any theory $T\,(\lambda \cup \mu)$ and any finite positive integer n the following conditions are equivalent:

(i)$_n$ for every $\mathcal{M}$, $|K_T\,(\mathcal{M})| \leqq n$;

(ii)$_n$ there are expressions S and G_i in $\mathcal{L}\,(\lambda)$ with the bindable individual variables $x_1, \ldots, x_k$ and $y, x_1, \ldots x_k$, respectively, such that

(a) $T \vdash (Ex_1) \ldots (Ex_k)\,(S\,(x_1, \ldots, x_k))$

and

(b) $$T \vdash (x_1) \ldots (x_k)\,(S\,(x_1, \ldots, x_k) \supset \bigvee_{1 \leqq i \leqq n} (y)\,(P\,(y) \equiv G_i\,(y, x_1, \ldots, x_k))).$$

We will below call the model theoretic condition $(\mathrm{i})_n$ the condition for the *finite identifiability* (or rather the *n-fold identifiability*) of P in terms of λ. The proof theoretic notion of definability expressed by $(\mathrm{ii})_n$ we will call *relative definability*. Kueker's above theorem is in an obvious sense a generalization of Beth's theorem. A corresponding generalization of Svenonius' theorem (IV.3.*) can be obtained from Kueker's theorem. There the semantic condition concerns $K(\mathscr{M}, P)$ rather than $K_T(\mathscr{M})$, and the proof theoretic condition says that some finite disjunction of the corresponding conditions of Theorem IV.8. follows from T.

Let us briefly indicate how the content of the above theorem can be seen within the theory of distributive normal forms (cf. Hintikka (1972a)).

The equivalence of finite identifiability and relative definability is manifested when expanding the theory $T(\lambda \cup \mu)$ into a disjunction of deeper and deeper constituents. This comes about in a closely analogous way to the manifestation of piecewise definability. The main difference is that in addition to the different constituents $C_i^{(d+e)}(\lambda \cup \{P\})$ of the expansion of $T(\lambda \cup \{P\})$ we also have to consider the shallower constituents $C_j^{(d+e-k)}(\lambda \cup \{P\}; x_1, \ldots, x_k)$ which occur in $C_i^{(d+e)}(\lambda \cup \{P\})$. From each such constituent $C_j^{(d+e-k)})(\lambda \cup \{P\}; x_1, \ldots, x_k)$ we may omit all the occurrences of P to get a constituent $C_j^{(d+e-k)}(\lambda; x_1, \ldots, x_k)$. Such a constituent $C_j^{(d+e-k)}(\lambda; x_1, \ldots, x_k)$ can of course be the reduct of several different constituents of the form $C_j^{(d+e-k)}(\lambda \cup \{P\}; x_1, \ldots, x_k)$ occurring in the same $C_i^{(d+e)}(\lambda \cup \{P\})$.

Consider now a constituent of the form $C_j^{(d+e-k)}(\lambda \cup \{P\}; x_1, \ldots, x_k)$ occurring in a $C_i^{(d+e)}(\lambda \cup \{P\})$. (Actually such a constituent does not normally occur as a consecutive part of $C_i^{(d+e)}(\lambda \cup \{P\})$. However, its attributive part $Ct_j^{(d+e-k)}(\lambda \cup \{P\}, x_1, \ldots, x_k)$ does so occur and here it is equivalent with the whole constituent $C_j^{(d+e-k)}(\lambda \cup \{P\}, x_1, \ldots, x_k)$.) If all but the outmost layer of P's are omitted in it we get in analogy with (4.1)

$$
\begin{aligned}
(4.6)\quad & \bigwedge_{m \in I_j} (Ey)\,(P(y)\ \&\ Ct_m^{(d+e-k-1)}(\lambda; y, x_1, \ldots, x_k))\ \& \\
& \bigwedge_{n \in I_j'} (Ey)\,(-P(y)\ \&\ Ct_n^{(d+e-k-1)}(\lambda; y, x_1, \ldots, x_k))\ \& \\
& (y)\,(\bigvee_{m \in I_j} (P(y)\ \&\ Ct_m^{(d+e-k-1)}(\lambda; y, x_1, \ldots, x_k)) \vee \\
& \bigvee_{n \in I_j'} (-P(y)\ \&\ Ct_n^{(d+e-k-1)}(\lambda; y, x_1, \ldots, x_k)))\ \& \\
& C_a^{(0)}(\lambda; x_1, \ldots, x_k).
\end{aligned}
$$

Here $C_a^{(0)}(\lambda; x_1, \ldots, x_k)$ is a conjunction which for each atomic sentence A in terms of λ and $x_1, \ldots, x_k$ contains either A or $-A$ as a conjunct.

Let us define

$$\alpha_j^k = \{Ct_m{}^{(d+e-k-1)}(\lambda; y, x_1, \ldots, x_k)\} \qquad m \in I_j$$
$$\beta_j^k = \{Ct^{n(d+e-k-1)}(\lambda; y, x_1, \ldots, x_k)\} \qquad n \in I_j'$$

The sets α_j^k and β_j^k are separated if and only if $\alpha_j^k \cap \beta_j^k = \phi$.

For all the different constituents $C_j^{(d+e-k)}(\lambda \cup \{P\}; x_1, \ldots, x_k)$ occurring in $C_i^{(d+e)}(\lambda \cup \{P\})$ and having the same λ-reduct $C_j^{(d+e-k)}(\lambda; x_1, \ldots, x_k)$ we may have this kind of separation, possibly due to different separating sets δ_j^k. HINTIKKA (1972a) shows that if and only if this kind of situation arises at some stage of the expansion for each of the constituents $C_i^{(d+e)}(\lambda \cup \{P\})$ (of $T(\lambda \cup \{P\})$ and for a suitable $C_j^{(d+e-k)}(\lambda; x_1, \ldots, x_k)$ we have finite identifiability. If the number of separating sets δ_j^k needed is at most n we have n-fold identifiability.

The following two cases are to be distinguished here (see HINTIKKA (1972a), p. 49):

(A) A separation is eventually effected in each branch of the expansion for *all* the constituents $C_j^{(d+e-k)}(\lambda \cup \{P\}; x_1, \ldots, x_k)$ which yield the same $C_j^{(d+e-k)}(\lambda; x_1, \ldots, x_k)$ such that n is the maximal number of different kinds of separation.

(B) A separation is eventually effected in each branch of the expansion for some constituent $C_j^{(d+e-k)}(\lambda \cup \{P\}; x_1, \ldots, x_k)$, but not necessarily for similar constituents yielding the same $C_j^{(d+e-k)}(\lambda; x_1, \ldots, x_k)$.

Condition (A) is shown in HINTIKKA (1972a) to express a necessary and sufficient condition of relative definability. On the other hand, (B) does not in general give relative definability, even if it represents the most straightforward generalization of piecewise definability (viz. separation in each branch, although not necessarily at the outermost level as in piecewise definability). Hintikka shows, however, that (B) is equivalent to the conditions in theorem IV.9. below.

The following theorem, due to CHANG and MAKKAI, generalizes theorem IV.8. (cf. KUEKER (1970)):

Theorem IV.9. For any $T(\lambda \cup \mu)$ the following conditions are equivalent:

(i) For every infinite model $\mathcal{M}$ with domain D, $|K_T(\mathcal{M})| \leqq |D|$;

(ii) for every infinite model $\mathcal{M}$, $|K_T(\mathcal{M})| < 2^{|D|}$;

(iii) for every infinite model $\langle \mathcal{M}, P \rangle$ of T, $|K(\mathcal{M}, P)| \leqq |D|$;

(iv) for every infinite model $\langle \mathcal{M}, P \rangle$ of T, $|K(\mathcal{M}, P)| < 2^{|D|}$;

(v) there are formulas $G_i(y, x_1, \ldots, x_k)$ $(i = 1, \ldots, n)$ in $\mathcal{L}(\lambda)$ such that

$$T \vdash \bigvee_{1 \leqq i \leqq n} (Ex_1)\ldots(Ex_k)(y)(P(y) \equiv G_i(y, x_1, \ldots, x_k)).$$

In this theorem conditions (i)—(iv) may be said to express *restricted identifiability*. Condition (v) gives a syntactical counterpart to restricted identifiability. It may be called *restricted definability*.

Taken together Kueker's and Chang-Makkai's results exhaust the search for proof theoretic counterparts for model theoretic notions of definability based on cardinality restrictions (of the above kind). We shall later apply these results to questions of identifiability of theoretical parameters within some theories in the social sciences.

We may finally notice that the above results of Kueker and Chang and Makkai may also be stated by using second-order sentences. For the model theoretic conditions in their theorems may be expressed by using numerical existential quantifiers. Thus we may add to Theorem IV.8. the following equivalent condition (in second-order logic):

$(\text{iii})_n \quad \vdash (E^{\leqq n} \Pi)\ T\ (\Pi)$

where Π is a predicate variable corresponding to P, and $T\ (\Pi)$ contains all the other members of $\lambda \cup \mu$ except P among its extralogical constants. The numerical quantifier reads 'there are at most n values for Π'. If $n \leqq 1$ we of course have explicit definability. For the Chang-Makkai case we have to put $|D|$ for infinite models instead of n.

We may go on to define new numerical quantifiers such as $E^n\ \Pi$ (there are exactly n values for Π) by:

$$E^n\ \Pi = E^{\leqq n}\ \Pi\ \&\ -E^{\leqq n-1}\ \Pi$$

When μ contains other members than P we may existentially quantify over them, too. Thus for all of our theoretical concepts we get corresponding numerical existential quantification ranging from $E\ \Pi$ (no restriction) through $E^n\ \Pi$ (exactly n values) to $E^1\ \Pi$ (always one value) and $E^{\leqq 1}\ \Pi$ (explicit definability), depending on the structure of the theory $T\ (\lambda \cup \mu)$ in question. The result may be called a *numerical Ramsey sentence*. Whereas the Ramsey sentence for a theory exists as a matter of logic, the existence of a numerical Ramsey sentence generally depends upon the nature of the extralogical axioms of the theory $T\ (\lambda \cup \mu)$. (These axioms have to satisfy $(\text{ii})_n$ of Theorem IV.8.)

1.3. We have so far been mainly concerned with the new notions of piecewise, relative, and restricted definability as well as their model theoretic counterparts. We do not want to completely ignore all the traditional logical types of definability. Explicit definability has already been discussed and will be discussed again in later chapters. Various "operational definitions" (e. g. Carnap's unilateral and bilateral reduction sentences) may still deserve some comments, as they represent *a* way of giving the structure of dispositional concepts (e. g. solubility).

Let us start with bilateral reduction sentence or conditional definition (cf. the standard formulation in PRZELECKI (1969), pp. 68—72). Within the theory of distributive normal forms it seems natural to begin with conditional definability within a constituent. Consider thus a theory $T\ (\lambda \cup \{P\})$ of depth $d+e$. We say that P is *conditionally definable* in terms of λ on the basis of a constituent $C_i^{(d+e)}\ (\lambda \cup \{P\})$ (of $T^{(d+e)}\ (\lambda \cup \{P\})$) if and only if $C_i^{(d+e)}\ (\lambda \cup \{P\})$ logically implies

$$(4.7) \qquad (x)\ (L_j\ (x) \supset (P\ (x) \equiv \bigvee_m Ct_m^{(d+e-1)}\ (x)))$$

for some L_j. Here the condition L_j is in the vocabulary λ, and so of course is the disjunction $\bigvee_m Ct_m\ (x)$. The disjunction may include Ct-predicates from the set α_i of P-positive Ct-predicates as well as Ct-predicates which do not occur in $C_i^{(d+e)}\ (\lambda \cup \{P\})$.

What can be said of the condition L_j? It has to be a condition which denies x having any of the Ct-predicates in the uncertainty set $\gamma_i = \alpha_i \cap \beta_i$. In other words, it includes at least a conjunction of negated Ct-predicates (of all the Ct-predicates in γ_i). This shows in which sense conditional definitions are generalizations of explicit definitions on the basis of a constituent. Our conditional definability on the basis of a constituent, however, turns out to be uninteresting. This is because one can always find a condition L_j for a C_j to make (4.7) true, provided that $\alpha_i, \beta_i \neq \phi$. Therefore we have to go to notions of conditional definability within the full theory.

The immediate generalization of conditional definability for the full theory $T^{(d+e)}\ (\lambda \cup \{P\})$ becomes this: A predicate $P \in \mu$ is said to be *piecewise conditionally definable* in terms of λ in a theory $T^{(d+e)}\ (\lambda \cup \{P\})$ if and only if for each constituent $C_i^{(d+e)}\ (\lambda \cup \{P\})$ in $T^{(d+e)}\ (\lambda \cup \{P\})$ (4.7) is true.

Analogously with piecewise definitions we now see that a P is piecewise conditionally definable in a theory if and only if the theory implies a finite disjunction of conditional definitions of form (4.7). Again, there is in general no way of putting together these conditional definitions to get one single conditional definition of the form (ii.b) of Theorem IV.8. for P in the theory. This happens only if the conditions L_j are the same for all constituents. In such a case we say that P is *simply piecewise conditionally definable* in the theory $T(\lambda \cup \{P\})$ (in terms of λ). We can see that even simple piecewise conditional definitions are logically weaker than relative definitions as they need not satisfy the existential condition (ii.a) of Theorem IV.8. Hence simple piecewise conditional definability does not imply finite identifiability. For the former kind of definability does not effect any restrictions on the interpretations of P in some models of T (while they fix its interpretation uniquely in the models in which the condition L_j is true).

If a simple piecewise conditional definition contains only one disjunct, that is, if $T^{(d+e)}(\lambda \cup \{P\})$ implies a single statement of the form (4.7), we have a *simple conditional definition* or a bilateral reduction sentence in Carnap's terminology.

Piecewise conditional definability, simple piecewise conditional definability, and simple conditional definability meet the criterion of noncreativity for definitions but fail to meet that of eliminability.

Let us next consider partial definitions or unilateral reduction sentences (cf. PRZELECKI (1969), pp. 72—78). In the case of a monadic predicate $P \in \mu$ a conditional definition gives a λ-condition for a positive instantiation of the predicate and another λ-condition for a negative instantiation of it. In the case of a constituent $C_i^{(d+e)}(\lambda \cup \{P\})$ of a $T^{(d+e)}(\lambda \cup \{P\})$ disjunctions of Ct-predicates of α_i qualify as the positive conditions whereas disjunctions of Ct-predicates of β_i can be conditions for an occurrence of $-P$. In analogy with conditional definability one can define a number of different notions of partial definability starting from partial definability within a constituent. We shall not, however, do it here but go directly to the traditional notion of (simple) partial definition or unilateral reduction sentence. We thus say that a $P \in \mu$ is *simply partially definable* in terms of λ in $T^{(d+e)}(\lambda \cup \{P\})$ if and only if $T^{(d+e)}(\lambda \cup \{P\})$ implies a conjunction of the form

$$(4.8) \qquad (x)\,((L_1(x) \supset P(x))\ \&\ (L_2(x) \supset -P(x)).$$

It is obvious that if $T^{(d+e)}(\lambda \cup \{P\})$ implies that the conditions L_1 and L_2 exclude γ_i for every C_i in $T^{(d+e)}(\lambda \cup \{P\})$, that is, if

$$(4.9) \qquad T^{(d+e)}(\lambda \cup \{P\}) \vdash (x) - (L_1(x)\ \&\ L_2(x)),$$

then we again get a case of simple conditional definability. But just because this does not generally happen, partial definitions fail to meet the criterion of noncreativity. (Obviously they do not satisfy the requirement of eliminability.)

2. Indeterminate Definability

2.1. In this section we shall investigate some other kinds of structural interwovenness which may be found to hold between the μ-predicates and λ-predicates in a scientific theory $T(\lambda \cup \mu)$. We shall now try to say something about the degrees of interwovenness in cases in which we do not generally have piecewise, relative, conditional nor even partial definability of the members of μ in terms of λ in the full theory $T(\lambda \cup \mu)$.

Let us thus start from a theory $T^{(d+e)}(\lambda \cup \{P\}) = C_1^{(d+e)} \vee \ldots \vee C_n^{(d+e)}$. Assume that $\gamma_i = \{Ct^*_{i1}, Ct^*_{i2}, \ldots\}$ is not empty in the case of some constituents $C_i^{(d+e)}$. Then P is not piecewise definable in terms of λ at depth $d+e$. But when this happens, we can still calculate how close γ_i is to being empty, and use the answer to define measures of *degrees of (piecewise) definability*.

To do this systematically, let us assume that a strictly positive probability measure is defined on all those consistent sentences of our language (whose nonlogical vocabulary is λ) which contain just one free variable, namely x. Let us denote this measure by p. This measure will be defined, in particular, on attributive constituents whose only free variable is x. Then we can call

$$(4.10) \qquad p(\bigvee_k Ct^*_{ik}),$$

where k runs over γ_i, a measure of the *indeterminacy* (4.1) leaves us with respect to P. *The (absolute) degree of definability* of P in $T^{(d)}(\lambda \cup \{P\})$ at depth $d+e$ will be defined so as to be proportional to the sum of all terms of the form

$$(4.11) \qquad p(C_i^{(d+e)})\,(1 - p(\bigvee_k Ct^*_{ik})),$$

where the first and the second p, of course, have arguments of different kinds. The different terms are obtained from the different constituents $C_i^{(d+e)}$ that occur in $T^{(d+e)}(\lambda \cup \{P\})$. The proportionality factor that preferably has to be used in (4.11) is $1/\sigma$ where σ is the sum of all the terms $p\ (C_i^{(d+e)})$ with $C_i^{(d+e)}$ in $T^{(d+e)}\ (\lambda \cup \{P\})$.

The following statement is a consequence of what has been said above:

Theorem IV.10. P is piecewise definable on the basis of $T^{(d)}\ (\lambda \cup \{P\})$ at depth $d+e$ if and only if the absolute degree of definability of P in $T^{(d+e)}\ (\lambda \cup \{P\})$ is 1.

It is obvious that such weaker kinds of definability (or interwovenness) as expressed by relative, restricted, conditional, and partial definitions usually receive degrees of definability less than one by (4.11).

It can be seen that in general the degree of definability of a concept at depth $d+e+1$ is at least equal to its degree of definability at depth $d+e$. Hence

(4.12) $\lim_{e \to \infty}$ (degree of definability of P in $T^{(d)}\ (\lambda \cup \{P\})$ at depth $d+e$)

is always well-defined, and can be used as an (unqualified) measure of the (absolute) degree of definability of P in $T^{(d)}\ (\lambda \cup \{P\})$ (or of any sentence of depth d whose distributive normal form this is).

If P is piecewise definable in terms of the members of λ, this degree is one. The converse does not always hold. Whether it holds or not depends essentially on the particular probability measure p used in (4.10) [3].

For many purposes, closely connected relative measures of partial definability seem more important. (The measures defined above cannot equal zero unless all attributive constituents of the given depth that are in the vocabulary λ occur in (4.2) and hence in (4.3).)

3 This dependence might seem to be a reason for doubting the general theoretical interest of our notion of "gradual" definability. However, this dependence may perhaps be viewed as a sign of flexibility rather than vagueness. By choosing the probability measure in different ways we can express different assumptions concerning the interest and importance of different kinds of individuals, and take these differences into account in evaluating degrees of definability. For instance, in some cases it is possible to choose the measure so that the degree of definability of a new term equals one if and only if this term is definable in an intended model or models. Thus a suitable choice of the probability measure may reflect our special interest in some intended models.

Instead of (4.10) we have now

$$(4.13)\quad p\,(\bigvee_k Ct^*_{ik}/\bigvee_l Ct_{il})\left(=\frac{p\,(\bigvee_k Ct^*_{ik})}{p\,(\bigvee_l Ct_{il})}\right),$$

where $l \in I_i \cup I_i'$ and relative probability is defined in the usual way.

Instead of (4.11) we then have a sum of terms of the form

$$(4.14)\quad 1/\sigma\, p\,(C_i{}^{(d+e)})\left(1-\frac{p\,(\bigvee_k Ct^*_{ik})}{p\,(\bigvee_l Ct_{il})}\right).$$

Here σ has the same meaning as before, and the sum is taken over all constituents occurring in $T^{(d+e)}\,(\lambda \cup \{P\})$. We shall call this sum the *relative* degree of definability of P in $T^{(d)}\,(\lambda \cup \{P\})$ at depth $d+e$. From what has been said it follows that for some sufficiently large e this equals one whenever p is piecewise definable in terms of the members of λ on the basis of $T^{(d)}\,(\lambda \cup \{P\})$.

We conjecture that the relative degree of definability at depth $d+e$ always converges when $e \to \infty$, but no proof is attempted here. If the conjecture holds, the limit serves as an unqualified measure of the relative degree of definability of P in terms of λ in $T^{(d)}\,(\lambda \cup \{P\})$ (or in any sentence having this as its distributive normal form). If the conjecture does not hold, this concept will not be defined in all cases.

In theory T_3 of our monadic example in the previous section P is not piecewise definable. Let us now measure its degree of definability using (4.11) and (4.14). For simplicity, we assume a uniform distribution of probabilities for constituents. Thus $p\,(C_1) = p\,(C_2) = p\,(C_3) = 1/16$. Hence $\sigma = 3/16$. Also assume even distribution over Ct-predicates. Then, by (4.10), the absolute degree of definability of P in T_3 on the basis of $\{O\}$ becomes

$$(4.15)\quad \frac{16}{3}\cdot\frac{1}{16}\cdot(1-0)+\frac{16}{3}\cdot\frac{1}{16}\cdot(1-0)+\frac{16}{3}\cdot\frac{1}{16}\cdot\left(1-\frac{1}{2}\right)=\frac{5}{6}.$$

The relative degree of definability of P again becomes

$$(4.16)\quad \frac{16}{3}\cdot\frac{1}{16}\cdot(1-0)+\frac{16}{3}\cdot\frac{1}{16}\cdot(1-0)+\frac{16}{3}\cdot\frac{1}{16}\cdot(1-1)=\frac{2}{3}.$$

Before going on there is one methodological remark to be made. Our measures of absolute and relative degrees of definability can be considered explicates for global probabilistic "correspondence rules". Thus (4.10) and (4.13) give global probabilistic correspondence rules with respect to constituents, while (4.11) and (4.14) are relativized to theories. These correspondence rules are global in the sense of being relativized to all the members of λ. More local probabilistic correspondence rules are obtained by defining analogous measures with respect to a subset of λ only.

The above considerations and measures for degrees of definability do not of course give an exhaustive qualitative and quantitative account of the nature of interwovenness between the concepts of a theory. Another interesting suggestion to characterize (in terms of "uncertainty descriptions") the indeterminacy of a $P \in \mu$ left by the terms of λ of a $T(\lambda \cup \{P\})$ has been made by HINTIKKA (1971)[4].

2.2. During our discussion in this chapter we have been concerned with the definability of an (atomic) monadic predicate P within a theory $T(\lambda \cup \{P\})$. It has been remarked, however, that the restriction to a monadic predicate is inessential. Furthermore, our main results (concerning the definability of P in terms of λ in $T(\lambda \cup \{P\})$ remain valid if we think that $T(\lambda \cup \{P\})$ is just a subtheory of a richer theory containing many other theoretical concepts in addition to P (cf. KUEKER (1970), p. 450).

In some cases it may, however, be of interest to consider the definability of complex theoretical predicates which are truth-functional combinations of atomary predicates. It suffices here to illustrate this with two atomary monadic theoretical predicates P_1 and P_2. Consider all the possible basic compound predicates which can be construed from P_1 and P_2:

$$Q_1 = P_1 \,\&\, P_2$$
$$Q_2 = P_1 \,\&\, -P_2$$
$$Q_3 = -P_1 \,\&\, P_2$$
$$Q_4 = -P_1 \,\&\, -P_2.$$

We can now consider, e. g., the definability of each Q_i in the theory $T(\lambda \cup \{P_1, P_2\})$ by using the method developed above. But we may

4 Let us mention here one result concerning Ramsey-eliminability in HINTIKKA (1971): A predicate P in $T(\lambda \cup \{P\})$ is semantically Ramsey-eliminable if there are no "singularities", i. e. certain kinds of principal types, in the uncertainty area described by all the sequences of uncertainty descriptions (with increasing depth) which are obtained from a complete consistent theory compatible with $T(\lambda \cup \{P\})$.

also want to consider the Q_i's (as well as the P_k's) together in some sense. (If we do this in full generality and allow truth-functional combinations of them we are of course back where we started, as P_1 and P_2 can be expressed as certain disjunctions of the Q_i's.) One case which has been investigated is the partial definability of the Q_i's and the conjunctions of their partial definitions (see STOPES-ROE (1958) and PRZELECKI (1969)). Consider thus a case where $T(\lambda \cup \{P_1, P_2\})$ implies an observational sufficient criterion for the negation of each of the Q_i's. We can transform these into the following form by the definitions of the Q_i's:

(4.17) $(x)(O_1(x) \supset (P_1(x) \vee P_2(x))$

(4.18) $(x)(O_2(x) \supset (P_1(x) \vee -P_2(x))$

(4.19) $(x)(O_3(x) \supset (-P_1(x) \vee P_2(x))$

(4.20) $(x)(O_4(x) \supset (-P_1(x) \vee -P_2(x))$.

Here $\lambda = \{O_1, O_2, O_3, O_4\}$ and $\mu = \{P_1, P_2\}$. These partial definitions for the Q_i's are a kind of reduction sentences for P_1 and P_2. More exactly, we say that each of the partial definitions (4.17)—(4.20) or any conjunction of them are called *generalized reduction sentences* for P_1 and P_2. Stopes-Roe has shown that every interpretative system (in the sense of HEMPEL (1958)) satisfying a certain rather restrictive condition can be transformed into a generalized reduction sentence. The condition in question is vaguely speaking that the prenex normal form of the interpretative system should not be "controlled" by an existential quantifier (see STOPES-ROE (1958), p. 145 for a sharp formulation).

What interests us more here is that considered from the point of view of the λ-definability of a single theoretical predicate P_i a generalized reduction sentence does not in general give a criterion of application for P_i (nor for $-P_i$). We have such a criterion of application for P_i (or $-P_i$) in terms of λ for an individual *a* only if we know that *a* has a certain other theoretical property. This reminds us of Carnap's "high probability"-criterion of theoreticity according to which there are always disturbing theoretical factors which prevent us from finding definite (i. e. more than "high probability") observational or λ-criteria of application for theoretical terms (cf. CARNAP (1956), p. 69 and PRZELECKI (1969), pp. 81—82). This seems plausible. But it has to be kept in mind that this kind of theoretical clause in a generalized reduction sentence is not the only theoretical presupposition involved. For as we have construed definability of theoretical concepts, *all* kinds of observational definitions (including explicit ones) presuppose the truth of a theory $T(\lambda \cup \mu)$, where e. g. highly theoretical statements may occur.

What kind of interpretative systems are there among those which cannot be represented as generalized reduction sentences? The most interesting ones are statements directly controlled by existential quantifiers (see STOPES-ROE (1958), pp. 154—155). A sentence contains an existential quantifier which directly controls a predicate $P \in \mu$ when one of the arguments of P is a variable bound by an existential quantifier (in the prenex normal form of the sentence). We shall below give a couple of examples of sentences controlled by existential quantifiers.

Assume that a textbook tells us that protons and electrons are the ultimate constituents of matter, such that a hydrogen atom has one electron and one proton, a helium atom has... (and so on for all basic chemical substances). (This example has been discussed in STOPES-ROE (1958).) Here we have a partial definition of 'proton' and 'electron' in terms of the basic chemical elements and some relations between them. For our theoretical purposes we can here simply assume that the list stops after the hydrogen atom. The partial definition for 'proton' and 'electron' can then be construed as the following sentence (assumed to be implied by a theory $T(\lambda \cup \mu)$):

$$(4.21) \quad (x)\,(H(x) \supset (y)\,((A(y)\ \&\ R_1(x, y)) \supset \\ \supset (Es)\,(Et)\,(P(s)\ \&\ El(t)\ \&\ R_2(s, t, y))))).$$

Here we take $\lambda = \{H, A, R_1, R_2\}$ and $\mu = \{P, El\}$. The symbols 'H', 'A', 'P', and 'El' stand, respectively, for 'hydrogen', 'atom', 'proton', and 'electron', '$R_1(x, y)$' reads 'x is part of y', and '$R_2(s, t, y)$' reads 's and t constitute y'.

While (4.21) obviously is a partial definition of H in terms of all the other concepts it is also clearly a kind of partially defining statement for P and El in terms of λ as well. An interesting aspect about (4.21) is that it swells the ontology of the original discourse assumed to be in $\mathscr{L}(\lambda)$. It invites us to take into consideration entirely new objects. Notice, however, that all of the basic types of definitions discussed in Section 1 of this chapter allow, of course, the introduction of new objects by existential quantifiers in the definiens. It is only that (4.21) represents so open or indeterminate a type of definability that it does not fit among the definitions discussed there.

In (4.21) the μ-ontology (represented by s and t) and the λ-ontology (represented by x and y) are connected by means of R_2. (Notice that also within the λ-ontology we have the two different types of entities x and y connected, through R_1). It is now more than conceivable that within intertheoretic reductions many of the "bridge-laws" are of the kind exemplified by (4.21) (cf. Chapter V). This aspect of course increases considerably the methodological importance of partially defining statements controlled by existential quantifiers.

WINNIE (1967) has argued that the correspondence rules connecting different ontologies should be of the form

(4.22) $$(x)\ (P\ (x) \supset (Ey)\ O\ (y)),$$

where $P \in \mu$ and $O \in \lambda$, and x and y range over disjoint domains of objects. Winnie comes to this conclusion from his untenable assumption that the μ-ontology and the λ-ontology have to be disjoint. (Cf. our criticism in I.2.) Irrespective of this criticism, (4.22) seems methodologically uninteresting as the μ-objects and λ-objects are not claimed to stand in any relation to each other. At least it is hard to find interesting scientific examples which would fit (4.22).

This concludes our systematic treatment of the logical questions of interwovenness (and definability) of concepts in scientific theories. Some additional types of interwovenness will still be discussed in Chapters VI and VII by using information-theoretic and probabilistic indicators of interwovenness. In Section 3. of this chapter as well as in Chapters V, VI, and VII various methodological and philosophical problems connected with the logical results of the present chapter will be discussed.

3. Openness vs. Definability of Theoretical Concepts in the Social Sciences

3.1. After the rejection of extreme positivism in the late 1930's it has become fashionable among philosophers and scientists to argue for the *openness* and "*surplus meaning*" of theoretical concepts. This is true especially in the social sciences. Usually openness is taken to mean something like noneliminability or nonreducibility on the basis of observational terms [5]. Mostly these arguments are of a semantical or methodological rather than a purely logical nature. Therefore one may at the same time accept the *logical* dispensability of theoretical concepts (e. g. in the Craigian sense) and the methodological desirability of (open) theoretical concepts.

What is or can be meant by the openness of theoretical concepts? First we have to notice that what empirically minded philosophers and scientists are interested in is only empirical or observational openness. As we shall argue in the next chapter, such openness cannot normally be regarded as openness of (semantical) meaning but rather as openness in an epistemological and methodological sense. Such empirical openness is related to questions of testability (truth values of theoretical statements in principle) and to the means for testing a theory (deciding these truth values). Secondly, generally only the extensional or structural aspects of the connections between theoretical and observational concepts are emphasized in the above kind of arguments. Hence the varieties of definitions discussed earlier in this chapter are highly relevant in clarifying what kinds of structural observational openness there are.

Let $T(\lambda \cup \mu)$ be a theory with λ interpreted as a set of empirical predicates and μ as a set of theoretical predicates. If the members of μ are not explicitly definable by means of λ in $T(\lambda \cup \mu)$ they are open (relative to λ) at least to some extent.

On the basis of our classification of definitions we get the following main kinds of *structural openness* of theoretical concepts in a theory $T(\lambda \cup \mu)$ and with respect to λ:

A. Openness left by *determinate* definitions:

(a) openness left by *noncreative* definitions

(i) openness with eliminability (piecewise definability excepting explicit definability);

(ii) openness without eliminability (e. g. conditional definitions such as bilateral reduction sentences, most generalized reduction sentences, some "existentially controlled" definitions, such as 4.22.);

5 See e. g. Carnap (1937), MacCorquodale and Meehl (1948), Feigl (1950), Braithwaite (1953), Pap (1958) and (1962), Popper (1959), Simon (1959), Nagel (1961), and Hempel (1965) for various kinds of arguments against the observational reducibility or eliminability of theoretical concepts.

(b) openness left by *creative* definitions (e. g. partial definitions, such as unilateral reduction sentences).

B. Openness left by *indeterminate* definitions.

Most types of interconnectedness belong to group B. For instance, generalized reduction sentences, "existentially controlled" definitions, Hempel's interpretative systems, various "contextual" definitions, and probabilistic definitions, all considered in their general forms, provide openness in this sense. The amount of this openness can be measured by means of our measures of degrees of definability.

At this point we can mention a psychological example to illustrate our two main kinds of openness. The *intervening variables* in the intervening variable-hypothetical construct dichotomy of MacCorquodale and Meehl seem to fit group A as far as their structural aspects are concerned whereas the *hypothetical constructs* fall within group B (cf. MacCorquodale and Meehl (1948), pp. 598—599)[6]. Hypothetical constructs have "*surplus meaning*" which intervening variables do not possess. It is mainly due to the alleged "*existential import*" of the hypothetical constructs. Logically speaking, this *may* involve that hypothetical constructs are introduced by something like "existentially controlled" definitions. In general this need not be so, but the claim of existential import may merely reflect the adoption of a *realist attitude* towards the role of concepts termed hypothetical constructs (cf. Tuomela (1971)).

Our classification of varieties of openness shows how the empirical openness of theoretical concepts is manifested. The next question to ask is why there is or should be such openness. A great part of this book consists of an attempt to answer this question. Let us here mention the main reasons for the empirical openness (here: non-eliminability) of theoretical concepts, to be discussed elsewhere in this book:

(1) The *meaning* (and use) of theoretical concepts require empirical openness (see Chapter V).

(2) Adequate "*theoretical generalization*" and *deductive systematization* presuppose open theoretical concepts (Chapter VI).

---

6 The logical characterization of this distinction offered by MacCorquodale and Meehl is, however, somewhat obscure, as we have argued elsewhere (see Tuomela (1968 b)). For a discussion of the definability and role of theoretical concepts within neobehavioristic theories see Tuomela (1971).

(3) *Deductive explanation* in science requires open theoretical concepts (Chapter VII).

(4) Even evolutionary *scientific change* may require open theoretical concepts (Chapter VI).

(5) *Inductive systematization* (and explanation) of empirical statements may presuppose open theoretical concepts (Chapter VIII).

We shall not here discuss these arguments. Instead we shall present some examples from the social sciences which illustrate the logical problems of definability and openness. Most of our remarks are related to piecewise definability and to various kinds of identifiability. These notions have hardly been discussed in philosophical literature to any extent (cf., however, TUOMELA (1968b), HINTIKKA and TUOMELA (1970)).

For metascientific purposes it is often appropriate and desirable to distinguish between the *core* of a theory $T(\lambda \cup \mu)$ (or, alternatively, a $T(\mu)$) and its various applied extensions. The core is the part of theory which remains unchanged or relatively constant in various empirical situations into which the theory is applied (to test it, to explain or to predict). The extensions are often given by means of some correspondence rules (restrictions or auxiliary hypotheses) C_i giving some new empirical content to the theory T relevant to a particular application. Thus conceived we get an open-ended *applied theory* T & C_1 & C_2 & ... (cf. e. g. Chapters V and VII).

We shall argue that often the following is the case. Within the core theory theoretical concepts are and should be open, whereas within the different applied extensions of it theoretical concepts should be somehow measurable or definable on the basis of observational concepts. This kind of methodological requirement can be regarded as appropriate at least for the kind of mathematical model building and theorizing that takes place in the mathematical portions of the social sciences, as we shall soon see. It seems to us that the adoption of this requirement for a kind of contextual definability of theoretical concepts can be closely related to our piecewise definability. Let us somewhat elaborate this.

The methodological requirement of contextual definability might be formulated as follows: Even if one cannot define a concept explicitly, it may still be defined by means of the context in which it occurs, perhaps so that different contexts define (in some sense) the concepts in different ways. (See, for example, PAP (1962), SIMON (1959), p. 446.) It seems to us that what can be meant by such *contextual definitions* has never been spelled out in a satisfactory way, even though some attempts to make it precise have been made. (See SIMON (1959), pp. 446, 449, SIMON (1970), p. 22.)

The basic idea behind these attempts to weaken the notion of (explicit) definability seems to have been to introduce a notion of definability which implies explicit definability provided that certain special cases or singularities are excluded. However, it may very well happen that these special cases are specifiable only by means of the theoretical concepts to be defined. Then we are led to piecewise definability rather than explicit definability. For one interesting feature of our notion of piecewise definition — one already commented on — is that its conditions themselves are stated in terms of theoretical expressions where the concepts to be defined occur. For instance, if we had piecewise definitions for, say, component forces in a first-order formalization of particle mechanics, the conditions in these definitions might be force laws. (See SIMON (1947), p. 903.)

This contextual feature is to be found also in Carnap's account for the openness of theoretical concepts. Contrasted with "purely dispositional terms" (see CARNAP (1956), pp. 66—69) theoretical concepts have a *nonconclusive* character. "Thus, if a scientist has decided to use a certain term '*M*' in such a way, that for certain sentences about *M*, any possible observational results can never be absolutely conclusive evidence but at best evidence yielding a high probability, then the appropriate place for '*M*' in a dual-language system like our system $L_O - L_T$ is in L_T rather than in L_O" (CARNAP (1956), p. 69). It is interesting to notice here that Carnap's characterization of theoreticity allows for piecewise, and even explicitly defined concepts, provided that the definitions are not finitely applicable; that is, provided that the definienses include quantifiers so that one cannot ascertain in a finite number of steps whether the theoretical concept is applicable.

According to Carnap there are two reasons for this nonconclusiveness of theoretical concepts. First, the interpretative sentences for a given theoretical term provide an observational interpretation only within a certain limited range, that is, only for certain empirically (or rather, technically) realizable circumstances. Secondly, a direct observational interpretation for a theoretical term always involves the tacit understanding that the occurrence or absence of the requisite observable response is to serve as a criterion only "unless there are disturbing factors" or "provided that the environment is in a normal state" (CARNAP (1956), p. 69).

The first of these reasons can be interpreted within our framework as saying that a theoretical concept usually is only partially defined, in the sense that it is at best explicitly defined on the basis of some constituents of a theory (but not all of them). Furthermore, this openness is desirable because it allows the growth of the theory. A scientist may later want to add new correspondence rules for a theoretical concept. This means that new axioms are added, and also that new observational concepts may be added.

The second of the above reasons may be taken to reflect the fact that a theoretical concept may be even piecewise defined, but still it is difficult to avail oneself of it as this would require asserting at each time the truth of the constituent whose truth is the condition. But — as we already mentioned — such a constituent is of a theoretical nature (that is, it contains theoretical terms, at least the definiendum). Furthermore, it naturally is much more demanding to assert the truth of a particular constituent than of the whole theory in which it occurs and which it implies. This actually gives another reason for saying that a theoretical concept may be piecewise defined in a theory. When an object satisfies the definiens of an explicit definition but not the definiendum, we may explain this away by saying that certain *ceteris paribus* assumptions failed, and that this had caused us wrongly to believe in the truth of the constituent on which the definition was conditioned.

Our discussion on the empirical openness of theoretical concepts may now be summarized by the following methodological rule of thumb for a (social) scientist building a theory: For certain central and often realized empirical circumstances there should be an explicit definition for a theoretical concept (in the *applied* theory), whereas for some other, so far empirically rare or technically unrealizable circumstances no definition is implied by the theory. In other words, the theoretical concept is definable in some or most (but not usually all) models of a theory. This represents an instance of weakly determinate or indeterminate definability. The more developed and grown a science is, the higher should the degree of definability of a theoretical concept be (in the fuller applied theory). This is one of the reasons why it is an interesting task to measure degrees of definability.

However, we notice that within the *core* theory theoretical concepts may retain their original openness while in the growing *applied* extensions of the theory they "behave" in the above manner.

3.2. Most of the technical results given in this book are presented within the framework of first-order or second-order predicate logic. In principle we can formalize most if not all existent scientific theories within such a framework and even within first-order logic only. This can be done either directly (cf. MONTAGUE (1961)) or indirectly. In the latter case we can first formalize a set theory (e. g. Zermelo-Fraenkel's) within first-order logic and then add the needed mathematical and scientific axioms. Apart from the presence of (mathematical) nonstandard models there are no serious *theoretical* disadvantages with this, we can argue. However, in actual practice this can never be fully carried out. Hence serious case studies of theories employing strong mathematical tools are difficult to carry out within "standard formalization".

Most or many *mathematical "models"* to be found in the social sciences are formulated by using (random) variables. Even if we do not in general employ these tools, most of the discussion in this book is directly relevant to theorizing within that framework. Of course there will be a number of specific problems that can in practice be stated and answered only by means of such a framework, but they will not be discussed here.

Let us now go on to discuss some questions of definability arising within some mathematical "models" or theories frequently employed in the social sciences (e. g. in economics, sociology, and politology). In these sciences it is common to view the object under study as a system of interacting components. For instance, man, social group or institution, or economic market can constitute such a system. The system receives inputs (e. g. stimuli) from its environment, manipulates these inputs by means of its internal mechanism (e. g. nervous system), and "acts" by means of some output (e. g. responses) to influence its environment. In most cases it is also assumed that the system can feed back into itself environmental information related to its own output.

Consider now abstractly and in an idealized way a factual system S with the components $s_1, \ldots, s_m$. Assume that the properties and ways of interaction of these components are represented and described by means of some real valued functions (variables) x_i $(i=1,$

$\ldots, n$) each of which may be vector valued. Now the vector $x = \langle x_1, \ldots, x_n \rangle$ can be employed to give (partial) state descriptions of the system. These state descriptions are only partial if there are some (latent) stochastic factors (called "disturbance" variables) affecting the behavior of the system. These disturbances (or rather their effects) are usually represented by a random vector $u = \langle u_1, \ldots, u_m \rangle$.

A theory (or "model") about the full behavior pattern of the system is generally given by a function

(4.23) $$f(x) = u.$$

Very often social scientists now make a greatly simplifying assumption and assume that f is a *linear* mapping. That is, it is assumed that f is representable by a system of linear equations given in matrix notation by

(4.24) $$Ax = u.$$

Here A is a $m \times n$ matrix of real parameters (constants), x is an n-component column vector and u is an m-component column vector. The elements of A can represent the intensities of the properties (represented by the x_i's), and their interaction. Important forms of such interaction between the variables are the relations of *causation* and *feedback* (cf. BLALOCK (1969)).

In the theory formalized by (4.24) the elements of x are usually considered directly observational. This is the case especially in econometric models which we mainly have in mind below (cf. HURWICZ (1962), FISHER (1966)). Some of them are *predetermined* or *exogenous* or input variables while the rest are *endogenous* or output variables. At least some parameters in A are regarded as theoretical (roughly in the sense of our characterization), and so are the disturbances (in principle and from the point of view of direct measurement).

It is generally assumed that in (4.24) the number of endogenous variables is m. Then we can partition the vector x into an m-component vector y and an n-m-component vector z. Similarly, A is partitioned into a $m \times m$ matrix B and an $m \times (n-m)$ matrix, that is, $A = [B\, \Gamma]$. Thus we get as an equivalent form for (4.24) this:

(4.25) $$By + \Gamma z = u.$$

(4.25) (and implicitly also (4.24)) defines the so called *structural form* of the theory (to use econometric terminology). Provided that B is a nonsingular matrix we can premultiply (4.25) by the inverse matrix B^{-1} to get

$$y = \Pi z + v \tag{4.26}$$

where $\Pi = -B^{-1}\Gamma$ and $v = B^{-1}u$. Notice that while Π can thus be explicitly defined in terms of B and Γ, neither of the latter can be defined in terms of Π (nor any other notions of (4.26)). The form (4.26) is called the *reduced form* of the theory. This form gives an explicit statement of how the values of the endogenous variables are determined by the predetermined variables and the disturbances. Despite the appearance of the disturbance vector v in (4.26) the reduced form is considered observational on the "population level" (i. e. considered apart from statistical sampling variation). That is, the probability distribution of y is considered estimable by means of measurements of the variables in y under fixed values of the predetermined variables and some specific assumptions concerning the joint distribution of the disturbances. The parameters of Π are therefore in principle estimable.

Speaking in general terms, (4.26) represents an observational or empirical law (observational subtheory of (4.24) and (4.25)) which describes how the factual system S acts upon certain stimuli. We explain this observational regularity by means of a theory of the form (4.25) (or (4.24)) which postulates an inner structure to account for the overt behavior of the system. As usual, there will be many (in general infinitely many) theories which potentially explain (or generate) the law (4.26). That is, there are generally many other theories which also account for the probability distribution of the endogenous variables y. To see this, let F be any nonsingular $m \times m$ matrix. Premultiply (4.24) by F to get

$$A^* x = u^* \tag{4.27}$$

where $A^* = FA$ and $u^* = Fu$. Correspondingly we have new partitions $A^* = [B^* \; \Gamma^*]$ such that $B^* \neq B$ and $\Gamma^* \neq \Gamma$ in general. Only when the permissible transformations are so restricted that F must be the identity matrix will there be a uniquely observationally identifiable explanatory theory for (4.26). Generally this requires that additional assumptions or restrictions $C_1, C_2, \ldots$ be added to the core theory (4.25) (or (4.24)).

Let us now examine more carefully the problem of identifying the assumed underlying explanatory structure. The (logical) models of the theory T formalized by (4.25) obviously consist of a domain D of objects and of the numerically specified interpretations for the variables z, y, and u as well as of the numerically specified values for the parameters in B and Γ. Given the structural form (4.25) of T the interpretations of z, y, u do not uniquely fix the parameters in B and Γ as we just noticed. On the other hand, the interpretations of z and u (thus including the specification of the probability distribution of u) suffice to define explicitly the probability distribution of y in accordance with (4.26). Let us therefore concentrate on the set of all the specific numerical probability distributions of the endogenous vector y which are generated by varying the interpretations of the predetermined z and v.

We say that two models $\mathscr{M}_1$ and $\mathscr{M}_2$ (with the same domain) of T (the structural equation (4.25)) are *observationally equivalent* if and only if they (for all interpretations of z) determine identical probability distributions $H(y)$ for the endogenous variables.

Now we are ready to define the basic notions of *unique identifiability* of a model of the theory T and of the theory T itself as well as of a (theoretical) parameter of T. Our definitions closely agree with the usual econometric definitions (cf. KOOPMANS (1953), FISHER (1966), TUOMELA (1968b))[7]:

A *model* $\mathscr{M}$ of T is *uniquely identifiable* if and only if $\mathscr{M}$ is the only member of the observational equivalence class determined by the probability distribution $H(y)$ of y that it generates[8].

A *theory* T is *uniquely identifiable* if and only if all the models of T are uniquely identifiable.

A *parameter* a_{ij} (occurring in a matrix $A = [B\ \Gamma]$) is *uniquely identifiable* in T if and only if for every (specified) probability distribution $H(y)$ it is the case that a_{ij} has the same value within all the $H(y)$-equivalence classes generated by the models of T.

---

7 The econometric notion of identifiability is easily seen to coincide with the notion of *observability* (of a state of a system) used within mathematical system theory. Hence the results of this chapter also apply to this notion, widely employed in engineering. See e. g. ZADEH and POLAK (1969), pp. 248—251.

8 Notice that $H(y)$ creates several observational equivalence classes with different domains, as models are grouped into them on the basis of their agreement on the value of $H(y)$ *and* their domain.

This definition generalizes to any partition of A and to A itself.

Let us illustrate our abstract discussion by a simple linear market theory from economics. The following linear market theory is constructed to account for the supply and demand of a given commodity at a particular moment of time. We take the following two sentences as the axioms of the theory (giving its structural form):

$$y_1 = a\, y_2 + b\, x + u_1 \qquad \text{(demand)}$$

$$y_2 = c\, y_1 + u_2 \qquad \text{(supply)}$$

where y_1 represents the quantity of the commodity;
y_2 represents the price of the commodity;
x represents personal income;
a, b, c are real valued free parameters;
u_1, u_2 are random variables (disturbances) with a specified joint probability distribution.

The quantity y_1 (endogenous variable) and the price y_2 (exogenous variable) are assumed to be directly observable. Here we want to account for the values of y_1 and y_2, not for those of x which is considered a predetermined observable variable. Sometimes we may want to add more axioms that give additional or "*a priori*" restrictions concerning the values of the parameters (e. g. $a > 0$, etc.).

When specific values are given to the concepts in this linear market theory we get a model for it, provided the axioms remain valid. Now we may calculate the probability distribution $H(y)$ of the endogenous variables and ask how many models there are that generate the same probability distribution of y_1. If this class has only one element $\mathcal{M}$, we call $\mathcal{M}$ uniquely identifiable. We call the economic theory uniquely identifiable if all its models are uniquely identifiable. A parameter is called uniquely identifiable if it has the same value in all the models within the same $H(y)$-equivalence class for all such equivalence classes. It can be shown, for instance, that in the linear market theory the parameter c is uniquely identified but not the others. (We can thus say that the supply equation is identified whereas the demand equation is not.)

Let us next translate the above definitions of identifiability into our logical framework by assuming a first-order reconstruction of the theory T representing the system S. According to our remarks above it suffices to consider the definability of $\mu = \{A\}$ in terms of $\lambda = \{z, H(y)\}$ in T. The problem of the unique identifiability of a model of T in terms of the interpretations of the members of λ is in fact seen to equal the problem of whether these interpretations (numerically) specify the interpretation of the matrix A. But if this is the case for all the models of T then (and only then) A is model theoretically definable in terms of λ in T. For our definition of model theoretic definability given in Section 1 of this chapter says essentially this: A predicate P of μ is model theoretically definable in terms of the interpretations (values) of the members of λ, given T, if and only if any two models of T which agree in their domains and in their interpretations of the members of λ also agree in their interpretation of P. The matrix A can be regarded as a complex theoretical predicate. In the econometric interpretation A represents the underlying explanatory mechanism *in re*. In other words, the identification of A (given some specification of the disturbances u) specifies the function f of (4.23) which represents the *full* behavior pattern of the system S under study. Using Beth's theorem (Theorem IV.1.) we can formulate our result as follows:

Theorem IV.11. The internal structure of a system S as described by a theory T (of the form (4.24)), possibly complemented with some auxiliary assumptions C, is uniquely observationally identifiable if and only if the matrix A is explicitly definable in terms of the probability distribution $H(y)$ of y (the endogenous variables) and of x (the predetermined variables) in T.

On the basis of our definition of the unique identifiability of parameters above Theorem IV.11. holds also for any parts of the matrix A and hence for parts of the internal mechanism of the system S.

Generally the structural form (4.24) is not uniquely identifiable, as we have noticed. The theorist has to add some extra information, e. g. concerning the values of some parameters in A, in order to make it uniquely identifiable. (For the well-known algebraic criteria of the unique identifiability of the equations in (4.24) see e. g. FISHER (1966).) Loosely speaking, the number of the observational terms (in z and y) must be great enough to enable one to solve the linear equation system for the unknown parameters in A. Generally this requires that the theory specifies a lower bound for the cardinality of the domains of its models. This cardinality corresponds to the number of components in the system S.

The additional restrictions C_i added to (4.24) often concern only specific circumstances and they identify A uniquely only for some important cases (in some models of T). Even their (usually open-ended) totality $C=\{C_1, C_2, \ldots\}$ does not in actual scientific practice suffice to give full unique identifiability of A (nor of its parameters). It only gives some kind of high degree of definability (cf. Section 3.1. of this chapter).

Suppose that the form (4.24) does not as such uniquely identify A but that it does uniquely identify it both when restricted by a condition C_1 and when restricted by a C_2. These two additional assumptions represent two distinct alternative ways of uniquely identifying A. We now say that A is *overidentified* in the applied theory T & C_1 & C_2 (cf. FISHER (1966), p. 29). In the special case when C_1 and C_2 are mutually incompatible they cannot be conjoined to T at the same time. Notice that if A becomes explicitly defined in T & C_1 and T&C_2 then the applied theory T & C_1 & C_2 serves to satisfy the above condition for overidentification.

In principle one can almost always overidentify any theory. (However, for a counterexample see our later Theorem VI.6.). The methodological importance of overidentifiability is that it makes possible a richer empirical testing of the theory. For in a merely uniquely identified theory T & C_1 all the empirical observations from an experiment are used for estimating the matrix A, and T cannot be noncircularly tested against the same data. But the parameters estimated with the help of C_1 can be used to derive predictions for some new situation or condition C_2 which serves to test the theory T.

Next we ask the following methodologically central question: Why should one require unique observational identifiability of the underlying mechanism (represented by the matrix A)? One answer to this is that *the parameters of A cannot statistically be estimated by a consistent point estimator unless A is uniquely identified* (see e. g. FISHER (1966) and also TUOMELA (1968b) for a discussion of this well-known result). The estimated parameters are of course assumed to be necessary for making observational predictions. However, here an instrumentalist may want to present the theoretician's dilemma argument, for in principle we are now exactly in the methodological situation discussed in Chapter I (cf. our quotation from SKINNER (1953) and HULL (1943)). However, econometricians in general seem to believe in the reality of an underlying explanatory structure and base their methodological arguments on that.

(Cf. especially the argument based on the changing of the underlying structure in HURWICZ (1962); also see Chapter VII.) We shall not here discuss them as they are just special versions of the arguments for the desirability of theoretical concepts, to which question most of this book is devoted.

So far we have mostly discussed cases of unique identifiability (of theories, their models and concepts) and mentioned the notions of unidentifiability and overidentifiability which are characterizable by means of unique identifiability. For theoretical purposes it is still interesting to consider a generalization of unique identifiability which can be termed *finite* or *n-fold identifiability* (cf. HURWICZ (1950)). We can generalize the above definition of the unique identifiability of a model $\mathcal{M}$ of T as follows:

A model $\mathcal{M}$ of T is *n-foldly identifiable* if and only if there are at most n models in the equivalence class determined by the probability distribution $H(y)$ generated by $\mathcal{M}$.

The n-fold identifiability of a theory T (or equivalently the matrix A associated with its form (4.24)) and the n-fold identifiability of a parameter a_{ij} of A are defined in an analogous way. In addition, we can define a notion of *restricted identifiability* by requiring that there are at most $|D|$ models in the same class, D being the domain of the models.

The logical remarks made above concerning unique identifiability have their generalized counterparts for n-fold identifiability and restricted identifiability. Analogously with the case of unique identifiability (Theorem IV.11.) we now have on the basis of Kueker's theorem (Theorem IV.8.) and Chang-Makkai's theorem (IV. 9):

Theorem IV.12. The internal mechanism of a system S as described by a theory T (of the general form (4.24), possibly complemented with some auxiliary assumptions C), is (a) n-foldly (observationally) identifiable, (b) restrictedly identifiable if and only if the matrix A is (a) relatively definable, (b) restrictedly definable in terms of $H(y)$ and x in T.

In general, matrices A in the equations (4.24) are not finitely identifiable, but they may be restrictedly identifiable and of course uniquely identifiable depending on how many and what kind of additional constraints are added to the theory T. Still there may be other kinds of behavioral theories (e. g. of the general form (4.23)) within which cases of finite identifiability can be found (cf. e. g. the simple example in RAMSEY (1931)).

As we have assumed above that our theories have been reconstructed in first-order logic the presence of nonstandard models may affect at least cases of restricted identifiability in ways which remain to be studied.

There is one final remark to be made in connection of theories of type (4.24) (and (4.25)). The parameters in the matrix A were said to be real valued constants. But it is important to notice that after all they are *free* parameters to be estimated. Therefore it may seem logically more appropriate to say that (4.24) is to be read

(4.24*) There exists a matrix A such that $A\,x = u$.

In other words, read this way (4.24) contains variables in A, and these variables are to be interpreted as real valued constants in the models of (4.24). Under this construal we are theorizing with a Ramsey-sentence and not with a theory with theoretical predicate *constants*. Notice, incidentally, that if A is identifiable to some degree, our *numerical* Ramsey sentences of Section IV.1. provide us with a neat descriptive device applicable here.

Notice, furthermore, that even if (4.24) is accepted in its original reading one treats the elements of A as uninterpreted dummies in the original phases of theory construction. Only later when the theory has been more widely used these dummies acquire (semantical) meaning such that (4.24) exceeds (4.24*) in its semantic content.

Especially clearly these difficulties can be seen within *factor analysis* which can in principle be represented by a theory of form (4.24). For in factor analysis not only A but also the predetermined variables z are theoretical. Even the number of variables in the vector z is initially unknown. Therefore the establishment of a proper psychological or sociological factor theory presupposes the fixing of the number of factors, identifying the loading matrix A and giving a proper semantical interpretation for all the components of the theory (see e. g. TUOMELA (1968 b) for comments on this).

Chapter V

Meaning and Interpretation of Theoretical Concepts

1. The Partial Interpretation View on Interpretation

1.1. The empiricist *partial interpretation view* on interpreting theories has been dominant in the last few decades, so dominant, in fact, that it has been called the *received view* on the interpretation and meaning of theories. The view is represented in the works of, for instance, CARNAP (1937), (1956), and (1966), HEMPEL (1958), ROZEBOOM (1960), (1963), and (1970), NAGEL (1961), PRZELECKI (1969), and STEGMÜLLER (1970). However, in recent years it has been heavily attacked by PUTNAM (1962), FEYERABEND (1965), ACHINSTEIN (1969), and HEMPEL (1970), among others.

It may seem that there must be some truth in the received view on the meaning of scientific concepts, for it has had so many outstanding representatives. We shall therefore start with a description and critical evaluation of this approach, from the point of view of semantical realism. The standard accounts of the partial interpretation view have quite often been discussed in the literature. Consequently, we have chosen to concentrate more on the fresh and clear accounts of PRZELECKI (1969), PRZELECKI and WOJCICKI (1969), WINNIE (1971), and the above mentioned works of ROZEBOOM. These works are also the most pertinent to the formal framework of this book.

A major standard feature in any empiricist epistemology and semantics is the following. It is assumed that the extralogical concepts of any (formal) scientific language can be dichotomized (by a semantical or epistemological criterion) into observational and theoretical concepts (see our discussion in Chapter I). A corresponding distinction is made between statements according to the terms they contain. Thus we have a division of the scientific language into an observational language and a theoretical language. (Sometimes it is in addition required that the logico-mathematical apparatus of the theoretical sublanguage be in some way richer than that of the observational sublanguage.) For an empiricist all factual knowledge is based on or inferred from some kind of "data basis" stated by means of the observational language.

An analogous thesis holds for empiricists' semantics. Observational statements are assumed to have "full meaning" or to be semantically fully interpreted. The observational sublanguage is accordingly assumed to be semantically (relatively) unproblematic, whereas this is not the case for the theoretical sublanguage. By analogy with the epistemological assumption of empiricism it is now assumed that the meanings of theoretical terms and statements are derived by means of correspondence rules or, rather, meaning postulates from the observational expressions. But the interpretation and meaning the theoretical expressions thus get is (in some sense) only partial. This is usually taken to be a consequence of the accepted "fact" (or assumption) that theoretical terms and statements are not in general translatable or reducible into the observational language by means of explicit definitions.

If it is thus accepted that the theoretical language is only a partially and indirectly interpreted calculus, then it may seem difficult to speak of the truth or falsity of purely theoretical statements; this again seems directly to lead one to scientific instrumentalism. However, as HEMPEL (1958) argues, in a suitably rich metalanguage one can give a Tarskian truth definition in order to have open the possibility for a realistic interpretation, in letter at least.

1.2. Carnap, Hempel and many other empiricists have taken the meanings of observational terms and statements to be relatively clear (often *per definitionem*). Most of them have not really given any detailed account of this matter (cf. CARNAP (1956), HEMPEL (1958)). On the other hand, Przelecki tries to give a clear and explicit semantical account of the (empirical) meaning of observational terms and statements in his recent book (PRZELECKI (1969)). Perhaps his view is not acceptable to many other empiricists. Be this as it may, his account is worth discussing in its own right as well, and our discussion will hopefully illuminate the problems involved in interpreting a formal language. Let us therefore go on to present and critically discuss the main features of Przelecki's semantics for an observational language.

The word 'interpretation' means for Przelecki interpretation in the model theoretic sense. Roughly speaking, the meaning of a predicate equals its denotation in each possible empirical state of affairs. The interpretations (i. e. the empirical truth conditions) of sentences are presumably obtained by means of the empirical interpretations of the primitive predicates and the grammar of the language. We shall below discuss only the empirical meaning (interpretation) of the primitive observational predicates of a given scientific theory.

Przelecki's formal framework is the usual kind of first-order predicate logic with a finite number of predicates as its only extralogical constants (cf. the previous chapters of this book). Przelecki assumes that this formal language, and theories formalized within it, can be given an empirical interpretation (in a semantic sense) through the *proper* or *intended models* of the language, but not verbally. Then the main problem for Przelecki is to define a set of intended empirical models (call it M^*) for his first-order language.

Can the family M^* be determined by verbal means only? By a verbal interpretation Przelecki means defining the family M^* to be the set of models for a certain set, MP, of meaning postulates stated in a first-order language $\mathscr{L}$ $(=\mathscr{L}(\lambda \cup \mu))$. Any other way of interpreting language is called nonverbal. Przelecki now argues, seemingly against the partial interpretation tradition, that the language of an empirical theory cannot be determined in a verbal way only.

Suppose it could be. The first obvious possibility that Przelecki considers is a definition of M^* by:

$$\mathscr{M} \in M^* \equiv MP \subseteq Ver(\mathscr{M}), \tag{5.1}$$

where $Ver(\mathscr{M})$ is the set of sentences of $\mathscr{L}$ true in $\mathscr{M}$. But this does not work, for the isomorphism theorem of first-order predicate logic implies that if $\mathscr{M}$ is an intuitively acceptable model of MP then all models isomorphic to $\mathscr{M}$ are also models of MP. Among them we have all kinds of unacceptable non-empirical, e. g. arithmetic, models. At best we get the structure of denotations of predicates by this method, and for infinite models not even that. Furthermore, it can be proved on the basis of the isomorphism theorem that under the present construal all the predicates of $\mathscr{L}$ will always either denote the empty set, or remain *completely vague* in the following sense:

(5.2) $(x)\ [(E\mathscr{M} \in M^*$ such that $x \in D_{\mathscr{M}}(P_i))\ \&\ (E\mathscr{M} \in M^*$ such that $x \notin D_{\mathscr{M}}(P_i))]$

where P_i is any predicate of $\mathscr{L}$ and $D_{\mathscr{M}}(P_i)$ its denotation in a model $\mathscr{M}$. What Przelecki requires as a necessary condition of an acceptable empirical interpretation is that

(5.3) $(Ex)\ [((\mathscr{M})\ (\mathscr{M} \in M^* \supset x \in D_{\mathscr{M}}(P_i)) \vee (\mathscr{M})\ (\mathscr{M} \in M^* \supset \supset x \notin D_{\mathscr{M}}(P_i))]$

will hold for some predicates P_i at least.

There is no essential improvement on the vagueness of predicates if instead of (5.1) it is required that

(5.4) $\mathscr{M} \in M^* \equiv U(\mathscr{M}) = U\ \&\ MP \subseteq Ver(\mathscr{M})$,

where '$U(\mathscr{M}) = U$' is read 'the domain of $\mathscr{M}$ is U'. Moreover, we do not see any additional philosophical reason for accepting (5.4) instead of (5.1); also see below.

Przelecki concludes on the basis of his rejection of (5.1) and (5.4) that at least some of the predicates P_i have to be interpreted nonverbally or *ostensively*, that is, by pointing out the objects to which they apply. It follows that there can be no meaning postulates for such predicates P_i.

However, Przelecki's conclusion is not warranted. From the fact that some types of verbal interpretation do not work we cannot conclude that no kind of empirical verbal interpretation could succeed. In fact we will below argue that we can interpret $\mathscr{L}$ by means of a suitable intensional metalanguage. But let us first see how Przelecki fares with his ostensive interpretation.

Przelecki calls *observational* exactly those predicates which are interpreted ostensively. Let the set of such predicates be λ. Thus an ostensive interpretation is given for the observational sublanguage $\mathscr{L}(\lambda)$ of $\mathscr{L}(\lambda \cup \mu)$. Przelecki assumes that $\mathscr{L}$ speaks about a fixed domain U of physical objects, $U_\lambda \subseteq U$ of which are observable and (presumably) ostensively determined (cf. PRZELECKI (1969), pp. 38—

39)[1]. (Notice that the nonobservable objects in $U - U_\lambda$ are in principle allowed to have observational properties even if there is no (observational?) criterion of application of such properties for unobservable objects (PRZELECKI (1969), p. 41)). I find an attempt like this to fix the reference class of a theory or language (i. e. a universe of objects) *extensionally* by cardinality unacceptable in case of universally applicable scientific theories, whose reference class is the class of *all possible objects* of a certain kind. Such theories deal with the properties of domains of almost any size. Furthermore, there is in general no extensionally fixed or fixable *maximal* domain of objects for a universal scientific theory. The domain or domains of objects are normally given by (intensional) descriptions, not by pointing at objects. In addition we have to notice that if the domain in question is infinite or indefinitely large it cannot be finitely specified by Przelecki's kind of ostension.

An ostensive method for determining a domain of objects might work in the case of some specific experimental situations or some special circumstances to which a theory is applied. It may also work for specifying *a* set or *some* sets of typical intended objects for a theory. It might, furthermore, succeed for cases where we are merely interested in (some specific kind of) objects existing in our actual world *at a specific time*. But all these situations give at most a small subset of the class of *all* the intended objects. This class is, however, to some extent unspecifiable and open *a priori*. Hence, as we said, there is no fixed "maximal" domain of a universal scientific theory.

1.3. Let us now consider the interpretation of observational predicates. Przelecki discusses two problems involved in an ostensive interpretation. One problem is that ostensively defined predicates are always *vague*, because there are always things such that the question whether they belong to the denotation of the predicate is basically undecidable. For instance, due to the vagueness of 'tall' there are always objects, e. g. people, who are doubtfully tall, and equally doubtfully not tall. Even if this point about linguistic (or conceptual) vagueness is acceptable to a certain extent within ordinary discourse, I suggest that we might try to make more exact such predicates for

1 Przelecki does not tell us *expressis verbis* how the domains U and U_λ are obtained, but we gather from his discussion that U_λ is ostensively obtained. As $U - U_\lambda$ cannot be obtained this way, Przelecki owes us a clarification on how it is.

the purposes of scientific observation, in order to minimize this kind of vagueness.

In any case Przelecki considers this vagueness unescapable and takes it into account when constructing his set M_λ of intended observational models (with domain U_λ) for $\mathscr{L}(\lambda)$. The above vagueness of observational predicates entails that the set M_λ contains more than one model. We can see why by means of an example. Consider some simplified anthropological theory about the interrelation of tallness and red-hairedness of presently existing (observable) human beings. We now have to give ostensively the denotation of the predicates 'tall' and 'red-haired' in the domain U_λ of presently living people. If there were no vagueness we would obviously get only one Przeleckian intended model. But due to the vagueness of 'tall' and 'red-haired' there will always be "border-line" cases for both of these predicates. These border-line people are taken into account by classifying them alternatively in all possible ways (respecting the definitely positive and negative cases of these predicates) into the extensions of 'tall' and 'not-tall', 'red-haired' and 'not-red-haired'. Thus a border-line case may belong to the denotation of a predicate P_i in one of the intended models whereas it does not belong to it in another one. Therefore we generally get more than one member in M_λ.

Now stretch your imagination to take into account the set $U - U_\lambda$ of unobservable existing human beings living, say, on some far-away inaccessible planet. According to Przelecki's account the predicates 'tall' and 'red-haired' remain totally indeterminate in the set $U - U_\lambda$. Therefore the number of intended $\mathscr{L}(\lambda)$-models (with domain U) in the family M_λ^* is still larger than that in M_λ.

The result that the ostensive method then gives us is that observational predicates of $\mathscr{L}(\lambda)$ generally remain vague. However, now the qualification is needed that criterion (5.2) for *complete* vagueness holds only for the border-line objects and for the unobservable objects (members of $U - U_\lambda$). Furthermore, Przelecki's necessary condition (5.3) for empirical interpretation will now presumably be satisfied, as there will in all likelihood be some predicates which are known *a priori* to apply to some observable objects which are not borderline cases. But it should be remembered that (5.3) is only a necessary condition and — I argue — a philosophically weak one.

I interpret the above result as saying that not very much was gained, after all, by resorting to a nonverbal method of interpretation. And that is not enough, as several new problems arise. Let us consider one such problem, which Przelecki overlooks. It is the following "fitting-together" problem. In any model of $\mathscr{L}(\lambda)$ we have to specify not only the denotations of the isolated primitive predicates but also how the denotations of different predicates relate to each other. Thus it does not suffice to know which people are tall and which are not and which people are red-haired and which are not. Every model of $\mathscr{L}(\lambda)$ says how the extensions of 'tall', 'not-tall', 'red-haired', and 'not-red-haired' are interrelated.

Przelecki does not explicitly tell us whether his ostensive interpretation method does this. Suppose it does. Then it certainly does more than a semantical interpretation method should do. For most of the above kind of relationships are *a posteriori* and synthetic, and it is indeed the task of science, not that of a semanticist, to find them out. They cannot be completely known before science has finished its task. Thus ostension cannot do so much as there would then be nothing left for factual scientific investigation. Hence we have to suppose that Przelecki's ostensive method specifies the denotations of the primitive observation predicates only in an isolated way. It follows that all the possible ways in which these predicates can be factually interrelated now have to be taken into account. This is done analogously to the above case of vagueness. Thus the size of both M_λ and M^*_λ increases considerably. To have an interpretation of $\mathscr{L}(\lambda)$ independent of experience, we obviously have to include all these models in M_λ and M^*_λ. (It follows that no contingent scientific theory formulated in $\mathscr{L}(\lambda)$ (or $\mathscr{L}$) can be true in all the models of our newly constructed families M_λ and M^*_λ.)

To summarize: 1) an ostensive specification of the domain about which a scientific theory speaks is inadequate; 2) an ostensive interpretation of the predicates of $\mathscr{L}(\lambda)$ also leads to great and, in our opinion, unnecessary difficulties. What our above criticism amounts to is that there is no such well-defined thing as the set of intended models for $\mathscr{L}(\lambda)$. It is relatively easy to specify a class of *typical* intended models but the class of *all* intended models is certainly "open-ended". But even if there were such a well-defined class it would create more problems than it solves when used for semantical interpretation. We claim that model theory as such is unable to handle questions of the empirical (or, rather, factual) interpretation (in a semantical sense) of scientific theories. While model theoretic methods, properly used, *may* suffice for questions dealing with the extensions (denotations) of expressions, truth of statements, and structural aspects of the world, they are insufficient for questions of meaning (intension). In interpreting the predicates of $\mathscr{L}(\lambda)$ we should proceed verbally (in a philosophically genuine sense) rather than ostensively, as we are generally in possession of intelligible communication devices for scientific purposes.

To elaborate one aspect of this, we should and generally can assume that $\mathscr{L}(\lambda)$ is semantically understandable in our metalanguage, which can well be intensional. Psychologically speaking, scientists often start their theorizing by communicating their observations and observational hypotheses by means of some (possibly enriched) fragment of the natural language which is understood at least by a certain scientific community. What we are doing here is to translate the formalized statements back into the same or into another pragmatically intelligible language. Then metastatements like

(5.5) The predicate '*P*' (of $\mathscr{L}(\lambda)$) means tall (or designates tallness),

which give senses of predicates, are understandable. (We shall discuss this matter below.) The word 'tall' *may* have been learnt by ostension but 1) *that* ostension is different from Przelecki's ostension, and in any case 2) no reference to ostension is needed after the meaning of 'tall' has been learnt. Furthermore, our traditional solution for interpreting observational predicates allows for the presence of analytic statements within $\mathscr{L}(\lambda)$ to connect the denotations of different observational predicates. (Such analytic statements may of course have clearly nonintended models, such as arithmetic ones, in addition to intended models. One way to exclude them is by means of intensional descriptions in the metalanguage.)

2. Meaning and Interpretation of Scientific Terms

2.1. The partial interpretation view on the interpretation of theories assumes that theoretical terms derive all their meaning from observational expressions on the basis of their connections with the latter. The observational language thus has to be semantically understood. This feature cannot easily be accounted for by the kind of intended-model approach Przelecki advocates, if our preceding criticisms are acceptable. Instead we may resort to semantic rules of the kind (5.5) (or other comparable formulations). To gain pragmatic (psychological) understanding of the observational language additional linguistic as well as nonlinguistic methods can of course be used.

In a typical partial interpretation account the theoretical language $\mathscr{L}(\mu)$, together with the axioms of a core theory $T^*(\mu)$ (cf. Chapter IV) and the rules of deduction, is an uninterpreted calculus (see CARNAP (1956), p. 46). Theoretical terms cannot be given (pragmatically?) intelligible semantic designation rules corresponding to (5.5). This follows at least in part from the dogma that theoretical terms designate and refer to unobservable entities. All the interpretation the theoretical terms and statements get is given to them through some *correspondence rules* (coordinating rules, interpretive postulates) connecting predicates of μ with those of λ in the full language $\mathscr{L}(\lambda \cup \mu)$ (cf. CARNAP (1956) and HEMPEL (1958)). (In the case of scientific languages of an ordinary kind these correspondence rules can be formulated either as rules of inference, or as postulates in the object language (cf. CARNAP (1956)). We shall here regard them as postulates.) Since the publication of Carnap's 'Testability and Meaning' (1937) the partial interpretation theoreticians have agreed that these correspondence rules do not in general explicitly define theoretical concepts in terms of observational ones (cf. CARNAP (1937)). Theoretical terms like 'magnetizability', 'electron', 'gene', and 'superego' do not admit of explicit definability in terms of observational terms by the property that for certain statements containing theoretical terms no possible observational results can ever be absolutely conclusive evidence but at best evidence yielding a high probability (see CARNAP (1956), p. 69). It follows that the theoretical language gets only a partial and indirect interpretation on the basis of the observational language.

Partial interpretation theoreticians differ somewhat on the issue whether correspondence rules are analytic or synthetic. If an analytic-synthetic dichotomy of scientific statements is accepted then it is required that some (but not all) of the correspondence postulates are analytic (i. e. meaning postulates). We shall below be concerned primarily with the views of those partial interpretation theoreticians who do accept such an analytic-synthetic division (e. g. Carnap, Winnie, Przelecki, Rozeboom). Notable exceptions to them are Hempel and Nagel.

Let us take a psychological example of partial interpretation:

"There is no itching without scratching, provided normal conditions obtain."

In the spirit of neowittgensteinians we might regard this correspondence rule as an analytic statement partially connecting the theoretical sensation term 'itching' with the observational term 'scratching'. Formally, we may write it as

$$(x)\ (I\ (x) \supset S\ (x)) \tag{5.6}$$

where '$I\ (x)$' translates 'x is an instance of itching under normal conditions' and '$S\ (x)$' is a translation of 'x is an instance of scratching'. The statement 5.6 is assumed to be a consequence of a psychological theory of sensations, and, furthermore, for Carnapians and neowittgensteinians a consequence of the meaning postulates of the theory. As (5.6) is only a conditional statement and as it cannot be strengthened into an explicit definition, 'itching' gets only a partial meaning.

As a physical example of the kind of correspondence rules considered by the partial interpretation theoreticians we may give the following (by CARNAP (1966), p. 233):

> "If there is an electromagnetic oscillation of a specified frequency, then there is a visible greenish-blue color of a certain hue."

In this statement, which is presumably synthetic, an observational visual sensation notion (designated by an observational expression *stricto sensu*) is connected with a theoretical microprocess.

On the basis of our discussion it can roughly be seen what is above meant by giving partial meanings or partial empirical interpretations for theoretical terms on the basis of observational terms. It is, first of all, important to distinguish between the following senses of interpretation of theoretical terms and statements in this context (recall our distinction between 'factual' and 'empirical' in Chapter I):

(a) interpretation as giving *factual meaning* (intension),
(b) interpretation as giving *factual denotation* due to i) semantical postulates or ii) semantical postulates *and* scientific theory.
(c) interpretation as giving *empirical* (or even *experiential*) *content* (import, "meaning")
(d) interpretation as giving *empirical* (or *experiential*) *denotation.*

Often these different senses of interpretation have not been kept distinct in the writings of empiricists. Quite commonly 'factual' and 'empirical' are treated as synonyms, which reduces (a) to (c) and (b) to (d). Moreover, our notion of empirical (=empirical or observational *lato sensu*) is sometimes not distinguished from experiential (empirical or observational *stricto sensu*). (The liberal version of partial interpretation by Rozeboom to be discussed does not completely conflate these notions.)

In any case the partial interpretation view does not consider (a) to make much sense and it rather seldom accepts even (b). Furthermore it is mainly concerned with the extensions of scientific terms and statements rather than with their intensions. (Intensions become involved in this kind of interpretation at most only through the semantic rules interpreting observational predicates.) The problem within the interpretation of theoretical terms and statements then, in complete parallel with the epistemological questions of truth and evidence, becomes how to fix or determine by observational procedures their extensions.

The extensions of observational predicates are assumed to become determined directly by means of the observer's senses or his measurement devices. In the case of theoretical terms this is not considered possible. Their extensions and meanings, therefore, have to be determined indirectly and, as we saw, at best partially by means of the observational terms. All correspondence rules (or systems of such) which do not satisfy the criterion of eliminability (see Chapter IV) accomplish only partial interpretation. For instance, conditional, partial, and "gradual" observational definability provide examples of partial empirical interpretation. (Operational "definitions", indicators, "objectifiers", and various measurement axioms belong here). Part of the partial interpretation thus obtained is semantical (and given by meaning postulates) while the rest is contingent.

Partial interpretation can in an obvious way be considered also from a model theoretic point of view. The formal connections between the proof theoretic and model theoretic notions of connectedness or definability have been discussed in Chapter IV and will be discussed again later in this chapter.

2.2. The most explicit and most carefully formulated liberal version of the partial interpretation view is that in ROZEBOOM (1960), (1963), and (1970). Using his formulation we can now summarize the main underlying semantical assumption in this approach by the following *Thesis of Semantical Empiricism* (ROZEBOOM (1963), p. 303): "The semantic properties, if any, of theoretical expressions, derive, in a potentially useful and syntactically general manner, wholly from their use with the observation language."

Rozeboom in fact allows this thesis to be characteristic of the (or a) theoretical/observational dichotomy. But because the rather full parallelism between epistemology and semantics within the kind of empiricism we are discussing, we may also characterize theoretical terms as follows (cf. ROZEBOOM (1970), p. 199). We say that the members of μ are theoretical with respect to the set λ of observational or "data" predicates if 1) they are not analytically definable in terms of the predicates in λ and if the credibilities of all the sentences $F_i(\mu)$ containing members of μ derive entirely from the credibilities of sentences $G_j(\lambda)$ containing only predicates in λ by way of the logical structure of the sentences $F_i(\mu)$ and their logical relationships to the sentences $G_j(\lambda)$.

Essentially on the basis of the Thesis of Semantical Empiricism and its rather obvious technical elaborations Rozeboom derives a number of interesting conclusions which characterize liberal versions of the partial interpretation view. Due to limitations of space we cannot here present any proofs and other details but only a few results which are interesting for our present purposes.

Let us examine the following statements which are essentially consequences of the Thesis of Semantical Empiricism (cf. e. g. ROZEBOOM (1960), pp. 360—361, 372—373 and (1970), pp. 216—217):

(1) Theoretical terms can have referents of their own and can thus be cognitively significant.

(2) Theoretical statements may signify states of affairs not signifiable by observational statements.

(3) The truth conditions of any theoretical sentence $F(\mu)$ can be expressed wholly in terms of the observational vocabulary relative to which $F(\mu)$ is theoretical.

(4) Theoretical predicates and expressions do not, in general, have unique referents. The semantic relation of designation is a many-many relation (and not a many-one relation as in traditional semantics.) Thus a theoretical predicate may simultaneously designate a variety of properties over and above its denoting the various parti-

culars which exemplify these properties. (According to Rozeboom the importance of this conclusion cannot be overestimated.)

(5) a) Two theories $T(\lambda \cup \mu)$ and $T'(\lambda \cup \mu)$ are incompatible if and only if they have incompatible consequences within $\mathscr{L}(\lambda)$ (cf. our Theorem III.6).

b) A theory is equivalent in meaning to its Ramsey sentence.

c) Two theories $T(\lambda \cup \mu)$ and $T'(\lambda \cup \mu)$ are equivalent in meaning if and only if they have the same observational consequences.

(The consequences (5.b) and (5.c) are for Rozeboom "intuitively inescapable" even if they do not follow rigorously from the Thesis of Semantical Empiricism and the auxiliary technical assumptions made by Rozeboom. If the Carnap sentence is assumed as an analytic postulate of the theory, they do follow rigorously; cf. our Theorem III.6.)

In this book we accept the viewpoint of *semantical realism* according to which theoretical terms and expressions may have designata and referents of their own independently of their relationships to an observational language (see the earlier formulation in Chapter I). Our Thesis of Semantical Realism (of Chapter I) is clearly incompatible with the Thesis of Semantical Empiricism. For instance, while semantical realism and liberal semantical empiricism agree on the above properties (1) and (2) (denied by stricter forms of semantical empiricism) they disagree on (3), (4), and (5).

Why are the properties (3), (4), and (5) unacceptable to the kind of realism adopted in this book? We cannot give a full and well-grounded answer before elaborating our version of semantical realism. But the following brief remarks can be made here.

First consider (3). It represents an unnecessarily strict requirement for a realist for whom theoretical statements have truth conditions of their own. For the theory to have observational content or import it is not necessary to give *full* truth conditions in the observational language. Many scientific theories do not even have any empirical content as such but acquire it only by the addition of special correspondence rules. Furthermore, in some situations even purely theoretical statements can play the role of evidence statements (a role usually reserved for the purely observational statements).

If the viewpoint of semantical realism is adopted then (most) theoretical terms can be given intelligible semantical designation rules (see V.2.3 below). As there is no reason why these rules should be given by means of antecedently understood *observational* expressions, all the properties a), b), and c) in (5) are of course denied by semantical realism.

Rozeboom attaches great importance to the result (4) as it implies the rejection of traditional semantics as far as the basic relation of designation is concerned. Why is a semantical realist then not compelled to accept (4)? Generally, of course, because he does not accept the philosophy underlying the Thesis of Semantical Empiricism. Speaking more specifically and in intuitive terms we can argue as follows.

Consider a simple theory $T(\lambda \cup \{P\})$ with P as the only theoretical predicate. Assume that the aspect of the world we are interested in has been modelled and idealized so as to be describable in model theoretic terms. Now consider an observational factual model $\mathscr{M}$ of the maximal subtheory $T'(\lambda)$ of $T(\lambda \cup \{P\})$. In general (i. e. when P is not piecewise definable; cf. Theorem IV.3.) when $\mathscr{M}$ can be expanded into a model $\langle \mathscr{M}, \mathrm{P} \rangle$ of $T(\lambda \cup \{P\})$ there is at least one other expansion $\langle \mathscr{M}, \mathrm{P}' \rangle$ with $\mathrm{P}' \neq \mathrm{P}$, which is also a model of $T(\lambda \cup \{P\})$. P and P′ are here assumed to be denotations of two different concepts C and C' both designated by the predicate P. A pure empiricist has to base his knowledge upon the information encoded solely in the observational models $\mathscr{M}$ (or in the subtheory $T'(\lambda)$). His knowledge thus never enables him to distinguish between the models $\langle \mathscr{M}, \mathrm{P} \rangle$ and $\langle \mathscr{M}, \mathrm{P}' \rangle$. If semantics is now based directly on this epistemological situation in accordance with the Thesis of Semantical Empiricism, Rozeboom's conclusion (4) follows rather immediately.

For a realist the situation is different. As the models $\langle \mathscr{M}, \mathrm{P} \rangle$ and $\langle \mathscr{M}, \mathrm{P}' \rangle$ are different and only one of them can then represent reality, the predicate P designates either C or C′ but not both; and it factually denotes either P or P′ but not both depending on how the world is. (The theory T may give us evidence as to how the world is but indeed it often leaves some openness, as here.) However, no resort to multiple designation is needed because our realist semantics is *not* based on epistemology in the way empiricist semantics is. The present theory T is not the *ultimate* criterion of how the world is.

Even if our realist semantics were thus based upon epistemology we would wait for additional knowledge or a sharper theory in order to distinguish between two different theoretical states of affairs. For us the world is not ultimately unknowable in any respect, or so we at last pretend.

2.3. Our basic standpoint on the philosophy of science is a synthesis of epistemological realism and semantical realism combined with an empiricist methodology for testing scientific theories. A few words to sketch and explain the semantical realism adopted in this book are now in order.

We shall assume that the (general) nonlogical terms occurring in scientific theories are normally capable of *designating* factual concepts such as the concept of specific gravity or that of latent aggression. Such concepts are to be construed as *objective*, at least in the senses of being non-experiential and, furthermore, generally accepted and internalized in a scientific community. They are to be understood as originally human creations developed in the course of time, and not as Platonic entities. Still they are not merely results of conventions which could easily be changed. For they usually belong to the ground stones of prevailing scientific paradigms (cf. KUHN (1962)).

We shall not here attempt a detailed philosophical justification of this kind of objectivistic view (cf. BUNGE (1972)). Rather we shall examine some of the consequences of adopting this position. We can first notice that our standpoint can be elaborated to give a criterion of cognitive significance of scientific terms. The general idea is this: A scientific term occurring in a theory has cognitive significance if it designates a factual scientific concept, which has been accepted by a scientific community to represent an objective aspect of the world. By saying this we rely on the capacity of scientists to form objectified concepts relevant to the gathering of knowledge concerning the external world. More generally, the cognitive significance of science ultimately comes about from scientists' continued confrontation with the world by means of their conceptual devices, such as theories, and not only by means of their senses.

Secondly, it seems that this kind of objectivistic realist semantics can avoid the worst pitfalls and difficulties of Platonism and Fido-Fido accounts because of its inbuilt historical pragmatic feedback mechanism. But a more detailed philosophical analysis of our evolutionary semantics and epistomology cannot be attempted here.

Let us now consider the following diagram which incorporates some of the semantic components relevant to interpreting a scientific term. In it '*L*' (or, as well, 'latent aggression') is assumed to occur in a formalized psychological theory (about human beings):

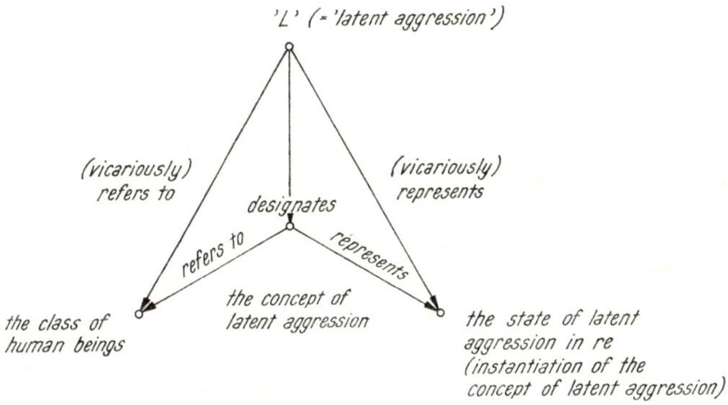

Diagram V.1

Diagram V.1 is an application of the general account of reference and designation developed in BUNGE (1972), which we accept here in its main lines.

In Diagram V.1. '*L*' can be a monadic predicate '$L\ (x)$' applicable to any person (subject) x, or a functor '$L\ (x, y)$' (or '$L\ (x) = y$') having some finite number of values; or a real-valued functor. This kind of diagram generally incorporates two kinds of semantic assumptions for the concept in question (cf. BUNGE (1972)):

a) a rule of denotation stipulating what the concept refers to;

b) a semantic assumption specifying which aspect of the referent the concept in question represents.

Correspondingly, the symbol designating the concept in question also gets a rule of (vicarious) reference and an assumption of (vicarious) representation:

(a′) '*L*' refers to human beings;

(b′) '*L*' represents (the state of) latent aggression.

To take a physical example of semantic rules, in the case of Maxwell's electromagnetic theory the symbol '$E\ (f, x, t)$' designates a concept which refers to an electromagnetic field f and represents the strength of the electric component of f at the point x and the instant t.

Having thus specified the reference class (domain) for the theory and having given rules of factual designation for all (or most) of the nonlogical constants of the theory in the manner of our Diagram V.1., have we given a satisfactory semantics? Not quite, as nothing specific has yet been said about how the meanings or intensions of the terms and statements become determined.

If we state which concept a symbol refers to we give its intension or meaning. But the problem here is really that the concepts referred to by semantic rules are often quite vague constructs and therefore they are not semantically (nor pragmatically) understandable. They are in need of semantic clarification and they must be made more exact. This is what the scientific theory in question does (at least in part). Maxwell's electromagnetic theory serves to clarify the concept $E(f, x, t)$ and a personality theory may help to clarify and give precision to the concept of latent aggression: these concepts are made semantically understandable. (We say that a term or concept is semantically understandable if a pragmatically justifiable meaning diagram of the above kind and corresponding semantic rules can be given for it. We shall later clarify the pragmatic underpinnings of semantics.)

As for the meanings of statements, we may for the present purposes simply assume that in scientific languages they become specified through the meanings of their components (words) and their structure. To take a very simple example, if we know what '*P*' represents and what '*a*' denotes, and understand what predication is, then the meaning of '$P(a)$' has been specified. The formation rules of the language suffice to account for the meanings of complex statements. We shall not attempt a detailed analysis of sentence meanings here. Furthermore, it is fairly clear that the above idea will not work for all languages outside science (e. g. for languages dealing with propositional attitudes).

Let us accordingly accept the following holistic thesis concerning the meanings of the extralogical predicates of a scientific theory, assumed to be in axiomatized form (cf. NAGEL (1961), GIEDYMIN (1970), BUNGE (1967b), (1972)):

(M) The meanings of the extralogical predicates of a formalized scientific theory $T(\lambda \cup \mu)$ are in general determined by the entire theory. That is, they are determined by the syntactical formation rules, logical and mathematical axioms as well as the rules of derivation of the language of the theory, by all the scientific axioms (and theorems) of the theory and by the adopted semantical rules.

The mathematical axioms, if any, of a scientific theory serve to give a (mathematical) structure to its extralogical concepts. For instance, if the theory deals with real-valued functors (e. g. mass, electric strength, or response strength), then the theory presupposes the axioms for real numbers among its mathematical axioms. Here we are not interested in the mathematical interpretations of a theory but only in its factual scientific interpretations. Furthermore, the reference to the mathematical axioms of a scientific theory can *normally* be suppressed because of the following result (cf. MONTAGUE (1961), pp. 357—358):

(5.7) $T \cup S \vdash F$ if and only if F holds in every mathematical standard model in which T holds.

Here T is a finite axiom set of a first-order theory, S is the set of mathematical axioms of the theory in question, and F is any statement in the language of the theory.

We shall accept thesis (M) and assume that usually at least some of the terms of a scientific theory are not semantically understandable without the "implicit definition" the theory gives to these terms. We shall assume that the predicates in λ have antecedent meaning which either alone, or together with some factual hypotheses independent of the theory $T(\lambda \cup \mu)$, are sufficient for determining the extensions of the λ-predicates so that all λ-predicates can be used in statements of direct report. Thus the predicates in λ are assumed to be directly "measurable" (i. e. measurable without reliance on the truth of $T(\lambda \cup \mu)$), whereas for the members of μ this is not the case. This is of course in accordance with our *methodological* characterization of observational and theoretical terms in Chapter I. Notice that we do not require that the λ-predicates be empirical even *lato sensu*, still less *stricto sensu*. Now we assume, according to (M), that at least some μ-predicates get their meanings on the basis of the meanings of λ-predicates and the interconnections between these kinds of predicates in $T(\lambda \cup \mu)$. This, together with the previous statement, gives another reason for the rejection of the Thesis of Semantical Empiricism. Empirical content or import and semantical meaning are distinct notions, and they need not even covary.

As has been frequently pointed out in the literature, a danger with holistic semantical theses, such as (M), is that they may lead to apriorism. (M) must therefore not be understood in a way which makes the theory $T(\lambda \cup \mu)$ true *a priori*. Every scientific theory must have some nonanalytic factual content. If we accept an analytic-synthetic division for scientific statements, we need a method for "factoring out" the analytic (or meaning) component and the synthetic component of a theory. We shall later discuss this problem in detail.

2.4. There are a number of other problematic issues connected with the holistic meaning thesis (M). To deal with some of them we shall give an illustration from psychology. We formulate in rather vague terms a small theory connecting latent aggression with sexual repression, frustration, and manifest aggression. Let us have $\mu = \{$'sexual repression', 'latent aggression'$\}$, $\lambda = \{$'frustration', 'manifest aggression', 'human being'$\}$. Let us assume, for simplicity, that the predicates in $\lambda \cup \mu$ are all monadic. (By frustration we mean *manifest* frustration.) Our axioms are:

(A1) Sexual repression leads to latent aggression for all human beings.

(A2) For all human beings, sexual repression presupposes frustration.

(A3) For all human beings, frustration leads to manifest aggression only when a person is latently aggressive.

This theory potentially explains, for instance, why frustration sometimes leads to manifestly aggressive behavior, sometimes not. The list of axioms should be continued, the number of relevant properties (of persons) discussed should be made much greater, and many qualifications should be made in A1, A2, and A3 in order to have a factually interesting theory. But for our present purposes the theory $T(\lambda \cup \mu)$ axiomatized by A1 & A2 & A3 is good enough. Let us now make our theory more precise by giving it the following axiomatization in monadic predicate logic. Let us make up the following semantical rules for our predicates:

(5.8) '$L(x)$' represents the latent aggression of subject x;

(5.9) '$S(x)$' represents the sexual repression of subject x;

(5.10) '$F(x)$' represents the frustration of subject x;

(5.11) '$M(x)$' represents the manifest aggression of subject x;

(5.12) '$H(x)$' refers to the class of human beings.

The interpretation of 'H' gives the reference class of the theory. By using this predicate we make it syntactically explicit that the aspects or properties (vicariously) represented by the terms 'L', 'S', 'F', and 'M' are aspects of human beings.

We may now formalize our idealized theory as follows:

(A1*) $(x)\,(H\,(x)\ \&\ S\,(x) \supset L\,(x))$

(A2*) $(x)\,(H\,(x)\ \&\ S\,(x) \supset F\,(x))$

(A3*) $(x)\,((H\,(x)\ \&\ (F\,(x) \supset M\,(x))) \supset L\,(x))$.

Forget now for a moment the origin of the resulting theory $T^*\ (\lambda \cup \mu)$ and try to interpret it in factual terms. That is, assume that we are given a formalism A1* & A2* & A3* and we wish to make it a factual psychological theory by adding some semantic assumptions. (Notice, incidentally, that T^* has no deductive observational content.)

We can now use as our semantic rules (5.8)—(5.12). These rules are stated in our metalanguage and they correlate our formal language with "scientific" English[2]. (For other ways of expressing semantic assumptions see SELLARS (1963); they do not make much difference for our purposes.)

Let us now concentrate on the meaning of the theoretical concept of latent aggression and the semantic assumption (5.8). The understanding of (5.8) involves a great deal. It presupposes the active mastery of the English language but also some assumptions and beliefs concerning the notion or concept of latent aggression and its (semantic and contingent) connections with other concepts. An important part of these beliefs is elucidated and exactified by science. Notice that objects have in principle indefinitely many aspects (properties). Any of them can in principle be ontically and semantically relevant to any other. But a theory deals only with a small finite number of aspects connecting them either semantically or contingently. Therefore a scientific theory can never give anything like the *full* meaning of its constructs. (The notion of *full* meaning and accordingly the notions of *full* semantic and pragmatic understanding seldom make any concrete sense, except perhaps in mathematics.)

In any case we should look for the meaning of the concept of latent aggression (and of any theoretical factual concept) in a theory

---

2 Notice that instead of using the symbol 'L' in (5.8) we could adopt a rule of the form

'latent aggression' represents the concept of latent aggression,

where only expressions from English occur. However, this rule is semantically about as problematic as (5.8).

involving it. Supposing it occurs in many scientific theories, all of them should somehow be taken into consideration. Let us here assume that our T^* is the only accepted scientific theory involving this notion, and let us pretend that it takes into account and connects an important part of our common sense assumptions and beliefs about latent aggression.

Accordingly, and following the thesis (M), we have to accept instead of (5.8):

(5.8*) 'L' designates (expresses) the concept of latent aggression as elucidated by the theory T^* *cum* (5.8)—(5.12).

The rule (5.8*) shows the strong theory-dependency of latent aggression. (This in part indicates why it is called a *theoretical* concept in our characterization in Chapter I.) In (5.8*) we have T^* rather than T because T^* is more exact with respect to the extensional aspects of the concepts designated by the predicates in $\lambda \cup \mu$. Intensionally T gives us about as much as T^*. Notice that neither T nor T^* as such makes a distinction between analytic designation (due to the meaning postulates) and synthetic designation (due to the contingent axioms of the theory).

Rule (5.8*) and generally rules of its kind refer us back to the theory from which we started our investigation. Is this a vicious circle? Not necessarily so. First, consider the following degenerate case of this kind of rule. The scientific concept in question (e. g. 'M') may be intensionally rather "primitive" and well understood. If needed, it can be extratheoretically and informally elucidated by means of other antecedently semantically or cognitively understood notions which do not belong to the theory T^*. Assume that this elucidation (possibly supplemented by some pure scientific assumptions not in T^*) suffices to determine conceptually, if not in terms of empirical procedures, the extension of the concept in all circumstances. Then T^* does not really contribute anything of its own to the meaning of the concept, and a rule like (5.8) would do as well as (5.8*). This is exactly the case with the λ-predicates as we characterized them in Chapter I.

But if the scientific concept is a new one (introduced by T^*) then we do need (5.8*). That is, it does not then help to say that 'L' represents latent aggression (or whatever concept is in question) as we just do not know what 'latent aggression' means, i. e. as we do not semantically and pragmatically understand the concept of latent aggression. (Here we have an important instance of the interplay between semantic and pragmatic meaning.)

In the spirit and letter of our thesis (M) we may thus accept rules of the kind (5.8*) to clarify the meaning of the concepts of a theory $T^* (\lambda \cup \mu)$. In effect, the formal axioms of T^* read in the light of its semantic assumptions determine the objective semantical meaning of its concepts. It should be noticed that the intuitive theory T can be formalized in different ways, which usually affect the meanings of the concepts.

For example, we might have chosen to represent latent aggression by a construct which has the mathematical structure of a real valued function. We might also have decided to construe our concepts as sets of acts and formulate the axioms by using their (relative) probabilities of occurrence. Aspects of reality can in general be "modelled" and represented in indefinitely many ways. Different ways of representing result in different formulations of theories and this often affects the meanings of concepts. A certain representation of an aspect of reality may be semantically clearer than another one. Thus a relatively coarse representation through a monadic predicate (binary-valued concept) may be semantically much clearer than a finer and more informative representation by a real valued function. Furthermore, the denotation of the monadic predicate is usually much easier to determine empirically than the denotation of the latter, even if this fact may not be directly related to the (semantic) meaning of the concept.

In this book we have discussed theories with fixed factual interpretations. We should notice, however, that the semantical assumptions of a theory may be changed without the formalism's being changed. Let us take a physical example of this. In Maxwell's time '$E(f, x, t)$' was often considered to refer to an aether particle f. Only after the adoption of the special relativity theory was it interpreted to refer to a field f (see BUNGE (1967b)). What is in question here is the realm of applicability of the formalism. One may use the word 'theory' so that such a switch of semantical interpretation means a change of theory.

As we noticed earlier, semantic rules of the kind (5.8*) do not yet as such say anything specific about how the μ-predicates get their meanings in terms of the λ-predicates in a theory. Furthermore, if nothing else is said, T^* *may* be true by *fiat* (or for purely *conceptual* reasons). That is, unless we can assume that T^* can be divided into an analytic and (nonempty) synthetic part it will be true *a priori*. For instance, if *all* the members of $\lambda \cup \mu$ were semantically connected with *all* the other ones in $\lambda \cup \mu$ then T^* would in all likelihood be true *a priori*. For then we could not probably "factor out" a synthetic part of T^*. Notice that the meanings of *all* the members of $\lambda \cup \mu$ may depend on *all* the axioms of T^* under some axiomatization of T^*. The question is whether there is at least one axiomatization of T^* under which T^* has some genuinely synthetic axioms. We shall discuss the problem of an analytic/synthetic division of this kind in the next section.

Let us now review our discussion from the point of view of the *openness* of meaning and extension of the concepts in a theory $T(\lambda \cup \mu)$[3].

Consider first the interpretation of the λ-predicates which we assumed to be antecedently understood and which are capable of being used in direct reporting to yield evidence statements. By saying that they are antecedently understood we assumed that their meanings are rather clear independently of the theory T. Ideally, if the intensional vagueness of an n-place λ-predicate 'P' is minimal we can characterize the situation as follows. The intension of 'P' (the concept represented by 'P') can *in part* be conceptually represented by a function f of the following kind. This function picks out from every factual domain of T (part of the reference class of T) exactly one n-tuple of objects. The function f might be called the (minimal) *sense function* of 'P'. It fixes completely the denotation of 'P' in all factual circumstances. This determination need not be empirical yet. But we also assumed of the λ-predicates that scientists should be able to "measure" them directly, at least in ideal cases.

As the predicate 'P' may denote unobservable objects in some cases, its empirical measurement presupposes additional knowledge and assumptions. If the sense function picks out a set of n-tuples (with several elements) for the denotation of 'P', 'P' is said to be intensionally open. By suitable factual hypotheses and assumptions (from outside T) such openness may often be reduced to the point of having factually (even empirically) fixed denotations. Thus λ-predicates are in general to be regarded as *extensionally determinate* and as having *determinate empirical import*, too. The determinateness of

3 We shall below disregard the "openness" resulting from the fact that the theory $T(\lambda \cup \mu)$ itself may model and represent reality rather poorly.

empirical import often comes about only by using additional scientific assumptions to complement *a priori* semantic rules.

We have assumed above that at least some μ-predicates of $T(\lambda \cup \mu)$ do not have clear antecedent meaning. The theory T is needed to give them meaning and to make exact their vague antecedent meaning. Assume now that we have distinguished the analytic component (meaning postulates) from its purely synthetic component. We then get, in the first place, some extensional or structural semantic interpretation for the μ-predicates in terms of the λ-predicates on the basis of the meaning postulates of T. (The forms various semantic postulates can have are discussed in Chapter IV and in the next section.) In general this interpretation is only partial. Therefore μ-predicates are *intensionally* and *extensionally open*, both when considered by themselves and relative to their semantic relationships to the λ-predicates. Furthermore, the synthetic component will usually give some additional determination to the extensions of the μ-predicates relative to the extensions of the λ-predicates. The theoretical predicates in μ have in general only *indirect* and *partial empirical import* through their connections with the λ-predicates, or with some entirely new observational concepts occurring in the assumptions added to T in testing.

In addition to being intensionally and extensionally open (both absolutely and relative to the λ-predicates), μ-predicates may also be *existentially* open. They may refer to different objects than do the λ-predicates, as we saw in Chapter IV. For instance, hypothetical constructs in the sense of MacCorquodale and Meehl (1948) can be construed as intensionally, extensionally, and existentially open. Furthermore, they are open with respect to their empirical measurability or empirical import. These features of openness account for the potential "surplus meaning" of hypothetical constructs. Their intervening variables again are best reconstructed as being existentially determinate, and extensionally and intensionally rather determinate as such; and their empirical import (or observational "anchorage") is rather determinate, too.

2.5. In discussing semantics above we have frequently employed pragmatic notions (in Morris's sense), such as understanding and intelligibility. Let us now try to say something about the connection between semantics and pragmatics, and especially about the pragmatic justification of semantic rules.

Consider our rule (5.8*) (or alternatively (5.8)) and the following proposed pragmatic criterion of adequacy for it:

(P1) (5.8*) is an acceptable semantic rule in a scientific community dealing with the theory T^* if and only if every representative scientist in that community understands the right hand side of (5.8*).

Here 'scientific community' may be elucidated in terms of sharing a common Kuhnian paradigm (see our Chapter I). The expression 'representative' represents a vague notion which may involve idealization and which need not thus be completely descriptive. Still, the right hand side of (P1) may be regarded as a factual scientific hypothesis that sociolinguistics should be interested in. (Notice that here 'understanding' has cognitive content and meaning which any sociolinguist has to respect and without which (P1) cannot be tested.) (P1) is just one possible suggestion for a criterion of adequacy that immediately comes up. Furthermore, it may seem too restrictive to impose it on *all* of the extralogical terms of a T $(\lambda \cup \mu)$. Some terms of a theory can thus remain without pragmatically acceptable semantic rules.

Earlier we noticed that the understanding of the rule (5.8) presupposes at least active linguistic knowledge of the expression occurring on the right hand side of this rule. This suggests a new criterion (P2) which is obtained from (P1) by substituting 'has active mastery of' for 'understands' in (P1). (P2) is implied by (P1) but the converse need not hold.

Our criteria (P1) and (P2) do not make any reference to various circumstances in which scientists describe the world (or the aspects of the world they are interested in). We think that in investigating somebody's active mastery and understanding of a (scientific) language we can get quite far just on the basis of various intralinguistic connections. That is, we investigate how well a person (scientist) can explain meanings of scientific terms by means of ordinarily understood expressions. Of course this may finally lead to a *cul de sac.* Then we have to investigate language usage as a response to extralinguistic circumstances. That is, we may have to resort to ostension and thereby to the investigator and the investigated's having sufficiently similar principles of thinking and ways of perceiving and "gestalting" the external world (cf. TUOMELA (1970b) on this point).

Some philosophers, e. g. Feyerabend, claim that in the case of interesting scientific concepts their meanings can only be elucidated or given by resorting to ostension. That is, for Feyerabend *et alii* the only way to learn the meanings of scientific terms and theories is to go into a laboratory, make experiments, and generally live the life of a scientist. Studying textbooks or, indeed, resorting to any verbal methods does not suffice. What is needed, in general, is a direct contact between scientific expressions and reality. The important thing then is to get the language of the theory connected with the sense impressions of the scientist and not with another language. The language of the theory is *about* the physical reality but it is brought into play or used via the perceptual responses of the scientist. In the spirit of Feyerabend we may then suggest the following rather demanding pragmatic criterion of adequacy for a semantic rule, such as (5.8*):

(P3) (5.8*) is an acceptable semantic rule in a scientific community dealing with theory T^* if and only if every representative scientist in that community can directly respond to appropriate sensual stimulation by the use of atomic expressions containing the phrase 'latently aggressive'.

Here "appropriate sensual stimulation" is, intuitively and extratheoretically speaking, stimulation prompted or evoked by a latently aggressive person (irrespective of however indirectly and ostensively this cause of stimulation has to be indicated in actual cases). The "atomic statements" of (P3) are of course of the form "Tom Jones is latently aggressive".

Incidentally, the requirement for the active use of *atomic* theoretical expressions can be regarded as a good criterion for a primary sense of existence or reality of theoretical entities. (Cf. SELLARS (1965) on this point.) A theoretical statement can be factually true in the full sense (in which observation statements are true) only if singular theoretical concepts are capable of being used in direct reporting at least in some contexts (SELLARS (1965), pp. 369).

If (P3) is taken seriously, it would have the consequence that no correspondence rules (or the like) are needed in science. For a scientist could then employ every descriptive part of his conceptual system evidentially in direct commerce with reality.

However, we consider (P3) too strict. First of all there is no mention in it of measurement instruments and the like. 'Responding directly' could (and should) at least be understood widely enough to include means and devices of this kind. But even if (P3) is so widely understood, I do not think it would be a good criterion. For I suspect the right hand side would turn out to be *factually* false and hence (P3) would have no applicability. To put it more strongly, I conjecture that it would not even be possible to train scientists to behave in accordance with the right hand side of (P3).

Somebody may object to (P3) on the grounds that it is based on unacceptable S-R-psychology which de-emphasizes the spontaneous activity of human agents. Such a theoretician should feel free to substitute his own favorite psychological assumptions on the right hand side of (P3). One possible candidate would be the following:

(P4) (5.8*) is an acceptable semantic rule in a scientific community dealing with theory T^* if and only if every representative scientist in that community can in his descriptions employ atomic expressions containing 'latently aggressive' in any (or most) scientific experiments or any other comparable scientific situations.

(P4) and our previous criteria obviously need some elaboration and qualifying. We shall not here attempt it. We conclude that, suitably elaborated, one of the rules (P1), (P2), and (P4) might provide a good beginning for displaying the pragmatic underpinnings of the semantics of scientific concepts.

3. Meaning Postulates and Correspondence Rules

3.1. The acceptance of the holistic meaning thesis (M) of Section 2. and the assumption that a scientific theory $T(\lambda \cup \mu)$ must have some factual content entail that the theory must have a (non-empty) synthetic and an analytic component. In the case the μ-predicates (or some of them) do not have any initial or antecedent meaning the analytic component, too, has to be non-empty.

Hempel, Quine and some other philosophers have argued against making an analytic-synthetic division. Either they have argued against it on pragmatic grounds, or they have opposed the division on the basis of its semantic vagueness. The pragmatic grounds usually amount to claiming that there are no statements in science that cannot ultimately be given up in face of strong factual evidence. To this one can first say that we are here after a semantic and not a pragmatic division of scientific statements. Secondly, semantic assumptions can be changed (and this does ultimately rely on pragmatic considerations). To the arguments concerning the vagueness of the division and the vast number of border-line cases one can say the following. First, there are some rather clear-cut elementary cases of analytic statements such as 'Nothing that is green all over is red', and so on. Secondly, one may take the border-line cases just to show that in most scientific statements analytic and synthetic elements are *almost* indistinguishably intertwined. Still there may be ways of "factoring out" the analytic and the synthetic components of a science or of a scientific theory.

We shall here accept the philosophical possibility and meaningfulness of an analytic-synthetic dichotomy of scientific statements. Given a first-order theory $T(\lambda \cup \mu)$ with the members of μ as *semantically new* concepts we shall look for its analytic and synthetic components as far as the predicates in μ are concerned. (We shall later discuss the case where the possible analytic connections within the language $\mathscr{L}(\lambda)$ are also taken into account.) The analytic component (T_A) will obviously include some correspondence rules (statements in the vocabulary $\lambda \cup \mu$), as the μ-predicates are to be given meaning on the basis of the *antecedently understood* λ-predicates[4]. However, as we shall see, (T_A) cannot include all of them, so that the synthetic component T_S of $T(\lambda \cup \mu)$ will include some of them. A statement of T is then called *analytic* (*synthetic*) if and only if it is, respectively, a consequence of T_A (T_S).

Let us first consider the solution to the problem of (theoretical) analyticity given by PRZELECKI and WOJCICKI (1969). Again, we shall below sometimes write $\mathscr{L}$ for $\mathscr{L}(\lambda \cup \mu)$ and $\mathscr{L}^*$ for the second-order language (with variables for the predicate constants in $\lambda \cup \mu$) corresponding to $\mathscr{L}$. We write $\mathscr{M}_\lambda$ for a model of $\mathscr{L}(\lambda)$ and $\mathscr{M}/_\lambda$ for the restrict $\mathscr{M}/\mathscr{L}(\lambda)$.

PRZELECKI and WOJCICKI (1969) require of the synthetic component T_S of T the following two properties:

(S1) T_S should not impose any conditions on the interpretation of the predicates in μ. This requirement can be formalized by requiring that for any two models $\mathscr{M}$ and $\mathscr{M}'$ of $\mathscr{L}$ for which $\mathscr{M}/_\lambda = \mathscr{M}'/_\lambda$ we have the following:

$T_S \subseteq Ver(\mathscr{M})$ if and only if $T_S \subseteq Ver(\mathscr{M}')$.

4 Notice that here we explicitly dichotomize our concepts on the basis of a *semantical* criterion whereas elsewhere in this chapter the dichotomy is made on the basis of our *methodological* criterion of Chapter I. These two dichotomies need not be coextensive, as we have emphasized.

(S2) T_S and T must not differ in what they say about reality described in terms of λ-predicates. This is formalized by requiring that, for every $\mathcal{M}_\lambda$ for $\mathcal{L}(\lambda)$, $\mathcal{M}_\lambda$ can be expanded into a model of T_S if and only if $\mathcal{M}_\lambda$ can be expanded into a model $\mathcal{M}$ of T.

The definition for T_S now becomes the following:

A set of sentences T_S in $\mathcal{L}^*$ is a *synthetic* component of T in the model theoretic sense if and only if for every model $\mathcal{M}$ for $\mathcal{L}$

$T_S \subseteq Ver(\mathcal{M})$ if and only if $\mathcal{M}/\lambda$ is expandable into a model of T.

Of the analytic component T_A of T Przelecki and Wojcicki require the following two properties:

(A1) T_A must endow the predicates in μ with the same meaning they have in virtue of T. When formalized this amounts to requiring that for every model $\mathcal{M}$ of $\mathcal{L}$, if $\mathcal{M}/\lambda$ is expandable into a model of T, then

$T_A \subseteq Ver(\mathcal{M})$ if and only if $T \subseteq Ver(\mathcal{M})$.

(A2) T_A is semantically noncreative with respect to $\mathcal{L}(\lambda)$.

Thus we get the following definition:

A set of sentences T_A in $\mathcal{L}^*$ is called an *analytic* component of T in the model theoretic sense if and only if

1) T_A is semantically noncreative with respect to $\mathcal{L}(\lambda)$ and

2) for every model $\mathcal{M}$ of $\mathcal{L}$, if $\mathcal{M}/\lambda$ is expandable into a model of T then

$$T_A \subseteq Ver(\mathcal{M}) \text{ if and only if } T \subseteq Ver(\mathcal{M}).$$

We can notice that the semantic interpretation given to the predicates in μ by the meaning postulates T_A is a) independent of experience, b) consistent with the language $\mathcal{L}(\lambda)$, and c) agrees with the theory T at least as far as its expandable $\mathcal{M}/\lambda$-models are concerned.

Let us now state some properties of the newly obtained analytic and synthetic components in the case of finitely axiomatizable theories (see PRZELECKI and WOJCICKI (1969), p. 388—389):

Theorem V.1 (a) $\models T \equiv T_A \,\&\, T_S$

(b) For every statement F in $\mathcal{L}(\lambda)$, $T \models F$ if and only if $T_S \models F$.

(c) For every F in $\mathcal{L}(\lambda)$, if $T_A \models F$ then $\models F$.

Here '$\models$' means semantical consequence. The analogous theorem with '$\models$' replaced by '$\vdash$' holds of course, too.

Let us now consider Carnap's proposal according to which $T_S = T^R$ and $T_A = T^R \supset T$. $T^R \supset T$ is called the Carnap sentence (T^C) of T. T^R and T^C do indeed qualify as the synthetic and analytic components of T in the above sense. In fact, as we have already seen in Chapter III (for '$\vdash$'), T^R and T^C do have the crucial properties (a), (b), and (c). Przelecki and Wojcicki have also shown that all the synthetic components T_S of a finite theory T are logically equivalent to T^R. On the other hand, they show that T^C is the weakest of all the analytic components T_A (of T), which need not be logically equivalent.

We may now ask whether there is any reason to prefer T^C over the stronger possible T_A-candidates. Carnap would in fact liberally allow one to choose any of the other ones as well. WINNIE (1971) has recently argued in an interesting paper that there is at least one good reason for adopting T^C rather than any other statement (or set of statements) as a T_A-component. His reason is that a T_A-component should be vacuous in T with respect to $\mathscr{L}(\lambda)$ in the following sense[5]. A statement S of $\mathscr{L}$ is *vacuous* in T with respect to $\mathscr{L}(\lambda)$ if and only if $T \vdash S$ and for any S' such that $T \vdash S'$, if $S \,\&\, S' \vdash F$ (F is any statement in $\mathscr{L}(\lambda)$) then $S' \vdash F$. In other words, the observationally vacuous statements of T are exactly those which are logically inessential in *any* deductions of observational consequences from T. This notion of λ-vacuity is obviously stronger than the notion of noncreativity with respect to $\mathscr{L}(\lambda)$. Now Winnie proposes that the condition

(A3) T_A should be vacuous in T with respect to $\mathscr{L}(\lambda)$

should be added as a requirement for T_A. Then he proves that the Carnap sentence T^C of a theory T and its logical consequences constitute exactly those statements which are λ-vacuous in that theory. Accordingly, here we have a nonarbitrary criterion for uniquely decomposing T into a T_A and T_S. A further consequence is that the adoption of T^C as the T_A-component leaves all the μ-statements ("pure" axioms) of T synthetic, whereas this need not be the case for other T_A-components.

---

5 Winnie, following Carnap, interprets $\mathscr{L}(\lambda)$ as an *observational* language; cf. our criticism below (and elsewhere).

What kind of statements of T become analytic if T^C is adopted as the analytic component of T? Let us illustrate this by the following simple example (cf. PRZELECKI and WOJCICKI (1969)). Let T be

(5.13) $(x)\,(O_1(x) \supset P(x))\ \&\ (x)\,(O_2(x) \supset \sim P(x))$.

The $\mathscr{L}(\lambda)$-consequences of T are axiomatized by

(5.14) $(x) \sim (O_1(x)\ \&\ O_2(x))$.

T^C is

(5.15) $(E\Pi)\,[(x)\,(O_1(x) \supset \Pi(x))\ \&\ (x)\,(O_2(x) \supset \sim \Pi(x)] \supset$
$\supset [(x)\,(O_1(x) \supset P(x))\ \&\ (x)\,(O_2(x) \supset \sim P(x))]$.

Now the antecedent of T^C is true whenever (5.14) is true, and conversely. (Every model $\mathscr{M}_\lambda$ of $\mathscr{L}(\lambda)$ in which (5.14) holds can then be expanded into a model of (5.13).) Thus we have

(5.16) $T^C \vdash (x) \sim (O_1(x)\ \&\ O_2(x)) \supset$
$\supset [(x)\,(O_1(x) \supset P(x))\ \&\ (x)\,(O_2(x) \supset \sim P(x))]$.

The statement (5.16) is a nontautological correspondence statement which does not have any consequence in $\mathscr{L}(\lambda)$ and which, in addition, is vacuous (in T) with respect to $\mathscr{L}(\lambda)$.

Obviously the following result holds in general:

Theorem V.2. If every model of a finitely axiomatizable maximal subtheory $T'(\lambda)$ of a finitely axiomatizable theory $T(\lambda \cup \mu)$ is expandable into a model of $T(\lambda \cup \mu)$, then

$$T^C(\lambda \cup \mu) \vdash T'(\lambda) \supset T(\lambda \cup \mu).$$

Recall from Chapter III that if $T'(\lambda)$ has only finite models then obviously the conclusion of Theorem V.2 holds without further assumptions.

It should be noticed that given a finite axiomatization of a theory $T(\lambda \cup \mu)$ with the axioms $A_1, \ldots, A_n$ (such that $T = A_1\ \&\ldots\&\ A_n$) it is quite possible that none, some, or all of these axioms are analytic under Przelecki's and Wojcicki's construal. Recall that no axioms solely in the vocabulary μ are analytic if $T_A = T^C$.

The Carnap-Winnie method of decomposing a theory into an analytic and a synthetic component can be applied effectively for finite theories in the above manner. As emphasized above, we do not for philosophical reasons here accept these authors' interpretation that the predicates of λ have to be observational; we only require that they are antecedently understood in a semantical sense. There is still another, more technical, reason against accepting Carnap's and Winnie's interpretation. It is that all scientific theories do not (by themselves) have observational content, i. e. they have tautologous Ramsey sentences. But in such cases the *whole* theory becomes analytic within the present construal (see Theorem V.1. (a)).

Another question is then whether the assumptions of Przelecki, Wojcicki, Carnap, and Winnie for an analytic-synthetic dichotomy are acceptable. One aspect of this problem comes up because of the property (a) of Theorem III.6. It says that the theory and its Ramsey sentence become logically equivalent upon assuming the truth of the Carnap sentence of the theory. (Still, they do not then have to be equivalent in meaning; cf. Section V.2.) The problematic aspect here is of course just the validity of the Carnap sentence. Why could the Ramsey sentence T^R not be true without T's being true? Could it not be argued that it is a task for scientific research to find out whether the entities postulated to exist by T^R are just those that the theoretical terms of T designate?

We argue that if and only if the predicates of μ are antecedently understood (e. g. on the basis of their external presystematic connections) a scientific realist will accept T^C as a contingent and thus as a nonanalytic scientific statement. ('Antecedently understood' means the acceptability of a semantic rule of the kind (5.8) to replace (5.8*).) At least within the present framework, the rejection of T^C as analytic would entail that all the statements of T become synthetic, as T^C here represents the minimal nonempty analytic component. However, if the predicates of μ are treated instrumentally in a purely syntactic manner as uninterpreted symbols then it seems better to treat T^C as a genuinely analytic statement.

As in this book we mainly have in mind scientific theories from the social sciences which do not usually have semantically completely unintelligible μ-predicates, Carnap's analytic-synthetic dichotomy is not of so much use for us. But let us here mention one interesting exception to this claim. In Chapter IV we discussed statistical factor analysis and noticed that to use it normally means to theorize with a Ramsey sentence. The "interpretation" of factors, formally speaking the rotation procedure, amounts to looking for a theory T such that

$T^R \supset T$ is valid. At least when such formal rotation techniques as varimax, etc., are used, $T^R \supset T$ is taken to be *always* valid, i. e. analytic.

We claimed earlier that meaning postulates for μ-predicates in terms of λ-predicates given within an extensional language in general accomplish only (partial) extensional interpretation for the μ-predicates, but fail to give direct intensional interpretation for them. This claim is neatly supported by the following simple theorem (cf. a related result by WINNIE (1967), p. 227):

Theorem V.3. Assume that a theory $T(\lambda \cup \mu)$ has a model $\mathcal{M}$ such that in the domain $D = V \cup U$ of $\mathcal{M}$ the subset V has the following property: no $x \in V$ belongs to the denotation of any λ-predicate. Then $T(\lambda \cup \mu)$ has a model $\mathcal{M}'$ which is isomorphic with $\mathcal{M}$ and in whose domain $D' = V' \cup U$ the subset V' is a set of numbers.

The theorem is proved by construing a model $\mathcal{M}'$ with a domain $D' = V' \cup U$. Here V' is a set of numbers with the same cardinality as V. In V' the counterparts to the relations (interpretations of theoretical terms) in V can be defined so that an isomorphism is established between the substructures in question. Then $\mathcal{M}$ and $\mathcal{M}'$ are easily shown to be isomorphic by using an identity mapping for the elements in U. Because $\mathcal{M}$ is a model of $T(\lambda \cup \mu)$ then $\mathcal{M}'$ is also since it is isomorphic with $\mathcal{M}$. $\mathcal{M}$ can now be an intended factual model while $\mathcal{M}'$ is a partly arithmetic model and hence nonintended. Of course the members of V' can be taken to be any other nonintended objects as well.

What Theorem V.3 thus shows is that when its conditions are satisfied no number of meaning postulates given within the (extensional) language of the scientific theory can directly guarantee more than an extensional interpretation for the members of μ. It seems to us that the unwanted model theoretic interpretations can be excluded only by *intensional* description. For instance, as shown in Section V.2, we may thus simply specify the reference class by stipulating in the metalanguage that the theory is about atoms, societies, red herrings, or what not.

When are the conditions of Theorem V.3 then realized? They are realized quite generally. They fail only when the theory $T(\lambda \cup \mu)$ entails that the denotations of all the μ-predicates include *only* objects which belong to the denotation of at least one λ-predicate. Consider now the above approaches to theoretical analyticity by Carnap,

Winnie, Przelecki, and Wojcicki. In these accounts there are no inbuilt conditions to exclude the conditions of Theorem V.3 from applying. Thus we have seen one important respect in which the current attempts to account for the semantical features of (new) scientific terms have failed.

One peculiar feature in the model theoretic approach of Przelecki and Wojcicki is that their basic conditions of adequacy (S1), (S2), (A1), and (A2) only concern expandable models of the theory T. (Here and below we assume that T is a deductively closed set of formulas.) We know from Chapter III that in some cases the models of $T \cap \mathscr{L}(\lambda)$ cannot be expanded into models of the full theory T without adding new elements into the domains. However, the conditions of Przelecki and Wojcicki (and hence of Carnap) leave completely open the model theoretic interpretation of the μ-predicates in such cases. If we also want to say something about these cases we might try their proof theoretic counterparts, which in fact have been discussed by PRZELECKI and WOJCICKI (1969). The essential change to be made in the previous model theoretic definitions of analytic and synthetic components is this: Whenever it was required in them that a restrict $\mathscr{M}/\lambda$ of a model $\mathscr{M}$ of $\mathscr{L}$ be expandable into a model of T we now require that

$$T'(\lambda) \subseteq Ver(\mathscr{M})$$

where $T'(\lambda)$ is the maximal subtheory of $T(\lambda \cup \mu)$ in $\mathscr{L}(\lambda)$. Then we obtain the following definitions for the proof theoretic analytic and synthetic components of T (see PRZELECKI and WOJCICKI (1969)):

A set of sentences T_S in $\mathscr{L}$ is a *synthetic* component of T in the proof theoretic sense if and only if T_S and $T'(\lambda)$ are proof theoretically equivalent.

A set of sentences T_A in $\mathscr{L}$ is an *analytic* component of T in the proof theoretic sense if and only if

1) T_A is proof theoretically noncreative with respect to $\mathscr{L}(\lambda)$.
2) T and $T_A \cup T'(\lambda)$ are proof theoretically equivalent.

These proof theoretic notions of analytic and synthetic components do not coincide with the semantic ones, as semantical noncreativity is a stronger notion than proof theoretic noncreativity (see our discussion in Chapter III). Notice also that while the semantic notions of analyticity and syntheticity do not deal with the nonexpandable models of T their proof theoretic counterparts do take account of them.

It can be shown that the properties given in Theorem V.1 for the semantic notions of analytic and synthetic components hold for the proof theoretic ones as well (cf. PRZELECKI and WOJCICKI (1969), p. 394).

It has been proved by PRZELECKI and WOJCICKI ((1969) and (1971)) that some sets do not even have analytic and synthetic components (neither proof theoretic nor model theoretic ones) and that they may not be effectively constructible when they exist. But if they exist then the synthetic component is unique but there are several nonequivalent analytic components both in the model theoretic and syntactic case. That severe logical problems concerning the existence, uniqueness, and effective construction of an analytic-synthetic dichotomy arise can be taken to reflect the logical side of the many philosophical difficulties of this issue.

Let us now face the problem of choice of T_A in the proof theoretic case. We suggest on the basis of our above considerations that the weakest of the T_A-components, corresponding to the Carnap sentence in the model theoretic case, should be taken as the analytic component of T, provided it exists. (That it need not always exist has been shown in PRZELECKI and WOJCICKI (1971).) Our suggestion can be motivated by considering the simplified case where the maximal subtheory $T'(\lambda)$ and $T(\lambda \cup \mu)$ are finitely axiomatizable. (Recall from Chapter II that $T'(\lambda)$ need not in general be finitely axiomatizable. Therefore we make here a clear restriction.) Then the statement

$$T^{C^*} = T'(\lambda) \supset T(\lambda \cup \mu)$$

is obviously the weakest T_A-component (for it is the weakest statement which together with $T'(\lambda)$ suffices to imply T). We know on the basis of our results in Chapter III that T^{C^*} is in general logically stronger than the Carnap sentence $T^C = T^R \supset T$. Nevertheless it shares some interesting features with it (cf. the analogous results for T^C in WINNIE (1971)). First, we shall prove that the choice of T_A as T^{C^*} leaves synthetic all those statements of T which contain only predicates of μ. Secondly, T^{C^*} captures exactly the statements of T which are vacuous with respect to $\mathscr{L}(\lambda)$.

The first of these results presupposes the following theorem which is interesting in its own right as well.

Theorem V.4. A statement F is analytically true in $T(\lambda \cup \mu)$ if and only if $T(\lambda \cup \mu) \vdash F$ and $\sim T'(\lambda) \vdash F$.

As we said above, we assume here and below that the theory $T(\lambda \cup \mu)$ and its maximal subtheory $T'(\lambda)$ are finitely axiomatizable in the cases we discuss. We say that a statement is *analytically true* exactly when it logically follows from T^{C*}. The proof of Theorem V.4 can now be given by the following logically equivalent steps:

(1) F is analytically true in T	(assume)
(2) $(T'(\lambda) \supset T) \vdash F$	((1), definition)
(3) $(-T'(\lambda) \vee T) \vdash F$	((2), prop. logic)
(4) $-T'(\lambda) \vdash F$ and $T \vdash F$	((3), prop. logic)

Now we can proceed to

Theorem V.5. If $T(\lambda \cup \mu)$ is a consistent theory which has nontautological consequences in $\mathcal{L}(\lambda)$, then: if $T^{C*} \vdash F(\mu)$ then $\vdash F(\mu)$, where $F(\mu)$ is a statement in $\mathcal{L}(\mu)$.

The proof of this theorem can be given as follows:

(1) $T \vdash G(\lambda)$	($G(\lambda)$ in $\mathcal{L}(\lambda)$, assume)
(2) not $\vdash G(\lambda)$	(assume)
(3) $T^{C*} \vdash F(\mu)$	(assume)
(4) $T'(\lambda) \vdash G(\lambda)$	((1), $T'(\lambda)$ maximal subtheory)
(5) $-G(\lambda) \vdash -T'(\lambda)$	((4), prop. logic)
(6) $-T'(\lambda) \vdash F(\mu)$	((3), Theorem V.4)
(7) $-G(\lambda) \vdash F(\mu)$	((5), (6), prop. logic)
(8) $-G(\lambda)$ is satisfiable	((2))
(9) $\vdash F(\mu)$	(Craig's interpolation theorem)

Theorem V.5 says that the μ-axioms of a theory $T(\lambda \cup \mu)$ with some $\mathcal{L}(\lambda)$-content remain synthetic if $T_A = T^{C*}$. Thus no axioms of the maximal subtheory $T^*(\mu)$ of $T(\lambda \cup \mu)$ are analytic. Only some correspondence statements in the vocabulary $\lambda \cup \mu$ connecting antecedently understood or λ-statements with theoretical or μ-statements are here analytic.

Our Theorems V.4 and V.5 correspond to Winnie's results obtained for the Carnap sentence (cf. Cor. 6 and Theorem 4 in WINNIE (1971)). This is of course a quite obvious consequence of the proof theoretic equivalence within $\mathcal{L}(\lambda)$ of the maximal subtheory $T'(\lambda)$ with the Ramsey sentence T^R. Hence the above proofs remain valid if we substitute 'T^R' for '$T'(\lambda)$' and understand '$\vdash$' as the sign for provability in second-order rather than in first-order logic.

An interesting feature in the minimal proof theoretic component $T_A = T^{C*}$ is that it comprises exactly all the λ-vacuous statements in

T — quite analogously with the minimal semantic component T^C (cf. WINNIE (1971)):

Theorem V.6. A statement S is analytically true in $T(\lambda \cup \mu)$ if and only if S is vacuous in $T(\lambda \cup \mu)$ with respect to $\mathcal{L}(\lambda)$.

We leave the simple but lenghty proof of Theorem V.6 to the reader.

In our discussion above it has been assumed that there are no analytic statements within $\mathcal{L}(\lambda)$. We would like to argue that if $\mathcal{L}(\lambda)$ is a well understood scientific language then the predicates in λ tend to get semantically separate so that finally there are no clear-cut meaning connections between them. Be this as it may, analytic postulates can be incorporated into the above approach both in the model theoretic and in the proof theoretic case. What has to be added is essentially that the theory $T(\lambda \cup \mu)$ be true in all models in which the analytic postulates of $\mathcal{L}(\lambda)$ are true. This has the consequence that the analytic components T_A now become logically weaker and the synthetic components T_S become stronger than in the earlier situation both in the semantic and in the proof theoretic case.

3.2. So far in this section we have discussed correspondence rules in $\mathcal{L}(\lambda \cup \mu)$ which are analytic (i. e. meaning postulates)[6]. In general there will also be *synthetic* or contingent correspondence rules, and some remarks concerning them will now be made.

In general, correspondence rules in $\mathcal{L}(\lambda \cup \mu)$ are needed to make possible the derivation of statements in $\mathcal{L}(\lambda)$ from statements in $\mathcal{L}(\mu)$, and conversely, in a theory $T(\lambda \cup \mu)$. If both λ-predicates and μ-predicates are semantically meaningful, then such correspondence rules are statements telling us something about the world. What else can be said about these correspondence rules depends crucially on the nature of the predicates in λ (and in μ, too).

According to our interpretation of λ-predicates as observational and μ-predicates as theoretical, which interpretation is applicable everywhere in this book except in parts of the previous section, the λ-predicates represent directly "measurable" concepts. They need not be empirical *stricto sensu*, nor even *lato sensu*, in an intuitive pre-

6 The semantic rules of denotation and designation discussed in connection with our Diagram V.1. have sometimes been called correspondence rules. Here, unless otherwise specified, we shall mean by correspondence rules only statements formulated in the language of the theory and containing nonvacuously both λ- and μ-predicates.

systematic characterization. Furthermore, they can have a rich mathematical structure, and be idealized and nonexperimental in this sense (e. g. continuous real-valued functions). Temperature, weight, manifest aggression, and voting behavior might be given as examples of our λ-concepts. Being measurable, these concepts have concrete experimental counterparts. In general (and to the extent this idealized-experimental distiction applies), scientific theories do not contain predicates representing concrete experimental notions.

Correspondence rules $C(\lambda \cup \mu)$, where the λ-predicates are understood in the above idealized sense, can be called *substantive correspondence rules* (cf. SELLARS (1961)). For example the following statements are such:

(i) The absolute temperature of a gas is proportional to the mean kinetic energy of its molecules.

(ii) Sexual repression presupposes (manifest) frustration.

(In (i) temperature is to be understood in the idealized sense and not in the pointer-reading sense.) The notion of substantive correspondence rule can be extended to cover the so called bridge laws used in intertheoretic reduction.

In the case where the λ-predicates are observational or empirical *lato sensu*, substantive correspondence rules serve to give *empirical import* (*empirical content* or *empirical "meaning"*) to the theory, and thus they serve to make it empirically *testable*. This shows their methodological importance. (Notice once more that such empirical substantive correspondence rules are not in general *semantical* meaning postulates but synthetic statements for connecting an empirical framework with a theoretical framework.)

As we have seen, the purely theoretical terms in μ cannot generally be used to form even idealized evidence statements, but they (though not necessarily all of them) are to be connected with empirical concepts (*lato sensu*) by means of substantive correspondence rules. When a theory is applied to new empirical areas, it usually has to be extended by incorporating new correspondence rules. This normally involves the addition of new empirical concepts in such new correspondence rules. However, it is usually convenient to separate the core content of the theory from these various applied extensions of the theory. If the predicates in λ are empirical (*lato sensu*) we shall call the maximal subtheory $T^*(\mu)$ (solely in $\mathscr{L}(\mu)$) a core theory. If they are not, then $T(\lambda \cup \mu)$ itself can be considered a core theory which needs to be supplemented by new substantive empirical correspondence rules to give it empirical content. (For a treatment of such new applied extensions and their role in testing, explanation, and prediction see e. g. Chapters IV, VI and VII and TUOMELA (1968a).)

There are also other kinds of contingent correspondence rules relating the theory to empirical matters. One such kind is needed for connecting a theory with concrete experimental situations and for measuring the values of the concepts of the theory. Such rules may be called *methodological correspondence rules* (the term is used e. g. by SELLARS (1961)). Connecting electron jumps with spectral lines can be taken as an example. Another example would be Carnap's correspondence rule for electromagnetic oscillation mentioned at the beginning of section V.2. Still another example would be a rule stating that intelligence can be reliably and validly measured by the WAIS-test. The so called "operational definitions" and various statements giving empirical indicators and objectifiers of scientific concepts are best classified as methodological correspondence rules. Methodological correspondence rules are often stated in a vague and hazy way, and they are not included in the scientific core theory nor in its applied extensions. In general they serve to give measurement procedures only for some special circumstances and do not amount to explicit definitions (cf. NAGEL (1961), p. 100). The possibility of applying the theory to new experimental situations is therefore left open.

What is the logical form of substantive correspondence rules? Nothing very determinate can in general be said about it. The form of meaning postulates has been partly discussed above. The various types of connectedness between scientific concepts in a theory discussed in Chapter IV are generally relevant here. Probabilistic correspondence rules should also be taken into consideration here (cf. Chapter VIII). In at least some interesting philosophical and methodological contexts it can be argued that correspondence rules are normally (extensionally and intensionally) "open". For instance, our arguments in Chapter VI and VII require that synthetic substantive correspondence rules $C(\lambda \cup \mu)$ in a theory $T(\lambda \cup \mu)$ be creative with respect to the (empirical) law (or laws) in $\mathscr{L}(\lambda)$ to be explained, but noncreative with respect to the core theory $T^*(\mu)$. On the other hand we saw above that analytic correspondence rules are noncreative with respect to the subtheory $T'(\lambda)$ and that minimal meaning postulates (Carnap sentences) are noncreative with respect to $T^*(\mu)$.

Chapter VI

Methodological Desirability of Theoretical Concepts

1. Gains Due to Theoretical Concepts

1.1. To introduce (new) theoretical concepts into a scientific theory means to enlarge the conceptual basis of the theory. In the cases of radical conceptual change either no old concepts are retained or they change their meanings to a great extent (cf. KUHN (1962), FEYERABEND (1965)). Especially in such cases conceptual change may involve an essentially new way of conceptualizing and modelling the world so that the interpretation and even the structure of the observational basis or data-basis of science is changed. This view is quite compatible with what we have said about the theory ladenness of scientific concepts, even if we will mostly deal with less radical forms of conceptual change in this book. Furthermore, we may recall that in any case conceptual change involves some growth of science, both with respect to its theoretical and its observational content (in our sense of these terms).

One may argue that if the change of the conceptual basis is of the above deep going nature, then it is presupposed that theoretical (or new) concepts can, so to speak, have a life of their own, viz. that they are semantically, epistemologically, and ontologically autonomous. (This autonomy would be strongly approved by a scientific realist.) If this presupposition is accepted then of course the question of the *entire* eliminability or dispensability of theoretical concepts is out of place. In fact, we do consider this kind of realistic attitude to be acceptable in the case of most established theories in the natural sciences. We then have a very strong reason against the eliminability of theoretical concepts in those sciences, as we have repeatedly argued before. (But recall that in this book we want to investigate the matter further, especially from a methodological standpoint, and fight the instrumentalist with his own weapons.)

However, in many young sciences, looking for their identity, an unqualified realistic attitude is not, in our opinion, equally acceptable, as conceptual artifacts seem to abound in them. For instance, in the exploratory and descriptive sciences, exemplified e. g. by most of the social sciences of today, a more instrumentalistic attitude may initially seem plausible. Consider, for instance, the reality of various systematizing "factors" that statistical factor analysis gives us in exploratory research. In this kind of abstract theorizing theoretical concepts, such as factors, may not be interpreted or interpretable in a proper way (see Chapter V). Or consider psychological terms such as motive terms which, according to neowittgensteinians, do not refer to any states (mental or physical) at all (cf. ANSCOMBE (1957), KENNY (1963)). To accept such an "Aristotelian" view concerning the nature of psychological concepts presents at least seemingly a difficulty for scientific realism. A (critical) realist's answer to this difficulty is to eventually reject the Aristotelian view in favor of a scientific image of man (cf. SELLARS (1965)).

In the last mentioned cases it is meaningful to discuss at least the various *methodological* advantages resulting from the introduction and use of theoretical concepts in a theory. If such advantages are found then an instrumentalist will find theoretical concepts (at least) desirable and a realist can take these additional reasons to strengthen his case.

Let us now briefly recall the reasons for employing theoretical concepts in science. These reasons are of course also reasons for rejecting the theoretician's dilemma argument in its original form. We group these reasons as follows. (Cf. FEIGL (1950), STEGMÜLLER (1970) for a discussion of them.) First we have various *semantical*, *epistemological*, and *ontological* arguments related to the nature of theoretical concepts. Secondly, we recall that theoretical concepts have been regarded as (logically) indispensable within *deductive* and *inductive systematization* (cf. Chapters II and VIII). Thirdly, fourthly, and fifthly we have arguments related, respectively, to the various kinds of *growth*, *economy*, and *explanatory power* of scientific theories. Finally there are a number of quasipsychological or *pragmatic factors* such as heuristical fertility and suggestiveness, perspicuity, and manageability of theories, which are all supposedly due to theoretical concepts.

Concerning the first group, in the previous chapters and above we have already discussed various philosophical reasons for employing theoretical concepts (recall e. g. the arguments for realism in I.1., II.1., III.2., V.1., and V.2. and for open theoretical concepts in IV.3.). Within the first group we still include some other arguments which we want to mention here, even if no further analysis of them is attempted in this book. These arguments try to show that there are special types of theoretical constructs in science which are not (in some sense) definable or reducible to observational concepts. (It is some kind of term-by-term reduction that is in question here, not the replacement of entire frameworks.) Among these constructs we have idealized constructs such as instant velocity, mass point and "ideal types" (e. g. *homo sociologicus*, free market) as well as various microphysical constructs. The reader is referred to STEGMÜLLER (1970) for a recent discussion of these arguments. (Stegmüller does not, however, take a definite standpoint as to whether this kind of theoretical terms can ultimately be defined in terms of observational terms.) Except for "ideal types" in Weber's sense, this kind of constructs are peculiar to the physical sciences, and we shall not discuss these constructs here, because our intended applications are mostly concerned with social sciences. As to the Weberian ideal types, such as *homo sociologicus*, it may suffice to point out that they refer to idealized theories which are at best very rough approximates to truth; but these theories contain only concepts ordinarily used in the social sciences.

As we discuss the logical dispensability of theoretical concepts (the second group of reasons) in Chapters II and VIII, we shall not comment on them here.

In the third group we have a number of arguments which purport to show that theoretical concepts are necessary or at least desirable for growth of science. These arguments try to show that observational growth is impossible without theoretical concepts. We shall below introduce one more explicate of observational richness in addition to that provided by non-Ramsey-eliminable theoretical concepts, and discuss the validity of a relevant thesis called the Braithwaite-Ramsey assumption in STEGMÜLLER (1970).

Fourthly, the notion of simplicity or economy is notoriously vague and ambiguous. We shall not try to clarify it here in a deeper sense but only give one partial explicate for it and briefly discuss the integrity of deduction.

It has often been said that theories containing theoretical concepts have more explanatory power than purely "phenomenological" (observational) theories. This matter will be taken up in the next chapter.

Finally, we have the various desiderata of axiom systems brought up by Craig's critics: finiteness, perspicuity, manageability, heuristical fruitfulness.

As far as the finiteness requirement is concerned, we argued that it is not a *sine qua non* condition; at least in some cases a finite set of axiom schemas, or even a clear-cut infinite basis, might do as well. On the other hand, it seems to us that the restriction to finite sets of axioms often dovetails neatly with the other desiderata, even if is not, strictly speaking, either a necessary or a sufficient condition for them. The other requirements (perspicuity, manageability, heuristical fruitfulness) are pragmatic in their nature, and on this ground they are often thrown out of philosophical discussion. This does not seem fair to us, as these notions are certainly philosophically important. However, a systematic discussion of these concepts belongs to philosophical pragmatics, which field cannot be seriously discussed within the scope of this book.

1.2. Let us now go on to discuss two types of methodological gains due to theoretical concepts: a gain in *observational richness* and a gain in *economy*. We consider a context of scientific discovery or *theoretical generalization* which starts from establishing one or more observational or empirical laws. Let us call the conjunction of these laws $S(\lambda)$. We now want to create a theory $T(\lambda \cup \mu)$ which, among other things, will explain S, give new observational predictions, and integrate and systematize the (observational) domain of discourse in general.

We shall investigate this methodological situation by employing the framework of distributive normal forms and by relying on the logical results described in Section II.3. (cf. especially Diagram II.2.). As we saw there, we can so to speak "improve on" or theoretically generalize $S\ (=S^{(d)})$ by creating a theory $T(\lambda \cup \mu) = T^{(d)}(\lambda \cup \mu)$ such that the direct reduct $r(T^{d}(\lambda \cup \mu)) = S^{(d)}$ with respect to $\mathscr{L}(\lambda)$[1]. Our Diagram II.2. gives an especially neat way of illustrating the gain in

1 We write simply r for the reduction operation with respect to λ. But if confusion can be expected we write r_{λ}.

observational power due to the deeper expansions $T^{(d+e)}$ $(\lambda \cup \mu)$ and the simplification due to "shallower" formulations of this theory. (We shall follow HINTIKKA and TUOMELA (1970) and TUOMELA (1969) in this and the next section to a great extent.)

Let us first elaborate our gain in observational power or information content. The new observational content due to T $(\lambda \cup \mu)$, and hence due to the new theoretical concepts in μ, is of course given by the sequence r $(T^{(d+i)})$ $(i=1,\ldots)$.

How can we measure the gain obtained by using auxiliary concepts? Natural ways of measuring the gain in information which one obtains by introducing auxiliary concepts, that is by moving from r $(T^{(d)}$ $(\lambda \cup \mu))$ to $T^{(d)}$ $(\lambda \cup \mu)$ (see Diagram II.2.), are obtained if we have a strictly positive probability measure defined for all the consistent closed sentences (sentences without free variables or constants) of our (fixed) first-order language. Let us assume that such a measure p is defined; using it, various information measures can be defined; e. g. $cont\ (S)=1-p\ (S)$.

In terms of some such measure of information the gain that accrues from the introduction of theoretical concepts into $S^{(d)}$ can be expressed in an obvious way. In the terminology of Diagram II.2., we can, for instance, identify it with

$$(6.1) \qquad \lim_{e \to \infty} cont\ (r\ (T^{(d+e)})) - cont\ (r\ (T^{(d)})).$$

Here the second term equals the informative content (substantial information) of the original sentence supposedly 'improved' by introducing the set μ of theoretical (or auxiliary) concepts. From (6.1) it is clear how the gain which the introduction of theoretical concepts yields can be understood as an increase in information.

What (6.1) thus gives us is the power of the subtheory obtained from $T^{(d)}$ over and above the logical power of r $(T^{(d)})$. Since this logical power comes from an involvement or interwovenness of the new concepts with the old ones in the richer theory, whose normal form is $T^{(d)}$ $(\lambda \cup \mu)$, (6.1) can also be thought of as a measure of this involvement. If this involvement is nil, then (6.1) becomes zero [2].

---

2 Actually the expression (6.1) is perhaps not the most natural measure for involvement here because it is asymmetric. Usually we do not think that it should make a difference whether we speak of the involvement of the members of μ with those of λ or vice versa. An explication for the symmetric

This does not yet exhaust the possible gains offered by theoretical concepts in the present context. In what follows we shall for brevity call the gain measured by (6.1) a *deductive gain in observational richness*. We may obtain another kind of advantage by going from the poorer theory (axiomatized by the sentence S, whose distributive normal form is $r\,(T^{(d)}\,(\lambda \cup \mu))$ to the richer one (axiomatized by $T^{(d)}\,(\lambda \cup \mu)$). Even when there is no sentence equivalent to S of a smaller depth than depth d of S, as we shall assume in what follows that there is not, there may very well be shallower sentences equivalent to $T^{(d)}\,(\lambda \cup \mu)$. Let the shallowest sentence of this kind be of depth $c \leqq d$. Then the situation can be represented (after all sentences are rendered into their distributive normal forms) by Diagram VI.1., which amplifies Diagram II.2.:

$$
\begin{array}{ccccccccccc}
T^{(c)} & \leftrightarrow & T^{(c+1)} & \leftrightarrow \ldots \leftrightarrow & T^{(d)} & \leftrightarrow & T^{(d+1)} & \leftrightarrow \ldots \leftrightarrow & T^{(d+e)} & \leftrightarrow \ldots \\
\downarrow & & \downarrow & & \downarrow & & \downarrow & & \downarrow & \\
r(T^{(c)}) & \leftarrow & r(T^{(c+1)}) & \leftarrow \ldots \leftarrow & r(T^{(d)}) & \leftarrow & r(T^{(d+1)}) & \leftarrow \ldots \leftarrow & r(T^{(d+e)}) & \leftarrow \ldots
\end{array}
$$

Diagram VI.1

The notation is here the same as in Diagram II.2.

In analogy with the gain in observational richness (6.1), the gain due to pushing down the depth of sentences (by means of theoretical concepts) may naturally be measured by

$$(6.2) \qquad cont\,(r\,(T^{(d)})) - cont\,(r\,(T^{(c)})).$$

This will be called a *gain in (descriptive) economy* due to using auxiliary concepts in $T^{(d)}\,(\lambda \cup \mu)$ (relative to $S^{(d)}$). As a rougher measure of this gain we could also use the difference $d-c$. Generally a richer theory can give us both kinds of gains. Their amounts depend, of course, crucially on the richer theory we are dealing with.

As pointed out earlier, the richer theory $T^{(d)}\,(\lambda \cup \mu)$ is not uniquely determined by S or $S^{(d)} = r\,(T^{(d)})$. A theoretician of course looks for

notion of involvement would in this situation be the following, where the *inf*-measure is used to measure the information content of the theory:

$$inf\,(T^{(d)}\,(\lambda \cup \mu)) - \lim_{e \to \infty} inf\,[r_\lambda\,(T^{(d+e)})\ \&\ r_\mu\,(T^{(d+e)})]$$

where $r_\lambda\,(T^{(d+e)})$ and $r_\mu\,(T^{(d+e)})$ denote the direct reducts of T into λ and μ, respectively.

the best $T(\lambda \cup \mu)$ compatible with the evidence. Criteria of adequacy relevant here are deductive and inductive power, economy, finite axiomatizability, deductive coherence and the like. As to axiomatizability, most of the logical results pertinent to it (and, as we will see, to deductive coherence and economy as well) are due to Kleene, Craig and Vaught (see, for example, CRAIG and VAUGHT (1958)).

To discuss axiomatizability, let us first define the notions of finite axiomatizability using additional predicates. A theory T' is *finitely axiomatizable by means of additional predicates* (*f. a.*+) if there is a theory T such that the nonlogical constants of T are those of T' together with some additional predicates, T is finitely axiomatizable, and T is a conservative extension of T'. Next, a theory T' is *finitely axiomatizable by means of additional predicates in the semantical sense* (*s. f. a.*+) if there is a number k and a theory T such that the nonlogical constants of T are those of T' together with k additional predicates, T is finitely axiomatizable, and an arbitrary realization $\mathcal{S}' = \langle D, O_1, \ldots, O_m \rangle$ of $\mathcal{L}(T')$ is a model of T' if and only if there exist relations $P_1, \ldots, P_k$ such that $\mathcal{S} = \langle D, O_1, \ldots, O_m, P_1, \ldots, P_k \rangle$ is a model of T. In the case of *s. f. a.*+ all models of T are expansions of models of T', and hence, according to Theorem III.3., T is even here a conservative extension. It is also clear that if the notions of second-order formula and satisfaction of second-order formulas in the standard sense are employed, then T' is *s. f. a.*+ if and only if there is a first-order theory T such that its Ramsey sentence T^R and T have the same observational models.

Let us state concisely some of the main results obtained in this field (see CRAIG and VAUGHT (1958)):

(1) For arbitrary theories in a language with or without identity which have only infinite models, the notions *f. a.*+, *s. f. a.*+ and (recursive) axiomatizability coincide.

(2) For arbitrary theories with identity, *f. a.*+ and *s. f. a.*+ become equivalent, and *f. a.*+ implies axiomatizability.

(3) There are axiomatizable theories with identity which are not *f. a.*+.

The following results hold only for theories without identity:

(4) Axiomatizability is equivalent to *f. a.*+.

(5) *f. a.*+ does not imply *s. f. a.*+.

A result of Tarski shows that the additional predicates can be reduced to one binary predicate in cases (1) and (4).

The above remarks show that among theories compatible with the evidence in most cases we may in principle choose as our extension a theory $T(\lambda \cup \mu)$ which is *s. f. a.*+ with respect to a given theory T' in $\mathscr{L}(\lambda)$. As we recall from Chapter III, our theoretical concepts will then really do some work for us by ruling out some observable states of affairs not ruled out by a *s. f. a.*+ theory. In other words, our theoretical concepts are then not semantically Ramsey-eliminable. Hence we can get the kind of *semantical gain in observational richness* of Chapter III. We might measure this gain by the cardinality of the set of models ruled out by our theory $T(\lambda \cup \mu)$.

What else can be gained when one moves to a theory that is finitely axiomatizable by means of additional predicates (*f. a.*+)? No deductive gain in observational richness ((6.1)) is obtained, but a gain in descriptive economy ((6.2)) will always be forthcoming. Assume that the sequence $S_1(\lambda), S_2(\lambda), \ldots$ is an axiomatization of the original nonfinitely axiomatized theory. The informative content of this axiom system is obviously

$$\lim_{i \to \infty} cont\,(S_1(\lambda) \;\&\; S_2(\lambda) \;\&\; \ldots \;\&\; S_i(\lambda)),$$

and the gain in economy thus becomes

$$(6.2^*) \qquad \lim_{i \to \infty} cont\,(S_1(\lambda) \;\&\; S_2(\lambda) \;\&\; \ldots \;\&\; S_i(\lambda)) - \\ - cont\,(r\,(T^{(d)}(\lambda \cup \mu))).$$

We can consider this as a *gain in deductive coherence* insofar as the finiteness of an axiom set reflects it.

Let us next discuss the special but important case of the introduction of new concepts by explicit definition (cf. Russell's maxim in Section 1 of Chapter II and Braithwaite's views discussed in Section 3 of this chapter). Assume that the richer theory is axiomatized simply by $S(\lambda)$ together with the explicit definitions of the members of μ in terms of those of λ. If none of the explicit definitions has a depth greater than the depth d of S, our richer theory $T^{(d)}(\lambda \cup \mu)$ may be simply the distributive normal form of the conjunction of all these definitions. Let us consider this possibility first. How does it fit into our discussion?

In virtue of the noncreative character of explicit definitions, we have for each sentence $v\ (\lambda)$ whose nonlogical constants are all in λ:

$$\text{(6.3)} \qquad \vdash T^{(d)}\ (\lambda \cup \mu) \supset v\ (\lambda) \text{ iff } \vdash S^{(d)}\ (\lambda) \supset v\ (\lambda).$$

Here $S^{(d)}\ (\lambda)$ is, of course, by assumption $r\ (T^{(d)}\ (\lambda \cup \mu))$. This means that all the implications of the lower row in Diagram VI.1. are equivalences from d on and that the maximal observational subtheory of $T^{(d)}$ is finitely axiomatized by $S^{(d)}$. The deductive gain in observational richness is then zero.

Does this mean that the introduction of new concepts by explicit definition is pointless? The answer is no, for it is perfectly possible that we obtain a gain in descriptive economy. In fact, there are interesting connections between this gain and the nature of the explicit definitions that mark the transition from S to the richer theory. For predicates, these definitions are of the form

$$\text{(6.4)} \qquad (x_1)\ (x_2) \ldots (x_k)\ (P\ (x_1, x_2, \ldots, x_k) \equiv v\ (\lambda, x_1, x_2, \ldots, x_k)),$$

where the definiendum $P \in \mu$ is a k-place predicate ($k \geq 1$); and where v (=the definiens) is a sentence whose extralogical constants are all in λ, and whose free variables are $x_1, x_2, \ldots, x_k$.

In the sequel we shall assume that in (6.4) the definiens v has been brought to a form in which its depth is minimal (i. e. that there is no shallower sentence equivalent to v with the same constants and free variables).

The simplest of the connections mentioned above is probably the inequality

$$\text{(6.5)} \qquad d - c \geq m,$$

where m is the maximum of the depths of the definienses of the definitions of the members of μ in terms of those of λ.

To show this, let us assume that in $T^{(d)}\ (\lambda \cup \mu)$ (see Diagram VI.1.) each member of μ is replaced by its definiens. The depth of the resulting sentence is at most $c + m$. This resulting sentence is clearly equivalent with the original S. Since it was assumed that S has no equivalents of smaller depth, we must have $c + m \geq d$.

As a corollary it follows that if each definiens of a member of μ in terms of those of λ is of depth zero ($m = 0$), as may very well be the case, $c = d$ and no gain in descriptive economy is obtained. Such definitions can be regarded as modern explicates of *nominal* definitions. No gain (in the above senses) accrues from such definitions. A gain can be expected from the introduction of explicit definitions only if at least one of these definitions presents a genuine quantificational analysis of the definiendum, in the sense that its definiens has one or more (irreducible) layers of quantifiers ($m \geq 1$). Such definitions seem to correspond to the old idea of *real* definitions. (This connection between modern and traditional ideas might merit some further attention.) It may be pointed out that our distinction between nominal and real definitions is analogous to Frege's distinction between trivial and nontrivial definitions in FREGE (1884), pp. 100—101.

Furthermore, from (6.5) it is seen that the deeper the analyses (deeper both in the literal and in the metaphorical sense) which our explicit definitions give of their definienda (in the sense that the definienses have greater depths), the greater is the gain in information that is likely to result from these definitions.

These observations can at once be generalized to serial definitions (where each new concept of a sequence is defined explicitly in terms of some of the earlier ones).

If the depth of the conjunction T of the explicit definitions of the members of μ in terms of those of λ is higher than that of S (whose depth is d), no gain in economy is obtained unless the conjunction S & T (of depth $e > d$) has an equivalent of depth less than d. In that case, the gain can be measured as above.

2. Methodological Illustrations of the Use of Theoretical Concepts

2.1. Let us next comment from a general methodological point of view on the gains in deductive observational richness and descriptive economy achieved by introducing theoretical concepts into a "phenomenological" theory $S^{(d)}(\lambda)$.

In both of these types of gain, and especially in a gain in economy, the crucial advantage which auxiliary concepts offer us is essentially due to the possibility of getting along with shallower axioms (and other assumptions). This is patent in the case of a gain of the second kind. But in the case of a gain of the first kind, too, we can in a sense say that the essential advantage is that we need only the sentence T (or its normal form $T^{(d)}(\lambda \cup \mu)$) of the fixed depth d so that we can obtain from it various consequences concerning the members of λ which not only did not follow from S (that is $r(T^{(d)})$) alone, but also could not, in many cases, be formulated without resort to much deeper sentences.

What is the intuitive meaning of this 'reduction' of the depth of one's axioms? It has been convincingly argued that the intuitive meaning of the concept of depth of a sentence *S* is essentially the number of individuals considered together (in their relation to each other) in the deepest part of *S*, of course over and above the individuals referred to by the individual constants (see HINTIKKA (1965 b), (1966 a)).

Now this notion of "considering so many individuals together" seems to have clear methodological significance. For one may argue that what an experimental scientist often does is to study the interrelations of a relatively small number of entities involved in an experimental situation which he can control. By discovering their interdependencies he hopes to obtain the means of theoretically mastering other, often much more complicated, situations.

To the extent that this enterprise can be described — even approximately — in first-order terms, it seems to amount to an attempt to discover relatively shallow (in the technical sense) laws whose deeper (technical sense again) logical consequences nevertheless match the behavior of more complicated situations (that is, situations involving more individuals). The (minimal) depth of the nonlogical axioms of a scientific theory thus becomes connected to the complexity of the empirical situations in which this theory can come into the play and in which it therefore can (in principle) be tested and perhaps corroborated. It is obvious that *ceteris paribus* it is highly desirable to have this number as small as possible. In fact, it is one of the main factors that seem to influence our ideas of the simplicity and easy testability of scientific theory.

Hence, if this complexity of a theory can be reduced by introducing new concepts, such reduction represents (*ceteris paribus* again) a definite and clear simplification in describing the world[3]. One might even go as far as to speak of a kind of ontological economy of a theory whose depth is small, though this sense has nothing to do with the size of the domain needed in order for the theory to be true.

The above argument may be highlighted by consideration of a hypothetical special case in which at any one time we can (perhaps

3 Therefore the gain measured by (6.2) was called a gain in descriptive economy.

because of restricted possibilities of experimentation) observe at most d individuals in their relations to one another. Then we have no possibilities of telling whether such hypotheses as can be distinguished from each other only by means of sentences of a depth $>d$ are true or not, unless we introduce new (theoretical) concepts. What we have seen is that by so doing we can, in fact, formulate hypotheses in which only d individuals are considered in their relation to each other and from which consequences nevertheless ensue concerning the old concepts which cannot be formulated otherwise except by going to depths greater than d. Thus the new concepts may bring essentially deeper hypotheses within the purview of testing and corroboration, even when this testing is of a restricted complexity.

Notice that our remarks above are not necessarily geared to the theoretical-observational interpretation of μ and λ. What we are trying to clarify here are the advantages of introducing new concepts of any kind. Moreover, our above three kinds of gains are methodlogical in their nature and they should be appreciated equally well both by scientific realists and instrumentalists.

As remarked in Chapter II, philosophers and scientists seem to think that "pure" theories (sentences containing auxiliary concepts only) play a special role in systems containing such terms. As we saw above, purely theoretical statements in a fixed and "finished" richer theory have a no more important function within deductive systematization than do "correspondence rules" (statements where members of both λ and μ occur). What is crucial here is as much the way old and new concepts are interweaved (involved with each other) in the richer theory as the assumptions concerning the auxiliary concepts alone (cf. Chapters V and VII).

Despite the generality and the somewhat restricted scope of our discussion above, we believe that we have brought out something interesting in this chapter. As we have mentioned, two important aims which theoretical (auxiliary) terms are typically supposed to serve are (observational) *richness* and *economy*. Our analysis shows that these aims can be achieved (in first-order theories). It also shows, to some extent, *how* they are achieved. In particular, our gains in deductive observational richness and in descriptive economy show that by means of theoretical concepts we can obtain (in the first-order case) something that Barker for one claims to be unattainable (see the quotation in Section 1 of Chapter II). We have arrived at a diametrically opposite conclusion by using essentially the same basic logical results due to Craig as Barker is there commenting on, both in the case of richness and economy.

Let us now see whether the arguments of the present chapter are sufficient to invalidate the theoretician's dilemma argument. Do not our deductive and semantical gains in observational richness (gain (6.1) and the gain due to not semantically Ramsey-eliminable theoretical concepts), our gain in descriptive economy as well as the welter of other reasons mentioned at the beginning of this chapter clearly show even for an instrumentalist that there is no real theoretician's dilemma?

First, it has to be noticed that the latest forms

$$\langle(1), (2'), (3'), (4'), (5''), (6')\rangle \text{ and } \langle(1), (2'), (3'), (4''), (5'''), (6')\rangle$$

still stand as valid as they stood previous to the arguments of the present chapter. That is, our present arguments clearly do not contribute to showing that theoretical concepts are *logically* indispensable for the deductive systematization (in our technical sense of Chapter II) of λ-statements. As far as one is concerned with this kind of deductive systematization, it is, in accordance with Craig's theorem (II.3.), *logically* possible to do as well by, so to speak, operating solely with the lower row of our Diagram VI.1. (although this may and will happen in a less economical way).

What our above arguments really contribute to show is this. First, some reasons mentioned at the beginning of this chapter (as well as in Chapters I and II) indicate that the scientific systematization of λ-statements by no means exhausts the tasks of a scientific theory. Secondly, the main purpose of this chapter has been to argue for the *methodological* indispensability (or desirability) of theoretical concepts (by actually using the same logical weapons an eliminationist or instrumentalist uses, but in an opposite way). If our arguments are acceptable at all they clearly indicate that the above strong forms of the theoretician's dilemma argument (concerning the *logical* dispensability of theoretical concepts) are *methodologically* uninteresting. By the same token, we have new additional reasons against accepting the original form of the argument (Chapter I). Indeed, we are now in a position to accept that theoretical concepts are (or, rather, can be) *methodologically desirable* for the deductive systematization of λ-statements.

2.2. Let us try to illustrate more concretely the usefulness of auxiliary concepts. First, we consider an artificial (but still instructive) example best described by reference to elementary arithmetics. Suppose that we are in a position to make observations concerning a single monadic property P of individuals in an ordering. The ordering is given by a two-place relation R to be interpreted as denoting immediate succession. The first-order axioms of R are given in a first-order language with identity as follows:

(A1) $(x)\ (Ey)\ R\ (x, y);$

(A2) $(x)\ (y)\ (R\ (x, y) \supset -R\ (y, x));$

(A3) $(x)\ (y)\ (z)\ (R\ (x, y)\ \&\ R\ (x, z) \supset y = z);$

(A4) $(x)\ (y)\ (z)\ (R\ (y, x)\ \&\ (z, x) \supset z = y);$

(A5) $(Ex)\ (y) - R\ (y, x);$

(A6) $(x)\ (z)\ (-(Ey)\ R(y, x)\ \&\ -(Ey)\ R\ (y, z) \supset x = z).$

These axioms describe an immediate succession-ordering with a unique first element but no last element. The immediate and distant (finite) successors of the first element can be correlated with the natural numbers 2, 3, 4, ...

Let us assume that a theorist can (directly or indirectly) "observe" which individuals have the property P. Assume that, starting from the beginning, individuals no. 2, 3, 5, 7, 11, and 13 are found to have this property out of the 13 first individuals. How can one try to "systematize" or to "explain" these observations? How can one obtain predictions concerning new individuals? It is intuitively obvious what the tempting suggestion here is, viz. that the predicate P belongs to those and only those distant and immediate successors of the first individual which are correlated with prime numbers. It is also clear that this conjecture cannot be expressed in finite terms solely by means of P and the successor relation. Hence we have here a clear-cut (though artificial) example of the need to resort to "theoretical" (auxiliary) concepts.

One thing our imaginary theoretician could do here is to expand our vocabulary so as to be able to formulate a fragment of elementary number theory. To our "observational" theory (formulated in the vocabulary $\lambda = \{P, R\}$) he adds a set μ consisting of two new three-place predicates A and M representing the addition and multiplication operations, and a few new axioms to obtain a richer theory $T\ (\{P, R\} \cup \{A, M\})$. Four of these axioms will state that A and M are functions defined everywhere, and the others can be modified versions of the usual recursion equations for addition and multiplication (let us call them (A7—A14) plus the following:

$$\text{(A15)} \qquad (x)\,(P\,(x) \equiv (y)\,(z)\,(y \cdot z = x \supset y = 1 \vee z = 1)\ \&\ x \neq 1).$$

Here we have, of course, used dot as a shorthand which can be eliminated in favor of the relation M. By means of axiom A15 we predict for any given future individual in our "observational" sequence whether it has the property P or not.

Our richer theory $T\,(\{P, R\} \cup \{A, M\})$ with its fifteen axioms (the deepest has depth 5) has thus been specified clearly enough. Here we will not undertake the laborious task of writing it out in its distributive normal form, nor is this needed for our purposes. Neither can the axioms of the 'observational' theory axiomatized by the successive reducts

$$r\,(T^{(d)}\,(\{P, R\} \cup \{A, M\})) \qquad (d = 5, 6, 7, 8, \ldots)$$

(into the language $\mathscr{L}\,(\{P, R\})$) be easily transformed into their distributive normal forms. However, we can see what their essential features would be like. In order to distinguish individual no. d from the others (so as to be able to say whether it has the predicate P or not) by means of the successor relation alone we need $d+1$ layers of quantifiers. Thus an essential part of what $r\,(T^{(d)}\,(\{P, R\} \cup \{A, M\}))$ says is to list which individuals among those numbered $1, 2, \ldots, d-1$ have P and which ones do not. In brief, the poorer theory $r\,(T^{(d)}(\{P, R\} \cup \{A, M\}))$ $(d = 5, 6, 7, \ldots)$ specifies which individuals have P, by enumerating them one by one, while the richer theory presents us with definite law governing the distribution of P.

It is striking how the introduction of "theoretical" (auxiliary) concepts can give us some real gain. The richer theory has deductive consequences concerning P and R beyond those of the reducts of any of its successive expansions. If one starts from any of these as one's poorer theory, a gain of the first kind is obtained. For instance, in the "experimental" situation described in our fictional example, a natural starting-point would have been $r\,(T^{(14)}\,(\{P, R\} \cup \{A, M\}))$. Furthermore, starting from any reduct with depth >5, a gain in economy (gain of the second kind) is obtained also, in that the richer theory can be axiomatized with fewer layers of quantifiers. It seems to us that the feeling of much greater "insight into" and "appreciation of" the situation that the richer theory seems to give us here is *partly* a reflection of these clearly definable features of the underlying logical situation.

Although the confirmation theory of relational (polyadic) generalizations is notoriously underdeveloped, it is clear that the poorer theory (lower row) in which we present our general hypothesis, so to speak, by enumerating the different cases cannot in any case be highly confirmed or corroborated by finite evidence, for such evidence cannot distinguish between this theory and a great many competing theories. In contrast, any adequate confirmation theory presumably ought to show how the richer theory is confirmed by its instances. Thus the gain obtained by enriching the conceptual basis may in the last analysis turn out to be as closely connected with the inductive properties of theories as with their purely deductive ones.

Recall that it is possible to axiomatize some standard version of set theory in first-order logic. As a great part of mathematics can be developed within set theory we can in principle formalize almost all actual scientific theories, even if the task may seem quite hopeless to carry out in practice. Therefore our above considerations are in principle applicable to real scientific theories.

An example from real science is offered to us by certain sociometric investigations (viz. attempts to explain the resulting sociograms) conducted by Sherif and Sherif. In these investigations contacts between individuals (a two-place relation) are recorded to form a sociogram, together with certain further properties of these individuals. Then new concepts incorporated in certain new axioms are introduced to explain these observations rather in the manner suggested above, so that our gains in observational richness and descriptive economy are obtainable (see SHERIF and SHERIF (1953)). However, in this connection, we cannot undertake a detailed methodological investigation of these sociometric studies.

As our second example we shall discuss a gain in descriptive power within a version of Ohm's theory circuits. We shall below mostly rely on Simon's axiomatization (SIMON (1970)), but some reformulation in translating the theory into our framework is needed. (Here we cannot even attempt a full and rigorous first-order standard formalization of the theory.)

We consider a theory $T(\lambda \cup \mu)$ where $\lambda = \{r, c\}$ and $\mu = \{v, b\}$. Here the observational terms r and c represent, respectively, *resistance* and *current intensity* of the components of any system or domain D to which the theory is applied. They are (mathematically) interpreted as non-negative real valued functions defined on such a D. The theoretical terms v and b represent, respectively, the *voltage* and the *internal resistance* of a system S. They are assumed to be mathematically interpreted as real constants. Our small theory $T(\lambda \cup \mu)$ of circuits is assumed to satisfy the following axiom

$$\text{(A)} \quad (x)\left[c(x) = \frac{v}{b + r(x)}\right].$$

Let us now consider the definability of voltage and internal resistance in terms of resistance and current intensity within T (cf. our discussion in IV.3. of linear equation systems). The definability of our theoretical concepts somewhat depends upon the cardinality of the domains D into which the theory is applied. If D contains one single element, v and b clearly remain undefined (and unidentified)as A now implies

$$\text{(A}'\text{)} \quad v = (b + r_1)\, c_1,$$

where r_1 and c_1 respectively designate the values of the resistance and current intensity of this single component. If D contains two elements with distinct r's and c's, then A gives us explicit definitions (and unique identifiability) for v and b in terms of r and c as follows:

$$\text{(A}''\text{)} \quad b = \frac{c_2 r_2 - c_1 r_1}{c_1 - c_2}; \qquad v = c_1\, c_2 \frac{r_2 - r_1}{c_1 - c_2}.$$

But in the general case when D contains more than two elements, to obtain explicit definitions for v and b (by formulas of type A″) A implies that for every x_j and with respect to any x_k, x_l (x_j, x_k, and x_l being variables valued over elements in D)

$$\text{(L)} \quad (x_j)\left[c_j(x) = \frac{c_k c_l\,(r_l - r_k)}{c_l r_l - c_k r_k + (c_k - c_l)\, r_j(x_j)}\right]$$

must hold. (In this case v and b are *over*identified in the sense of Chapter IV.) Notice that L is an observational law statement. Let us denote the requirement (statement) that D contain at least two elements with distinct c's and r's by B.

Now consider the extended or full Ohmic theory $T'(\lambda \cup \mu)$ axiomatized by the conjunction of A and B. In this extended theory the theoreticals v and b are eliminable by explicit definitions (of form A″) in terms of c and r. However, the observational subtheory L obtained from the full theory $T'(\lambda \cup \mu)$ is in a clear sense theoretically complex and uneconomical relative to the full theory where b and v are present. For within T' $(\lambda \cup \mu)$ we can, for those purely theoretical purposes where we operate solely or primarily with b and v, get along with the formula A, whose quantificational depth is 5 (in a first-order standard formalization)[4]. But if we eliminate b and v from the full theory T' $(\lambda \cup \mu)$ then we for all purposes have to go back to the complex formula L, whose depth is 15.

In other words, for some theoretical purposes at least, we obtain a definite *economy gain in depth* (of the magnitude $15 - 5 = 10$, if you like) due to the employment of the theoretical concepts v and b in this Ohmic theory T' $(\lambda \cup \mu)$.

3. Scientific Growth and Explicitly Defined Theoretical Concepts

3.1. It has often been argued that theoretical concepts which are *not* explicitly definable in terms of observational concepts are necessary for the growth of a scientific theory. BRAITHWAITE (1953) and STEGMÜLLER (1970) can be cited as representatives of this view. We shall below first consider Braithwaite's argument and then Stegmüller's discussion of what he calls the Ramsey-Braithwaite assumption.

Braithwaite's main argument, which he attributes to Ramsey, is that if the theoretical terms of a theory are defined explicitly in terms of its observational concepts the theory becomes incapable of growth, as stated in the following paragraph:

"A little reflection, however, makes it clear that if the theoretical terms are defined in such a way as to make the theory logically equivalent to the facts it explains, the theory becomes merely an alternative way of stating these facts. The hypotheses of the theory become translations of the empirical generalizations rather than, in any important sense, explanations of them; they do not stretch out beyond the limited number of generalizations; not

---

4 To compute the depth of formula A we formalize it by the following statement:

$$(y_1)\ (y_2)\ (y_3)\ (y_4)\ (x)\ [S\ (y_1, y_2, v)\ \&\ M\ (y_3, b, y_1)\ \&\ M\ (y_3, y_4, y_2)\ \&\ c\ (x) = y_3\ \&\ r\ (x) = y_4].$$

Here

$$S\ (y_1, y_2, v) \text{ if and only if } y_1 + y_2 = v$$

$$M\ (y_3, b, y_1) \text{ if and only if } y_3 \cdot b = y_1$$

Formula L is treated analogously.

only do they have exactly the same field of application, but they say exactly the same things about this field. A definition of the theoretical terms would thus sacrifice one of our principal objects in constructing a scientific theory, that of being able to extend it in the future, if the way opens, to explain facts about new things by incorporating the theory in a more general theory having a wider field of application." (BRAITHWAITE (1953), pp. 67f.)

As we have understood Braithwaite, he clearly claims that explicit definitions are the kind of definitions which "make the theory logically equivalent with the facts it explains" (see especially BRAITHWAITE (1953), pp. 62 and 67).

The above passage and Braithwaite's discussion leading to it can be taken to give us the following theses:

If the theoretical or μ-concepts of a theory $T(\lambda \cup \mu)$ are explicitly defined in terms of its observational or λ-concepts, then

(1) $T(\lambda \cup \mu)$ becomes an alternative way of describing the conjunction of the generalizations $E_1, \ldots, E_n$ in the vocabulary λ it explains;

(2) $T(\lambda \cup \mu)$ does not really explain the generalizations it entails;

(3) $T(\lambda \cup \mu)$ cannot be extended to apply to new (kinds of) objects;

(4) $T(\lambda \cup \mu)$ says exactly the same things about the old objects as the empirical generalizations $E_1, \ldots E_n$ the theory purports to explain;

(5) $T(\lambda \cup \mu)$ does not entail any new generalizations in terms of λ beyond $E_1, \ldots, E_n$ (and the logical consequences of them).

Braithwaite argues for the above theses by means of some artificial theories stated in terms of various class calculi. Hence his theo retical and observational concepts are only monadic. But Braithwaite argues for the generality of his theses: "... the theoretical terms can only be defined by means of observable properties on condition that the theory cannot be adopted properly to apply to new situations. *Still more* will this be the case with a theory using a more complicated mathematical apparatus" (BRAITHWAITE (1953), p. 76; our italics).

We claim that, strictly speaking, all of the above theses (1)—(5) attributed to Braithwaite are false when taken as *general* theses and that Braithwaite has simply been mislead by his special examples. Moreover, these theses can be shown to be false by the same kind of simple monadic theories Braithwaite uses to argue for his theses.

Let us start our discussion by considering some of Braithwaite's examples. His first theory (call it T), constructed within the calculus of classes, has as its logico-mathematical symbols $=$, $\cap$, (,) and as its descriptive symbols A, B, C, k, m, and n. Of these symbols $=$ stands for the identity, (,) for the parentheses, and $\cap$ for the intersection of classes. As the set of theoretical terms we have $\mu=\{k,m,n\}$ and as the set of observational terms $\lambda=\{A, B, C\}$. The members of both μ and λ are interpreted as classes. The intersection operation is assumed to be associative, commutative and idempotent. Identical classes are substitutable for each other in this calculus. The inclusion operation $\subseteq$ is defined by the schema

$$X \subseteq Y = (X \cap Y = X).$$

The descriptive axioms of T are the following three:

(G1) $A = m \cap n$

(G2) $B = k \cap n$

(G3) $C = k \cap m.$

The theory T is assumed to have been introduced to explain the following two empirical generalizations:

(E1) $A \cap B \subseteq C$

(E2) $B \cap C \subseteq A.$

The theory T entails these generalizations, and for Braithwaite this also means T explains them. Furthermore, T has predictive power in the sense of entailing still a third analogous empirical generalization

(E3) $A \cap C \subseteq B.$

Generalizations $E1$, $E2$, and $E3$ together give the observational or λ-content of T.

The theoretical terms of T are open in the sense that they are not explicitly definable in terms of λ. In addition, we cannot even, consistently with T, formulate explicit definitions for the theoretical terms k, m, and n. To be able to do this, let us add the symbol $'$ for complementation to the underlying calculus to have a Boolean algebra. We then assume that for all classes X, Y

$$(X' \cap Y')' \cap (X' \cap Y)' = X.$$

Now we can define the union operation $\cup$ as follows:

$$X \cup Y = (X' \cap Y')'.$$

In the resulting calculus it is possible to formulate the following explicit definitions for the theoretical concepts in terms of the observational ones:

(D1) $k = B \cup C$

(D2) $m = A \cup C$

(D3) $n = A \cup B$.

Let us denote by T_1 the theory consisting of the axioms G_1, G_2, and G_3 and the definitions D_1, D_2, and D_3. The new theory T_1 is a conservative extension of T (with respect to the vocabulary $\lambda \cup \mu$). It is also easily seen that

$$E_1 \,\&\, E_2 \,\&\, E_3 \,\&\, D_1 \,\&\, D_2 \,\&\, D_3 \vdash G_1 \,\&\, G_2 \,\&\, G_3.$$

This Braithwaite takes to show that theses (1) and (4) (which is entailed by (1)) are correct. But (1) is not true, not at least in the form Braithwaite has stated it in the quoted passage. Consider the following counterexample. Let us form a theory T' by taking as its axioms the generalizations E_1, E_2, E_3 and the theoretical statement

(H) $k \subseteq n$.

Now this theory has as its observational content the subtheory axiomatized by $E_1 \,\&\, E_2 \,\&\, E_3$, which it trivially "explains" (entails). Next we add to T' the definitions

(D4) $k = A$

(D5) $m = B$

(D6) $n = C$.

Call the resulting theory T''. Now, clearly it is *not* the case that

$$E_1 \,\&\, E_2 \,\&\, E_3 \,\&\, D_4 \,\&\, D_5 \,\&\, D_6 \vdash E_1 \,\&\, E_2 \,\&\, E \,\&\, H.$$

Furthermore, T'' entails a new observational law

(E4) $A \subseteq C$,

and hence it has predictive power. This seems to show that not only are theses (1) and (4) false in general, but so is (5), too.

But perhaps Braithwaite meant something else by his theses (1), (4), and (5), after all. One immediate solution to the above dilemma seems to result from asking whether the full observational content of T'' (and not T') together with the above definitions implies T'. If we consider the observational content of T'' (which equals $r_\lambda (T'' (\lambda \cup \mu))$ then we see that it includes E_4. Therefore it is easily seen that Braithwaite's theses (1), (4), and (5) are true on this construal. On the other hand, they now become completely trivial. For they amount to saying that explicit definitions satisfy the criteria of eliminability and non-creativity, which is a trivial well-known truth.

Braithwaite's thesis (2) claims that no real explanation is obtained by using theories with explicitly defined concepts. There is certainly much truth in this, but still it may not always be true if the explaining theory initially has sufficiently much theoretical content. Then explicit definitions with quantificationally deep definientia may perhaps provide the required openness and generality (e. g. such definientia are usually not finitely verifiable; cf. Section VI.2). As Braithwaite has studied monadic theories only, features like this seem to have escaped him.

Furthermore, and, what is more important, Braithwaite clearly seems to identify deductive explanation with plain deduction. This makes his arguments concerning explanation somewhat uninteresting (cf. Chapter VII).

Let us next examine the remaining thesis (3). This is best done by following Braithwaite's argumentation. He constructs two new theories out of T and T_1 by extending their vocabulary and axioms in the same way. To λ he adds D and E and to μ a term r, and as new axioms Braithwaite takes

(G4) $D = m \cap r$

(G5) $E = n \cap r$.

These new axioms are introduced to explain the generalizations

(E4) $A \cap D \subseteq E$

(E5) $A \cap E \subseteq D$.

In addition to entailing these generalizations, (G1)—(G5) conjunctively also entail

(E6) $E \cap D \subseteq A$ and

(E7) $B \cap D = C \cap E$.

Let us denote by T_2 the extension of T and by T_3 the extension of T_1 obtained by adding the axioms G_4 and G_5. T_3 is stronger than T_2. T_3 implies

(E8) $D=(A\cup C)\cap r$

(E9) $E=(A\cup B)\cap r$

which are not deducible from T_2. The generalizations E_8 and E_9 express the fact that none of the observational statements of T_3 can speak about objects that the statements of T and T_1 say nothing about. By objects that T and T_1 speak about we simply mean objects belonging to at least one of the classes A, B, or C. Braithwaite's *new* things or objects are such that they belong to none of these classes. (Notice that this notion of a new object is different from the usual model theoretic one which simply refers to increasing the domain of a model.)

Braithwaite's thesis (3) is too strong. (This has been shown in KAKKURI-KETONEN (1972).) For we can extend the theory T_1 consistently in another way so that Braithwaite's thesis (3) becomes false. Let us thus add t as a new theoretical term and F as a new observational term to the descriptive vocabulary of T. Then we add to T_1 the following two axioms

(G6) $t=A\cup F$

(G7) $t\cap F=(A\cup B\cup C)'$.

Call this extension T_4. Now T_4 implies

(E10) $F=(A\cup B\cup C)'$.

This generalization says that the members of the class F are new objects in Braithwaite's sense.

We can conclude our discussion on Braithwaite's analysis by saying that he has not been able to give logical reasons for the indispensability of theoretical concepts within the context of the growth of science, which was the aim of his analysis. This finding is consistent with our earlier conclusions. It seems to be extremely hard to find purely *logical* reasons for employing (open) theoretical concepts in scientific theories, if only questions of scientific systematization in the broad sense of Chapter II are considered. The reasons to be found are usually methodological and philosophical and related to some more restricted scientific tasks and situations.

3.2. Braithwaite's (and Ramsey's) main claim, according to which explicit definitions of theoretical concepts prevent the growth of theory, has been interpreted in ways differing from ours. Let us first take up Hempel's interpretation. He argues for the partial definability of theoretical concepts somewhat in the spirit of thesis (5) above. If theoretical concepts are only partially interpreted then we have the possibility of adding new partial interpretations. Thus e. g. the observational interpretation of 'temperature' or 'neurotic' should be open so that new ways of measuring them may be accounted for. This means that it should be possible to add new correspondence rules (perhaps by adding new observational concepts) to the theory. On the other hand, if these kinds of theoretical concepts are explicitly defined in terms of observational concepts their interpretation is completely fixed, and no growth in (structural) interpretation is possible. (See HEMPEL (1958), pp. 204—205.) Hempel's argument is acceptable and sound at least as far as the correspondence rules in question are not meaning postulates, but his analysis clearly does not exhaust what Braithwaite has tried to say.

In his recent book Stegmüller discusses the following thesis which he calls the *Braithwaite-Ramsey thesis* (STEGMÜLLER (1970), p. 289): *In all interesting scientific theories there are at least some theoretical terms which are not explicitly harmless and not even implicitly harmless.*

Let us first give Stegmüller's definitions for the basic notions occurring in this thesis. Theoretical terms are said to be *explicitly harmless* in a (partially interpreted) theory T exactly when T is only a conservative extension of a given set of empirical generalizations (STEGMÜLLER (1970), p. 285). An extension T^* of a theory T is a *mathematical extension* if it can be obtained from T by strengthening the logico-mathematical apparatus of T in the sense of adding to T new logical or mathematical symbols plus axioms for these new symbols (STEGMÜLLER (1970), p. 287). The theoretical terms of a theory T are said to be *implicitly harmless* if there is a mathematical extension of T where explicit definitions for the theoretical terms of T can be given (STEGMÜLLER (1970), p. 287). By the phrase '*can be given*' Stegmüller simply means the same as Braithwaite above, viz. that explicit definitions consistent with the theory can be formulated and added to the theory. By an *interesting* theory Stegmüller means a theory which has predictive power over and above the given set of empirical generalizations the theory was introduced to explain.

Stegmüller shows next that in Braithwaite's theory T the theoretical terms k, m, and n, are not explicitly harmless (with respect to the two given empirical generalizations E_1 and E_2). This is because T is not a conservative extension of E_1 & E_2, that is, because the new E_3 is deducible from T. However, the terms k, m, and n are implicitly harmless. This is proved by constructing the theory T_1 (with $'$ as the new mathematical primitive). As we saw, the definitions (D_1), (D_2), and (D_3) serve as the required explicit definitions for k, m, and n.

Notice that if the theory T were a *scientific* theory in Stegmüller's sense it would represent a counterexample to the Braithwaite-Ramsey thesis. What Stegmüller means by 'scientific' over and above that it has to entail that T is somehow *factually* interpreted, is not clear. It is likely that he refers to real existing theories in science. If so, the truth of the Braithwaite-Ramsey thesis is not a matter of logic only.

We also have to notice here that while Stegmüller in the above example judges only the original theory T (on the basis of T_1), Braithwaite always considers a theory "on its own merits", so to speak. Thus for Braithwaite T would be a perfectly acceptable theory, while T_1 is not.

Stegmüller does not present any proof for his Braithwaite-Ramsey thesis but leaves the issue completely open. It is obvious to us that the thesis has to be relativized to some well-defined logical framework before it (or its logical part) can be seriously discussed.

We shall now briefly and inexhaustively examine the thesis in the case of first-order theories. We present a sufficient logical condition for a first-order theory's having theoretical terms which are neither explicitly nor implicitly harmless. Provided that such a theory is scientific (in Stegmüller's sense), the following result shows that there are "interesting" first-order theories of the required kind:

Theorem VI.1. Consider two finitely axiomatized first-order scientific theories $T(\lambda \cup \mu)$ and $T'(\lambda)$. $T(\lambda \cup \mu)$ contains theoretical terms which are neither explicitly nor implicitly harmless if the following conditions are satisfied:

(A) $T(\lambda \cup \mu)$ is a creative extension of $T'(\lambda)$ with respect to $\mathscr{L}(\lambda)$.

(B) $T(\lambda \cup \mu)$ has a model $\mathscr{M}$ such that

(1) The domain of $\mathscr{M}$ contains a subset $V \subset D$ which has at least two members and which is such that no $v \in V$ belongs to the interpretation of any λ-predicate.

(2) In $\mathcal{M}$ the interpretation of some monadic μ-predicate includes at least one $v \in V$ but not all $v \in V$.

Proof. Condition (A) guarantees by definition that the members of μ are not explicitly harmless. Condition (B) implies that they are not implicitly harmless either. The proof of this is sketched as follows.

Let us assume that $\lambda = \{O_1, \ldots, O_n\}$ and $\mu = \{P_1, \ldots, P_i, \ldots, P_k\}$ and that the interpretation P_i of P_i satisfies B.2. in a $\mathcal{M} = \langle \mathrm{D}, \mathrm{O}_1, \ldots, \mathrm{O}_n\, \mathrm{P}_1, \ldots, \mathrm{P}_k \rangle$. Assume that $V = \{v_1, v_2, \ldots\}$ and that $v_1 \in \mathrm{P}_i$ and that $v_2 \in \mathrm{P}_i$. Now we construct a model $\mathcal{M}' = \langle \mathrm{D}, \mathrm{O}_1, \ldots, \mathrm{O}_n, \mathrm{P}_1, \ldots, \mathrm{P}_i', \ldots, \mathrm{P}_k \rangle$ which differs from $\mathcal{M}$ only in its interpretation of P_i and which is isomorphic to $\mathcal{M}$. We define an automorphism

$$f : \mathrm{D} \rightarrow \mathrm{D}$$

carrying $\mathcal{M}$ into $\mathcal{M}'$ such that

$f\,(v_1) = v_2$
$f\,(v_2) = v_1$
$f\,(x) = x$ for all other elements in D.

The resulting interpretation P_i' of P_i thus includes v_2 but not v_1 in difference to P_i. As $\mathcal{M}'$ is isomorphic to $\mathcal{M}$ it is a model of $T\,(\lambda \cup \mu)$ by the isomorphism theorem of first-order predicate logic. By Beth's theorem of definability we now immediately see that the predicate $P_i \in \mu$ is *not* explicitly definable in terms of the predicates in λ, given $T\,(\lambda \cup \mu)$. An explicit definition of an n-place predicate P_i in $T\,(\lambda \cup \mu)$ would mean that $T\,(\lambda \cup \mu)$ logically implies a sentence of the form

$$(\alpha) \quad (x)\,(P_i\,(x) \equiv M\,(\lambda, x)),$$

where $x_1, \ldots x_n$ occur free in the definiendum M. Any logico-mathematical extension $T^*\,(\lambda \cup \mu)$ of $T\,(\lambda \cup \mu)$ would have to entail a sentence of the form (α) in order to make P_i implicitly harmless. But given the truth of (B) we see on the basis of Beth's theorem of definability that the addition of (α) (or a theory entailing (α)) would lead into logical contradiction. This suffices to prove our theorem.

Notice that Theorem VI.1 obviously generalizes to hold for any n-place predicate P_i.

Let us consider the following simple monadic application of our theorem VI.1 with $\lambda = \{A, B\}$ and $\mu = \{P\}$. Take the initial observational theory $T'\,(\lambda)$ to be

$$\text{(L)} \qquad (x)\,(A\,(x) \supset B\,(x)).$$

Let $T\,(\lambda \cup \mu)$ be axiomatized by the conjunction of the following axioms

(A1) $(x)\,(P\,(x) \supset -A\,(x)\ \&\ -B\,(x))$

(A2) $(Ex)\,P\,(x)\ \&\ (Ex)\,(-P\,(x)\ \&\ -A\,(x))$

(A3) $(x)\,(A\,(x) \equiv B\,(x))$.

In $\mathscr{L}\,(\lambda)$ clearly $T\,(\lambda \cup \mu) \vdash T'\,(\lambda)$ but not conversely. Hence $T\,(\lambda \cup \mu)$ is a creative extension of $T'\,(\lambda)$ and thus condition A of our theorem is satisfied. Axiom (A1) guarantees that condition B.1. is satisfied and (A2) accounts for the truth of B.2.

Our example theory $T\,(\{A, B\} \cup \{P\})$ is methodologically rather uninteresting as the theoretical concept does not seem to do any work at all when the theory is employed for explanation and prediction. Still there may quite well be cases of methodologically interesting applications of Theorem VI.1. For instance, it would be interesting to have applications of our theorem (or of other cases with theories containing implicitly harmful theoretical concepts) in which $T\,(\lambda \cup \mu)$ really *explains* $T'\,(\lambda)$, which is not the case in the above examples. Explanation could be characterized, for instance, in terms of our DEL-model to be formulated in Chapter VII.

It seems to us appropriate to reinterpret the word 'scientific' in the Braithwaite-Ramsey thesis to mean only 'factually interpreted' rather than to take it to mean something like 'extant in science'. Under our reinterpretation this thesis is purely logical.

To summarize, we have shown by a counterexample that within first-order logic the Braithwaite-Ramsey thesis is false as we interpret it. However, by our Theorem VI.1. there are certain kinds of first-order theories with implicitly and explicitly harmful theoretical terms. We have thus found one more reason for the *desirability* of open theoretical terms. However, this reason need not be accepted by an instrumentalist, if he is only interested in the *logical* indispensability of theoretical concepts for scientific systematization (in the sense of Chapter II). For Craig's theorem II.3. is applicable in all the cases discussed above. On the other hand, for a realist who wants to speak about unobservable objects (in the sense of condition B. of theorem VI.1.) our theorem VI.1. is of course most welcome.

Chapter VII

Deductive Explanation and Theoretical Concepts

1. Deductive Explanation and Information

1.1. We shall in this chapter focus on the logic and methodology of the deductive explanation of scientific laws and generalizations and on the role of theoretical concepts within such explanation. We also have something to say about the explanation of singular events and facts (or, rather, statements about them). This latter topic has been discussed much more in contemporary philosophy of science than the explanation of scientific laws and theories[1]. However, at least theoretical science is primarily concerned with *general* knowledge and only secondarily with knowledge about singular facts. That is, it is concerned with discovering general patterns and regularities and explaining them (by means of theories) rather than with describing and explaining singular events (by means of single laws).

As a well-known classical example of a deductive explanation of an empirical law we may consider the explanation of Galilei's law of falling bodies. Using familiar symbols, this explanation consists of the (many-step) derivation of Galilei's law ($s(t) = {}^1/_2\, gt^2 + v_0\, t + s_0$) from the following premises: the general law of gravitational force

1 For instance, the classical paper by HEMPEL and OPPENHEIM (1948) and the works prompted by it have concentrated on the explanation of *singular* events. Even the recent extensive treatise by STEGMÜLLER (1969) neglects the explanation of laws. There are, however, some works treating the deductive explanation of laws; e. g. the book by CAMPBELL (1920), NAGEL (1961), BUNGE (1967a), and the recent articles by ACKERMANN (1965), ACKERMANN and STENNER (1966), OMER (1970), and TUOMELA (1972).

$\left(F = G\frac{mM}{r^2}\right)$, the auxiliary hypothesis that r is constant, and the general law of motion ($F = m\,a$). Here g is defined to be $\frac{GM}{r^2}$.

Let us start our discussion with some general problems that any philosopher of science dealing with explanation has to face. First there is the question whether our intuitive notion(s) of explanation can be given any formal structure at all.

It has often been argued that the concept of (scientific) explanation is a pragmatic notion which does not have a clear-cut objective formal structure. Sometimes these arguments purport to show that the relation of explanation holding between an explanans and an explanandum ceases to hold under the substitution of logically equivalent explanantia or explananda; or then some other commonly accepted formal invariance conditions are claimed to fail (cf. our Theorem VII.1 below). Usually this type of argumentation is invoked to show the intensional (non-truthfunctional) character of the notion of explanation which then, so the argument goes, *qua* intensional cannot be clarified by an explicate (or explicates) within standard extensional logic. But as we do not know of any convincing arguments to substantiate this conclusion we shall below proceed under the working hypothesis that, for the time being, it is meaningful to look for logical criteria that acceptable scientific explanations should satisfy.

On the other hand, it seems clear to us that the enormously difficult and complex notion of explanation will have a number of different objectified and idealized explicates — and not only one. This partly follows from the contextual characteristics of ordinary common sense explanations from which the notion or rather the various notions of scientific explanation have been obtained by the processes of abstraction, idealization, schematization, and objectification, and so forth. Common sense explanation seems to be dependent on the properties of the explainer and the explainee as well as on many other aspects of the context. All this is part of what is often meant by referring to explanation as a *pragmatic* notion. There are a number of pragmatic features which cannot be abstracted away in a full-blown theory of scientific explanation without too great a philosophical loss. Lacking a developed adequate pragmatics for the philosophy of science — which would be needed — something like Kuhnian paradigms (constellations of group commitments) presently seem to provide the best pragmatic background frame for a theory of scientific explanation (cf. the postscript of KUHN (1969)).

Indeed, the general framework within which the problems of the present chapter can be embedded is briefly this. Consider a fixed Kuhnian paradigm and within it a research programme incorporating a temporal sequence of theories T_1, $T_2, \ldots$, T_n, $T_{n+1}, \ldots$ We shall assume that the paradigm "determines" which (essentially general) statements qualify as scientific laws and which (sets of) statements represent acceptable theories. We shall here say of lawlike statements only that they have to be essentially *general* with respect to some logical individuals. We shall not attempt to provide a sufficient condition of lawlikeness[2]. We also assume that the paradigm specifies the philosophical purposes of a scientific explanation. Unless these conditions are fulfilled it does not seem meaningful to ask for a clarification of the logical and methodological features of scientific explanations.

Within the present frame one can start asking various questions pertaining to the growth of science as seen from the point of view of the present paradigm. For instance, one may ask what kind of philosophically, methodologically, and logically interesting transitions from some T_n to T_{n+1} can be found? In answering this question obviously some rational reconstruction and idealization of actual scientific practice is to be made. Scientific change can then, for instance, be looked upon from the point of view of pure accumulation of ideas and facts at one extreme, or from the point of view of successive mutually inconsistent and incommensurable theories at the other extreme. In this book we have adopted an evolutionary point of view which is closer to the former than to the latter of these viewpoints. Still there is no doubt that the history of science abounds with genuine revolutions which no amount of rational reconstruction can make into cases of pure accumulation of knowledge. However, as we said earlier, we do not in this book attempt a detailed analysis of extreme scientific revolutions.

In the present chapter we shall consider only one special type of scientific growth occurring within this scheme, viz. that where T_{n+1}

2 For a generalization to be a lawlike statement *systemicity* (occurrence in an established broader theory) and direct and indirect empirical *corroboration* are often required as two other necessary conditions (cf. BUNGE (1967b, vol. I, p. 361). A third commonly accepted criterion is *supporting counterfactual conditionals* (Goodman). However, our analysis can proceed without a discussion of these features.

(deductively) explains and thus supersedes T_n. Here T_n can be an empirical law or theory and T_{n+1} a more comprehensive theory, often introducing new explanatory ideas.

It has often been contended that in actual science a superseding theory T_{n+1} almost never deductively implies T_n. Rather T_{n+1} implies a theory or law T_n^* which can be considered an *approximation* of T_n and which is at least initially in experimental agreement with T_n [3]. (The explanation of Kepler's laws by Newtonian mechanics is often mentioned as an example at this point.) Another way of putting this is to say that T_{n+1} explains T_n by correcting it at the same time. Undoubtedly this kind of correction process often takes place in science. Nevertheless, one may argue that this does not basically contradict the very idea of deductive explanation. For a scientific realist may always argue that what one really aims at in this situation is an explanation and deeper understanding of the (extralinguistic) regularity or law allegedly described by T_n. However, in the process of explanation it is found that T_n^* rather than T_n seems to be a correct description of this regularity, i. e. T_n^* is found to represent the law *in re* better than T_n does.

If this characterization of the situation is accepted there is nothing seriously wrong with deductive explanation, not at least on this point, even if deductive explanation alone does not then seem capable of accounting for transitions within actual scientific research programmes. (It should be remarked here that our notions of paradigm and research programme are to be understood in such a way that really revolutionary transitions always involve abandoning a paradigm and a research programme associated with it. Hence we do not have to take stand to questions of meaning variance, etc., which seem to involve a change of paradigm.)

Apart from some comments later, we shall in this chapter concentrate on the logical and methodological (rather than on the epistemological and metaphysical) aspects of deductive scientific explana-

---

3 The general question of whether a theory or a law can be considered an approximation of another one is difficult. Its solution obviously depends both on the extensional closeness and the "conceptual" closeness of the two theories. In many cases a lawlike statement T_n is accepted on purely inductive grounds whereas T_n^* is obtained by theoretical considerations and is at best *compatible* with the evidence. This distinction corresponds, respectively, to the second and first kind of "observational framework counterpart" in SELLARS (1965), p. 359.

tion, especially the explanation of empirical laws and generalizations [4]. Our starting point will be to regard explanation as an informative or information-providing argument. Unless considerably explicated and developed this idea is of course platitudinous. Explanation of laws (and other explananda as well) can and has been regarded, for instance, as aiming at finding hidden causes for observable phenomena, or alternatively a deeper description of reality. Both of these basic types of explanation give us reasons for believing in the explananda. At the same time an explanation (such as each of the above kinds) always carries a proper amount of relevant information concerning the explanandum, and this piece of information indeed constitutes (the) grounds for our believing in the explanandum. In this chapter we shall mainly discuss information as measured by the logical (and especially quantificational) strength of statements. The sense or senses of information due to the introduction of new explanatory and perhaps ontologically more basic theoretical ideas (concepts) will be emphasized, too.

1.2. Let us start our discussion on models of explanation from a general information-theoretic principle. (We shall describe the results of TUOMELA (1972).) We propose that the following general information-theoretic condition be accepted:

(I) An explanans should contain a (qualitatively and quantitatively) proper amount of relevant information concerning the explanandum.

As it stands, (I) is so general that it is hard to find any objections to it (except its generality), once it has been accepted that explanation can be regarded as an information providing argument. (I) obviously has to be precisized in order to make it informative and interesting.

---

4 As we said above, among the previous attempts to give exact formal criteria of adequacy for deductive explanation, only those by ACKERMANN (1965), ACKERMANN and STENNER (1966), OMER (1970), and TUOMELA (1972) were also concerned with the explanation of general explananda in addition to singular ones. ACKERMANN's 1965 paper has been criticized and shown to be faulty in ACKERMANN and STENNER (1966). The latter paper again has been criticized by OMER (1970) and by KÄSBAUER (reported in STEGMÜLLER (1969)). Omer also presented a model of explanation of his own, based on general information-theoretic considerations, and his paper has again been criticized by TUOMELA (1972).

Before going on to discuss (I) specifically and in detail let us mention briefly what is involved in (I) as we shall understand it. First, (I) will be taken to say that an explanans should contain more information than the explanandum. Secondly, we shall assume of the notion of information involved that the information content of a statement increases with its logical strength. Thirdly, we shall in general require that one and the same explanandum can have several explanantia differing in their quantificational strength (and hence in their information content in one sense of 'information'). There is then no unique proper amount of information an explanans candidate has to contain in order to qualify. We shall, furthermore, regard an explanans the better the more information it contains, *ceteris paribus*. Fourthly and fifthly, there are two senses of relevancy that are important in speaking about relevant information. One will be explicated by our "noncomparability" condition below. This condition guarantees that the explanans and the explanandum do not contain too much common content which would lead to viciously circular explanations. The other sense of 'relevant' guarantees, for instance, that an explanans does not explain any intuitively irrelevant logical consequences of any explanandum it explains. (This relevancy requirement then amounts to requiring that among quantification-theoretically equally strong explanans candidates one should choose the logically weakest one as the explanans.)

Let us now go into some details. As we saw, one important question left open by (I) is how to measure the information content of a sentence. We shall below use essentially the logical content explicate due to Carnap's theory of semantic information. According to it, the content of a statement is identified with its logical strength (and formally measured as one minus the logical probability of the statement). However, we do not below need to utilize the metrical *cont*-measure at all. The only information-theoretic notion concretely needed is that of noncomparability of statements. We shall say that two statements p and q are *noncomparable* with respect to their information content if and only if not $\vdash p \supset q$ and not $\vdash q \supset p$.

It is important to notice what is involved in this notion of noncomparability. Two statements are noncomparable exactly when each of them includes some content-elements not included in the other one. Thus it is quite possible that they contain common content-elements. Indeed, unless this were the case within deductive explanation, the requirements concerning the noncomparability of the elements of the explanans and the explanandum to be considered below could not be reconciled with the idea of the explanans logically implying the explanandum. (Consider e. g. Craig's interpolation theorem from which it follows that there has to be some amount of common content between two statements one of which implies the other.)

It can be pointed out here that within nondeductive explanation (cf. Chapter VIII), measures of transmitted information (the *inf*-, *cont*- and *entropy*-measures) can and have been used to measure the goodness of an explanation. The more an explanans transmits or conveys information concerning the explanandum, the better is the explanation. However, in this sense all deductive explanations are maximally good. For if the explanans logically implies the explanandum, our coming to know the explanans completely relieves us of our ignorance or uncertainty (these notions understood in the sense of the semantic theory of information) concerning the explanandum. Thus within deductive explanation this kind of information-theoretic explicate of explanation is of no help.

As we said above, we shall understand the requirement (I) to imply that the explanans and the explanandum of an explanation should in a certain sense be noncomparable. Let us discuss this requirement briefly before stating it in a more precise way. Consider the following simple example where T is a theory and L is a law or generalization:

$$\frac{\begin{array}{c} T \\ T \supset L \end{array}}{L}$$

This most trivial deduction should not qualify as an explanation. One reason for this is that the second premise in the explanans cannot be verified or confirmed without knowing the truth value of L. But if so, this putative explanation could not be considered a potential prediction, which we in general require of good deductive explanations. Now, if we require that the statements occurring in the explanans should be noncomparable with the explanandum, then the above deduction disqualifies as an explanation. This is because L entails $-T \vee L$ (which is logically equivalent to $T \supset L$).

Next consider the following example:

$$\frac{K \; \& \; B}{K}$$

Here K may stand for Kepler's laws and B for Boyle's law (cf. HEMPEL and OPPENHEIM (1948), p. 273). This example is a self-explanation which cannot be accepted. But, we may argue, the noncomparability condition clearly blocks this as K & B logically implies K. But now something is clearly wrong, as within deductive explanation the explanandum should of course be deducible from the explanans. Apparently the noncomparability condition has to be formulated in a different way so that it blocks the above kind of viciously circular explanation while allowing the explanans to entail the explanandum. We shall now go on to make this improvement which obviously depends on the notion of a *component* of the explanans. The condition of noncomparability should hold between different components of the explanans and the explanandum but not between the explanans as a whole and the explanandum. We cannot simply formulate this condition by referring to *any* statements of the explanans as clearly the conjunction of all component statements is itself a statement. The reader is referred to ACKERMANN and STENNER (1966) and TUOMELA (1972) for a discussion leading to and motivating the refined construction to be discussed next.

First we shall have to introduce some technical apparatus. Let us consider some factually interpreted scientific language $\mathscr{L}$ with specified logical and extralogical vocabulary, well formed formulas, logical axioms and rules of inference. In the manner of ACKERMANN and STENNER ((1966), p. 160) we now define the notions of a sequence of truth functional components and a set of ultimate sentential conjuncts of a given formula (sentence) T.

A sequence of statemental well formed formulas $\langle W_1, W_2, \ldots, W_n \rangle$ of $\mathscr{L}$ is a *sequence of truth functional components* of T if and only if T may be built up from the sequence by the formation rules of $\mathscr{L}$, such that each member of the sequence is used exactly once in the application of the rules in question. The W_i's are thus to be construed as tokens. Thus, for instance, $\langle (x)\, F(x), (x)\, F(x) \rangle$ and not $\langle (x)\, F(x) \rangle$ is a sequence of truth functional components of the formula $(x)\, F(x)$ & $(x)\, F(x)$. The formation rules of $\mathscr{L}$ naturally have to be specified in order to see the exact meaning of the notion of a sequence of truth functional components of a theory finitely axiomatized by a sentence T.

A *set of ultimate sentential conjuncts* Tc of a sentence T is any set whose members are the well formed formulas of a longest sequence $\langle W_1, W_2, \ldots, W_n \rangle$ of truth functional components of T such that T

and W_1 & W_2 &...& W_n are logically equivalent. If T is a set of sentences then the set Tc of ultimate conjuncts of T is the union of the sets of ultimate sentential conjuncts of each member of T. We may notice here that although by definition the Tc-sets of two logically equivalent theories are logically equivalent they need not be the same.

Now we are ready to state the final version of the noncomparability requirement for a Tc of a theory T constituting an explanans (cf. OMER (1970), p. 424 and TUOMELA (1972), p. 376):

(R) For any Tc_i in Tc, Tc_i is noncomparable with the explanandum.

The requirement (R) seems to avoid at least the paradoxical examples of self-explanation concerned with singular explananda to be found in the literature (cf. ACKERMANN and STENNER (1966) and OMER (1970) for a discussion of them). Furthermore, it seems to do the same in the case of the explanation of laws as well (cf. the example by Hempel and Oppenheim given above).

Now we can go on to state some necessary conditions for an explicate of deductive scientific explanation. Let us write $E(L, T)$ for 'L is potentially explained by T'. Here T and L are contingent statements of our scientific language $\mathscr{L}$. (Sometimes we shall also denote by T and L sets of statements, which does not make any essential difference as long as these sets are finite.) As above, Tc is a set of ultimate sentential conjuncts of T. For simplicity, in the sequel we shall be concerned with $E(L, Tc)$ rather than $E(L, T)$. (Recall that Tc and T are logically equivalent. When speaking of $E(L, Tc)$ Tc is to be understood as the conjunction of its members rather than a set.) Now we are ready to give some logical conditions for an explanatory relation $E(L, Tc)$ to hold between Tc and L:

$E(L, Tc)$ satisfies the *logical* conditions of adequacy for *deductive explanation* only if

(7.1) $\{L, Tc\}$ is consistent;

(7.2) $Tc \vdash L$;

(7.3) some Tc_i in Tc is a universal law;

(7.4) for any Tc_i in Tc, Tc_i is noncomparable with L.

In view of what was said earlier in this chapter, (7.1) seems acceptable. Requirement (7.2) is obvious. In (7.3) we shall here require of a law only the syntactic feature that it essentially contains at least one universal quantifier. Requirement (7.4) is just our (R). Notice that in this model L can be either a singular or a general statement.

Can the conjunction of the conditions (7.1)—(7.4) be regarded as a sufficient condition of explanation as well? It seems that the resulting model of explanation is too wide. For if we have found an explanans for a statement, say $G(a)$, within this model, the same explanans will also be allowed to be an explanans for all the disjunctions in which $G(a)$ occurs as a disjunct and which do not contradict condition (7.4). We are here inclined to consider this consequence undesirable and even unacceptable, as such disjunctions might be intuitively irrelevant to the explanans.

To illustrate, if we have such a disjunction, say $G(a) \vee H(a)$, as our explanandum, and $F(a)$ as an initial condition statement, then in the explanans we should have the law $(x)(F(x) \supset G(x) \vee H(x))$ (rather than $(x)(F(x) \supset G(x))$) which (together with $F(a)$) does explain $G(a) \vee H(a)$. As the latter law is logically stronger than the former, this suggests that we should look for the "minimal" or "minimally informative" law among those which together with the initial conditions satisfy the conditions (7.1)—(7.4). Thus to explain something would be to give, in the above sense, a specific *minimal* amount of information concerning the explanandum. This is indeed what Omer (1970) required of an explanation, even if he did not succeed in building a coherent model out of this idea (see Tuomela (1972)). We do not, however, find this idea of explanation satisfactory. For it does not allow us to have several different (perhaps incompatible) explanantia for an explanandum. More specifically, it does not allow for a hierarchy of increasingly stronger and more informative explanantia for an explanandum.

Let us illustrate the last point by the following proposed explanations for the same singular explanandum:

$$(*)\qquad \frac{\begin{array}{ll}(x)(y)(F(x,y) \supset G(x,y)) & Tc_1{}^*\\ F(a,b) & Tc_2{}^*\end{array}}{G(a,b)}$$

$$(**)\qquad \frac{\begin{array}{ll}(y)(F(a,y) \supset G(a,y)) & Tc_1{}^{**}\\ F(a,b) & Tc_2{}^{**}\end{array}}{G(a,b)}$$

The more general proposal (*) is not accepted as an explanation in a "minimal law" model, but (**) is. Now one may argue that there is a sense of explanation in which (*) counts as an explanation of $G(a, b)$, perhaps even as a much better one than (**). In this sense of explanation the information provided by the additional quantificational generality of the law Tc_1^* over and above the generality of the law Tc_1^{**} may be considered *relevant* (redundant) information (in the sense of (I)). (Cf. e. g. HINTIKKA (1970b) for an argument concerning the increase of "surface" information with quantificational depth, and cf. Chapter VI of this book for an argument concerning how observational information content increases with quantificational depth due to the introduction of new explanatory concepts.)

Let us thus accept that there is a sense of information in which the increase in quantificational generality provides relevant information. It follows that there is no unique proper amount of relevant information an explanation should provide, as we can have several increasingly more informative explanantia for an explanandum. How can our observations be taken into account in a more technical fashion? According to our arguments we want to have minimal explanation within each level of quantificational depth to exclude explanations of irrelevant explananda, but we also want to consider as relevant and acceptable the information provided by increasingly deeper theories and laws. We then propose the following. Let us write $p \vdash_p q$ when q is deducible from p by using sentential logic only. Conditions (7.1)—(7.4) for explanation now have to be augmented by the following condition (cf. TUOMELA (1972)):

(7.5) It is not possible, without contradicting any of the previous conditions for explanation, to find sentences $S_i, \ldots, S_r$ $(r \geqq 1)$ at least some of which are essentially universal such that for some $Tc_j, \ldots, Tc_n$ $(n \geqq 1)$:

$Tc_j \,\&\ldots\&\, Tc_n \vdash_p S_i \,\&\ldots\&\, S_r$

not $S_i \,\&\ldots\&\, S_r \vdash Tc_j \,\&\ldots\&\, Tc_n$

$Tc_s \vdash L$

where Tc_s is the result of the replacement of $Tc_j, \ldots, Tc_n$ by $S_i, \ldots, S_r$ in Tc.

Conditions (7.1)—(7.5) can be regarded as severally necessary and jointly sufficient to the logical form of the relation $E(L, Tc)$. In other words, the resulting model of deductive explanation — call it the *DE-model* — explicitly defines the logical properties of the relation $E(L, Tc)$ by the conditions (7.1), (7.2), (7.3), (7.4), and (7.5). One might also consider a *"minimal law"* model which results from the DE-model by substituting '$\vdash$' for '$\vdash_p$' in condition (7.5)[5]. We shall alternatively call this model *Omer's corrected model,* as it seems to formalize what Omer (1970) was after. For the reasons stated above we do not, however, consider Omer's corrected model acceptable.

Our DE-model accepts both (*) and (**) as explanations. In principle the explananda *L* can again be either singular or general. To get a simple example with a general explanandum we can change (**) by adding a third argument to the two-place predicates *F* and *G* and by universally quantifying over the new argument (say *z*). The resulting explanation (call it (″)) qualifies in our present model but not in Omer's corrected model. The same holds true for the analogue (′) of (*). The only explanatory argument which in the present frame would be accepted both by our present DE-model and Omer's corrected model is the one in which only *z* is quantified. (Call this explanation (‴).)

We now propose that the DE-model is to be accepted as adequate for determining the logical structure of the explanation of at least singular explananda. It may also be considered adequate for a "*phenomenological*" explanation of scientific laws (i. e. for explanations where the explanans contains only "molar" concepts of the same kind occurring in the empirical laws to be explained). (Below we shall still require something more of good explanations of scientific laws and theories.) It should be noticed that conditions (7.1)—(7.5) are not restricted to any specified formal language, as most of the previous models of explanation have been. Therefore they should be widely applicable. In addition, we have not made any philosophical restrictions as to the substantial content of explanation, but have restricted our analysis to the purely formal aspects of explanation. (These formal aspects will be further clarified in the next section.)

2. Theoretical Concepts and Deductive Explanation of Scientific Laws

2.1. The main thesis of this book is to emphasize the importance and desirability of theoretical concepts in the various functions into which

---

5 Both the DE-model and the minimal law model seem to be able to handle the paradoxes of singular explanation directed against previous models of explanation (see OMER (1970) and TUOMELA (1972)).

scientific theories are put. But we have not yet explicitly discussed the role of theoretical concepts within scientific explanation. This is what we shall do now.

When we characterized theoretical concepts in the first chapter of this book we stated that they are concepts which have been introduced into theories to explain the behavior of objects. On the other hand, it has been claimed that scientific explanation involves theoretical concepts. Campbell, for instance, has frequently emphasized that an explanatory theory shall "add to our ideas", with the precaution that "the ideas which it adds shall be acceptable" (CAMPBELL (1921), p. 83)[6].

Sellars' view, to cite another author on explanation, is that "microtheories containing theoretical concepts not only explain why observational constructs obey inductive generalizations, they explain what, as far as the observational framework is concerned, is a random component in their behavior, and, in the last analysis it is by doing the latter that microtheories establish their character as indispensable elements of scientific explanation and ... as knowledge about what *really* exists" (SELLARS (1963), p. 122).

Thus "theories explain laws by explaining why the objects of the domain in question obey the laws that they do to the extent that they do" (SELLARS (1963), p. 123). To illustrate Sellars' view — which we accept — let us describe his own example on the explanatory power of theoretical concepts. Let us thus assume that it has been discovered that gold dissolves in *aqua regia* sometimes at one rate, sometimes at another rate. Assume furthermore that no observational circumstances have been found to account for this phenomenon. Now our explanatory theory, a microtheory of chemical reactions, posits two different structures of microentities. Each of them corresponds to gold as an observational construct but they also correspond to the differences in the dissolution rate of gold, and hence explain its variation and "randomness"[7]. In other words, theoretical concepts here

6 This notion of "acceptability" seems to be almost synonymous with that of cognitive significance of theoretical constructs. It is hard to give *general* criteria of cognitive significance, and we shall not discuss this problem here; cf. our comments in Chapter V. Still we hope it can be solved *in casu*, at least in most cases of interest.

7 Examples of this kind are easily multiplied. An interesting psychological case is discussed in FODOR (1968). In this example an experiment shows that some perceived pauses of human talk may not have any physical (acoustic)

serve to show that observational variation is in a sense spurious when viewed from a deeper level. (Cf. the analogous problem of explaining spurious statistical correlations in the social sciences.)

In general terms, explanation by means of theories containing "acceptable" theoretical concepts correspond to *interpretative* theorizing, whereas explanation by means of observational theories corresponds to *phenomenological* theorizing (cf. BUNGE (1968)). An explanation of observational laws (and theories) by theories introducing new ideas (hidden causes, etc.) can be regarded as ontologically and epistemologically deeper. It can also be considered to add to our understanding of the world more than mere phenomenological explanation does. As we have indicated and as will be seen in more detail later, this kind of penetration into deeper levels of reality is in part made possible by condition (7.5) or our DE-model of explanation, which gives a hierarchical structure to explanations. (In a model of explanation based only on minimal theory explanations — such as Omer's corrected model — this would not be possible.)

So something essential still remains to be done: to add to the DE-model a requirement that the explaining theory has to contain (acceptable) theoretical concepts. We shall hence assume that our explanandum laws contain only members of λ (the set of observational predicates), and that the explanantia always contain at least some statements in which members of μ (the set of theoretical predicates) occur.

In the explanation of a law $L(\lambda)$ the explanans will be a theory axiomatized by a sentence $T(\lambda \cup \mu)$ (or, alternatively, a $Tc(\lambda \cup \mu)$ corresponding to $T(\lambda \cup \mu)$). One can now distinguish the following three parts in the theory:

(1) the Campbellian part (sometimes called the core theory) which consists of those statements of $T(\lambda \cup \mu)$ which are solely in the vocabulary μ;

(2) the observational content of $T(\lambda \cup \mu)$ which consists of those statements of $T(\lambda \cup \mu)$ which contain members of λ only;

(3) the correspondence rules of $T(\lambda \cup \mu)$ which consist of all the other statements of $T(\lambda \cup \mu)$ and are in the vocabulary $\lambda \cup \mu$.

---

counterpart. The existence of such perceived pauses is explained by assuming that the subjects have internalized certain grammatical rules (which function as theoretical concepts here).

Let us here denote the deductively closed sets comprising the components (1), (2), and (3) by $H(\mu)$, $O(\lambda)$, and $C(\lambda \cup \mu)$, respectively. For convenience we frequently use the same symbols for the axioms (or axiom sets) for these components. (Recall that in previous chapters we in general used $T'(\lambda)$ for $O(\lambda)$ and $T^*(\mu)$ for $H(\mu)$.) For first-order languages, the decomposition of a sentence $T(\lambda \cup \mu)$ can be done by using, for instance, the reduction operation defined in Chapter II. More generally, as we saw in Chapter II, Craig's general replacement method shows how this can be done for deductive systems in the case of practically any formal system. We shall below denote by $Cn(T(\lambda \cup \mu))$ $(= H(\mu) \cup O(\lambda) \cup C(\lambda \cup \mu))$ the deductive closure of $T(\lambda \cup \mu)$, and by the Craigian μ-reduct of a deductive system we shall mean the recursively axiomatizable part of $Cn(T(\lambda \cup \mu))$ solely in the vocabulary μ.

When we below investigate how a theory $T(\lambda \cup \mu)$ explains a law $L(\lambda)$ this problem can thus also be considered as how a core theory $H(\mu)$ conjoined with some suitable correspondence rules $C(\lambda \cup \mu)$ explains the law $L(\lambda)$ belonging to $O(\lambda)$[8].

As we have repeatedly pointed out, there are many ways to explicate the notion of explanation. Furthermore, one may argue about which properties of the relation $E(L, Tc)$ are analytic and which are synthetic. We shall not take a definite standpoint to this here but we shall rather liberally try to take into account various logically and methodologically important features of $E(L, Tc)$.

In the DE-model of explanation a number of important aspects of explanation (e. g. proper informativeness, prohibition of completely circular explanation, etc.) are already incorporated. But in the explanation of laws there are still at least two logically explicable properties that have to be considered (other properties will be discussed

---

8 We may interpret this still somewhat differently. When using the core theory $H(\mu)$ for explanation and prediction, or when testing it, we give it empirical content by embedding it into a broader "applied" theory $T(\lambda \cup \mu)$, which can in principle be divided into the above three parts. This applied theory $T(\lambda \cup \mu)$ is assumed to contain all the additional auxiliary hypotheses or theories and initial condition statements, etc., needed for the purposes of explanation, prediction, and testing.

The λ-predicates in $\mathscr{L}(\lambda)$ are usually *idealized* rather than concrete in the sense of Chapters I and V, and they correspond to the first type of "observation framework counterparts" of SELLARS (1965), p. 359. Similarly, the correspondence rules are more often *substantive* rather than methodological (see Chapter V).

later). These are the requirements of observational creativity of the explanans over the explanandum law and the theoretical noncreativity of the explanans with respect to its Campbellian part.

As to the first of these let us quote Nagel.

"At least one of the premises in the explanation of a given law will meet the following requirements: when conjoined with suitable additional assumptions the premise should be capable of explaining other laws than the given one; on the other hand it should not in turn be possible to explain the premise with the help of the given law even when those additional assumptions are adjoined to the law". (NAGEL (1961), p. 36).

We shall accept a strengthened form of this condition, and its formalized version will appear below as condition (7.6) among our additional desiderata for explanation.

The theoretical noncreativity condition has been formulated by Nagel as follows: "the introduction of new correspondence rules does not change either the formal structure or the intended meaning of the theory, though new rules may enlarge the theory's range of application" (NAGEL (1961), p. 102; also see CAMPBELL (1920), p. 133). In HINTIKKA (1972b) this condition has been dubbed the theoretical adhockery condition, as it requires that no *ad hoc* theoretical principles, but only (or at most) new correspondence rules, may be added when applying the theory to explain new laws. (If it is needed for the application in question, correspondence rules can here be taken to include many kinds of auxiliary hypotheses "borrowed" from other theories.) However, this condition cannot be applied unqualified to all explanation as clearly the core theory $H(\mu)$ must be allowed to grow if this growth takes place "in a fruitful way". We shall not include the theoretical noncreativity (or adhockery) requirement among the conditions of our model proper but as a separate condition ((7.7) below) to be applied when the above qualification can be accepted. (After thus accounting for this requirement, all of Nagel's logical conditions of adequacy for the explanation of laws are taken care of by our conditions; cf. NAGEL (1961), p. 33 ff. and p. 102).

Now our final model of the explanation of scientific laws can be stated. As before, let T be a contingent statement, Tc a set of ultimate sentential components of T (or actually a conjunction of components in the context $E(L, Tc)$), and L a contingent statement to be explained. Then we propose:

The relation $E(L, Tc)$ satisfies the *logical* conditions of adequacy for the *deductive explanation of scientific laws* if and only if

(7.1) $\{L, Tc\}$ is consistent;

(7.2) $Tc \vdash L$;

(7.3′) Tc contains essentially universal statements at least some of which contain members of μ and L contains only essentially general statements in the vocabulary λ;

(7.4) for any Tc_i in Tc, Tc_i is noncomparable with L;

(7.5) it is not possible, without contradicting any of the previous conditions for explanation, to find statements $S_i, \ldots, S_r$ $(r \geqq 1)$ at least some of which are essentially universal such that for some $Tc_j, \ldots, Tc_n$ $(n \geqq 1)$:

$Tc_j \,\&\ldots\&\, Tc_n \vdash_p S_i \,\&\ldots\&\, S_r$

not $S_i \,\&\ldots\&\, S_r \vdash Tc_j \,\&\ldots\&\, Tc_n$

$Tc_s \vdash L$,

where Tc_s is the result of the replacement of $Tc_j, \ldots, Tc_n$ by $S_i, \ldots, S_r$ in Tc.

As an additional desideratum we consider Nagel's composite requirement:

(7.6) If $Cn\,(Tc) = H\,(\mu) \cup O\,(\lambda) \cup C\,(\lambda \cup \mu)$, then there is a $L' \neq L$ $(L \in O\,(\lambda),\ L' \in O'\,(\lambda))$ such that not $\vdash L \supset L'$ and such that $E\,(L', Tc')$, for some Tc' (of a T') for which $Cn\,(Tc') = H'\,(\mu) \cup O'\,(\lambda) \cup C'\,(\lambda \cup \mu)$ and $H \subseteq H'$; in addition, not $\{L\} \cup (H' - H) \cup (O' - O) \cup (C' - C) \vdash H$.

The optional theoretical adhockery condition, to be applied if no fruitful growth is present, is:

(7.7) If $H\,(\mu)$ is an established core theory, and if, for some L, $E\,(L, Tc)$ with $Cn\,(Tc) = H_r\,(\mu) \cup O\,(\lambda) \cup C\,(\lambda \cup \mu)$, then the difference $H - H_r = \phi$. (H_r is the Craigian μ-reduct of $Cn\,(Tc)$)[9].

It can be noticed that none of the above conditions is restricted to a specific formal system (such as first-order predicate calculus). Therefore they should have a wide area of application.

Let us call a model of deductive explanation of laws for which (7.1), (7.2), (7.3′), (7.4), and (7.5) hold the *DEL-model*. If it is not

9 By an *established* core theory $H\,(\mu)$ we roughly mean a theory which has been empirically and, perhaps, purely theoretically corroborated to the extent as to become accepted by a scientific community as a part of a paradigm.

required that theoretical concepts be essential for the explanation of laws, our old (7.3) can be substituted for (7.3′) in the above model (and the appropriate notational changes can be made elsewhere) and we get the DE-model discussed in Section 1. (An analogous remark holds for the situation where one is not willing to dichotomize the extralogical concepts in the manner assumed here.)

Earlier we described three simple law-explanations (′), (″), and (‴) which all qualified as explanations within the DE-model. If, in addition, the three-place predicate F is theoretical, all these explanations are accepted by the DEL-model, too. Explanations (′) and (″) carry more relevant and deeper (quantificational) information than (‴). One consequence of this is that they in addition satisfy (7.6) which (‴) fails to satisfy. (Notice that the fate of condition (7.7) cannot be determined before fixing an initial core theory $H(\mu)$.)

As an additional example, consider the following simple monadic chain explanation:

$$\frac{\begin{array}{c}(x)\,(G_1(x) \supset F(x))\\ (x)\,(F(x) \supset G_2(x))\end{array}}{(x)\,(G_1(x) \supset G_2(x))}$$

where $\lambda = \{G_1, G_2\}$ and $\mu = \{F\}$. (Here G_1 and G_2 might be observable symptoms of a theoretical virus F.) This explanation is accepted by the DEL-model. But its shallowness is reflected by the fact that it does not satisfy (7.6).

As a scientific illustration of the DEL-model we may still consider, for instance, the explanation of the well-known probability matching law. This law is explained by the linear learning theory of Bush and Mosteller. But it is also explainable by the general stimulus sampling theory of Suppes and Estes, which in turn explains the linear learning theory as its special case.

Let us next state some formal properties of $E(L, Tc)$ in the DEL-model. Most of them will also apply to the DE-model, as can easily be seen.

First, it is easy to verify that in the DEL-model

(a) $E(L, Tc)$ is asymmetric;
(b) $E(L, Tc)$ is irreflexive;
(c) $E(L, Tc)$ is not transitive.

In the DE-model $E(L, Tc)$ is easily seen to be irreflexive and neither symmetric not transitive. To see that it is not transitive assume that $E(L, Tc)$ and $E(Tc, Tc')$ for some L, Tc, Tc'. Then we may possibly have $\vdash Tc_i' \supset Tc_j$, though not $\vdash Tc_j \supset L$, for some $Tc_i' \in Tc'$, $Tc_j \in Tc$. Thus, even if not $\vdash Tc_j \supset L$ it may happen that $\vdash Tc_i' \supset L$. Hence condition (7.4) fails to hold. But still $E(L, Tc)$ is not intransitive in the DE-model.

Next we observe that:

(d) If $E(L, Tc)$ and if, for some Tc', $\vdash Tc' \supset Tc$ (assuming not $\vdash_p Tc' \supset Tc$), then $E(L, Tc')$, provided every $Tc_i' \in Tc'$ is noncomparable with L.

(e) If $E(L, Tc)$ and if for some T' such that $\vdash T \equiv T'$, T and T' posses identical sets of ultimate sentential components (i. e. $Tc = Tc'$), then $E(L, Tc')$.

(f) If $E(L, Tc)$ and for some L, $\vdash L \equiv L'$, then $E(L', Tc)$, provided that, for all Tc_i in Tc, Tc_i and L' are noncomparable.

It should be noticed, however, that a DEL-explanation is not invariant with respect to the substitution of logically equivalent explanantia or explananda. This lack of linguistic invariance may be taken to reflect the *pragmatic* nature of our notion of explanation: How you *state* your explanatory argument makes a difference.

The properties (*d*), (e), (f) above and (g) below hold for the DE-model as well.

For some purposes it may be appropriate to define a notion of indirect explanation. We may say that if $\vdash T \equiv T'$, $E(L, Tc)$ for some Tc of T and $Tc \neq Tc'$ (for all Tc'-sets of T'), then T' explains L *indirectly.*

It is easily seen that the explanatory relations of the DEL- and DE-model do *not* satisfy the following debated subset and conjunction properties:

If $E(L, Tc)$ and L' is a conjunct of L, then $E(L', Tc)$.
(Subset property)

If $E(L_i, Tc)$ for all L_i of an $L = L_1 \,\&\ldots\&\, L_i \,\&\ldots\&\, L_n$, then $E(L, Tc)$.
(Conjunction property)

This means that the explanandum can be neither weakened nor strengthened without the explanation possibly ceasing to be valid.

We have already noticed that in the DEL-model a law L may have explanantia differing in their quantificational strength (and information content). The DEL-model does require minimal explanation only within explanans candidates of the same quantificational strength. Thus we have a *tree-structured hierarchy* of explanations such that on each level of this quantificational hierarchy the minimality principle is satisfied. We can finally notice that the branches of the explanation-tree for an L may be created in diverse logically incompatible ways (cf. HEMPEL (1965), p. 147, footnote 17):

(g) If $E(L, Tc)$ and $E(L, Tc')$, then it is possible that Tc and Tc' (and hence the corresponding theories T and T') are mutually logically incompatible.

The explanantia in one and the same branch are of course logically compatible, as the deeper explanantia quantification-theoretically imply the shallower explanantia for L.

Let us sum up the above formal properties of $E(L, Tc)$ in our DEL-model as a theorem:

Theorem VII.1. The relation $E(L, Tc)$ of the DEL-model has the above properties (a)—(g). That is, $E(L, Tc)$ is asymmetric, irreflexive, and not transitive. It has the strengthening property (d) and the equivalence properties (e) and (f) as well as the branching property (g).

2.2. Conditions (7.6) and (7.7) were above considered to be only optional desiderata for good explanations of (empirical) laws and theories. They are nevertheless philosophically and methodologically important. Some of their importance can be brought out within the framework of distributive normal forms. Instead of our diagrams II.2. and VI.1. we may now consider a diagram of the following kind (cf. HINTIKKA (1972b)):

$$\begin{array}{llll}
r_\mu(T^{(c)}(\lambda\cup\mu)) \leftarrow\ldots\leftarrow & r_\mu(T^{(d-1)}(\lambda\cup\mu)) \leftarrow & r_\mu(T^{(d)}(\lambda\cup\mu)) & \leftarrow \\
\quad\uparrow & \quad\uparrow & \quad\uparrow & \\
T^{(c)}(\lambda\cup\mu) \leftrightarrow\ldots\leftrightarrow & T^{(d-1)}(\lambda\cup\mu) \leftrightarrow & T^{(d)}(\lambda\cup\mu) & \leftrightarrow \\
\quad\downarrow & \quad\downarrow & \quad\downarrow & \\
r_\lambda(T^{(c)}(\lambda\cup\mu)) \leftarrow\ldots\leftarrow & r_\lambda(T^{(d-1)}(\lambda\cup\mu)) \leftarrow & r_\lambda(T^{(d)}(\lambda\cup\mu)) & \leftarrow
\end{array}$$

$$\begin{array}{lll}
r_\mu(T^{(d+1)}(\lambda\cup\mu)) \leftarrow\ldots\leftarrow & r_\mu(T^{(d+e)}(\lambda\cup\mu)) & \leftarrow\ldots \\
\quad\uparrow & \quad\uparrow & \\
T^{(d+1)}(\lambda\cup\mu) \leftrightarrow\ldots\leftrightarrow & T^{(d+e)}(\lambda\cup\mu) & \leftrightarrow\ldots \\
\quad\downarrow & \quad\downarrow & \\
r_\lambda(T^{(d+1)}(\lambda\cup\mu)) \leftarrow\ldots\leftarrow & r_\lambda(T^{(d+e)}(\lambda\cup\mu)) & \leftarrow\ldots
\end{array}$$

Diagram VII.1

In Diagram VII.1. symbols have the same meaning as earlier. In addition, r_λ and r_μ are the (direct) reduction operators into the vocabularies λ and μ, respectively. The validity of Diagram VII.1. follows immediately from the results given in Chapter II, Section 3.

In Chapters II and VI we were mostly concerned with the following kind of situation of discovery or "theoretical generalization". We considered a given empirical generalization $S^{(d)}$ $(=r_\lambda\ (T^{(d)}\ (\lambda\cup\mu)))$. On the basis of $S^{(d)}$ the theory $T^{(d)}\ (\lambda\cup\mu)$ was then assumed to have been invented. But if we are concerned with explanation rather than with this kind of discovery, a somewhat different conceptual scheme has to be adopted. Then we think that a core theory, axiomatized by $H=H^{(d)}=r_\mu\ (T\ (\lambda\cup\mu))$, is given, and possibly there is also an empirical law $L=L^{(d)}=r_\lambda\ (T^{(d)}\ (\lambda\cup\mu))$ to be explained. (H, T, and L are now, for simplicity, all regarded as statements, not as sets.) In order to be able to explain L by means of H some correspondence rules is needed. Now, the content of these correspondence rules over and above H is

$$(7.8)\qquad cont\ (T^{(d)}\ (\lambda\cup\mu))-cont\ (H)$$

and their content over and above H and L is

$$(7.9)\qquad cont\ (T^{(d)}\ (\lambda\cup\mu))-cont\ (H\ \&\ L).$$

Let us now see what can be said about the desiderata (7.6) and (7.7) for explanation within this framework. Consider the following two key expressions (cf. HINTIKKA (1972b)):

$$(7.10)\qquad \lim_{e\to\infty} cont\ r_\lambda\ (T^{(d+e)}\ (\lambda\cup\mu))-cont\ (L)$$

$$(7.11)\qquad \lim_{e\to\infty} cont\ r_\mu\ (T^{(d+e)}\ (\lambda\cup\mu))-cont\ (H).$$

Our desideratum (7.6) clearly implies that (7.10) should be nonzero; and it is in the spirit of (7.6) to require (7.10) to be as large as possible within explanation. (In Chapter VI we accepted this desideratum for theoretical generalization and called (7.10) a measure of observational richness due to theoretical concepts.) The theoretical adhockery condition (7.7) again implies that (7.11) should be zero, provided that no fruitful theory-growth is present (or that H is a "grown-up" theory). We may here relax this requirement a little and require only that (7.11) be small. In any case (7.11) may be taken to measure the amount of purely theoretical growth in the course of the explanation of L. If no fruitful growth (=growth leading to other new corroborable predictions) is present, then (7.11) can be considered a measure of theoretical adhockery within this explanatory situation.

Some observations concerning the present situation can now be made. First we may ask under what circumstances (7.7) can be satisfied or (7.11) be made zero. This will happen when the maximal subtheory of $T^{(d)}$ $(\lambda \cup \mu)$ in $\mathscr{L}$ (μ) is finitely axiomatizable at a depth not greater than d. A sufficient condition for this is the definability of the members of λ in terms of those of μ within $T^{(d)}$ $(\lambda \cup \mu)$ by means of noncreative definitions of depth less than or equal to d. For instance, explicit definitions of the members of λ in terms of those of μ (at a depth less than or equal to d) would be such definitions. This is in effect how HINTIKKA (1972b) argues. See e. g. RAMSEY (1931), BRAITHWAITE (1959), SELLARS (1963), and CARNAP (1966) for different kinds of arguments leading to the same recommendation, viz. that observational terms should at least in the last analysis be (theoretically) eliminable by means of explicit definitions in terms of theoretical concepts. One should especially notice that the methodological requirement for avoiding theoretical adhockery dovetails neatly with the general philosophical idea of explanation as redescription or reinterpretation of the world. For ideally such a redescription just means replacing the "common sense" framework given in observational or λ-terms by means of a scientific framework stated in theoretical or μ-terms.

While interpretative theorizing (especially explanation) by means of established theories thus seems ideally to require explicit definitions of observables in terms of theoreticals, phenomenological theorizing seems to imply the reverse. As we have argued in previous chapters, within cases of theoretical generalization (theory-formation) it is desirable to keep (7.10) large for the invented theory T, which presupposes ideally that the members of μ are not explicitly definable in terms of the members of λ at any depth. (However, in the case of the "applied" extensions $T' = T \;\&\; C_1 \;\&\ldots\&\; C_n$ it is in many methodological situations desirable to strive for a high degree of observational definability of the theoretical terms; see Section IV.3.)

The avoidance of theoretical adhockery seems to be connected with many other interesting philosophical and methodological issues. Let us take up some of them.

Nagel has required that in the explanation of laws the explaining theory should be more *general* than the explanandum law (NAGEL (1961), pp. 37—38). As the generality in question is denied to be proportional to logical strength, the following suggestion seems to be at hand. A sufficient, though perhaps not necessary, condition for arriving at Nagel's generality would be to define explicitly the concepts occurring in the law in terms of theoreticals such that each definiens is a conjunction of at least two theoreticals. For then one can in an obvious sense say that observational concepts are applications of theoretical concepts and that every theoretical concept is more general and broader in its scope than each observational concept in whose definiens it occurs.

One important point to notice in connection with the theoretical adhockery condition is that even if (7.11) is zero or very small, (7.8) and (7.9) may still be relatively large. As we noticed, (7.8) (and perhaps (7.9), too) may be taken to measure the contribution of the correspondence rules to an explanation. Thus the correspondence rules may contribute rather much to an explanation even when no theoretical adhockery is present. After requiring that the correspondence rules satisfy (7.8) and (7.9) and are well confirmed, it may seem somewhat difficult to find other general additional criteria to guarantee that the contribution of the correspondence rules is genuine and fruitful. However, our general information theoretic principle (I) (or actually its consequence (7.5)) gives us one more criterion provided that of two otherwise equally good explanatory theories the logically stronger one is preferred. For then in Diagram VII.1. a core theory $H^{(d+e)}$, $e>0$, is a better explainer of an L than $H^{(d)}$. Then, *ceteris paribus,* the content of the correspondence rules for $H^{(d+e)}$ (which belong to $T^{(d+e)}(\lambda \cup \mu)$) is smaller than the content of the correspondence rules for $H^{(d)}$. Thus there is less chance for adhockery in giving observational content to $H^{(d+e)}$ than in giving it to $H^{(d)}$.

What can we say about the involvement or interwovenness of the members of μ with the members of λ within good explanatory theories? It can be measured by the difference between the content of the full theory $T(\lambda \cup \mu)$ and the content of the conjunction of its maximal subtheories or reducts in $\mathscr{L}(\lambda)$ and in $\mathscr{L}(\mu)$. Within the framework of distributive normal forms the latter can be obtained as a limit of the content of the conjunction of $H = H^{(d+e)}$ and $L = L^{(d+e)}$ when $e \to \infty$. Thus we get as a kind of measure of involvement between λ and μ in $T^{(d)}(\lambda \cup \mu)$ (cf. Chapter VI):

$$(7.12) \quad cont\,(T^{(d)}(\lambda \cup \mu)) - \lim_{e \to \infty} cont\,(r_\lambda (T^{(d+e)}(\lambda \cup \mu))\ \& \\ \& \ r_\mu (T^{(d+e)}(\lambda \cup \mu)).$$

The index (7.12) is positive between the limits zero and one. It is zero, for instance, when $T(\lambda \cup \mu)$ is equal to the conjunction of its maximal subtheories in $\mathscr{L}(\lambda)$ and $\mathscr{L}(\mu)$. As the behavior of (7.12) obviously very much depends on the probability measure used in defining *cont*, one cannot prove many interesting theorems about (7.12). We should notice that, as the maximal subtheories of $T(\lambda \cup \mu)$ in question are not in general logically exhaustive, the measure *cont* does not distribute over their conjunction in (7.12) to yield the minimum

$$(7.13) \qquad cont\, T^{(d)}(\lambda \cup \mu) - (\lim_{e \to \infty} cont\, (r_\lambda\, (T^{(d+e)}(\lambda \cup \mu))) + \\ + \lim_{e \to \infty} cont\, (r_\mu\, (T^{(d+e)}(\lambda \cup \mu)))).$$

Instead of the *cont*-measure we might have used the *inf*-measure in the formulas (7.8)—(7.13). Still we should not in general strive for the additivity required by the analogue of (7.13), for this implies inductive independence of these (logically independent) maximal subtheories of $T(\lambda \cup \mu)$; and this inductive independence would usually diminish the methodological import of the theory $T(\lambda \cup \mu)$.

The following inequalities are seen to be valid:

(7.8) ≧ (7.9) ≧ (7.12) ≧ (7.13). If the maximal λ-reduct and μ-reduct of $T(\lambda \cup \mu)$ are both finitely axiomatizable at depth d (as is the case when the members of λ are explicitly definable in terms of μ, and conversely) we have (7.9) = (7.12). This means that the interwovenness is increased as compared with the general case. But as we have seen, in this case (7.10) becomes zero. But as it should be large in a good explanatory theory, this amount of interwovenness is too great. Small values of (7.12) approaching (7.13) are not acceptable either, as then the amount of theoretical adhockery (7.11) increases. The optional amount of interwovenness between λ and μ for a good explanatory theory has to lie between these limits, as both (7.10) and (7.11) have to be satisfied. Of our conditions of DEL-explanation only (7.1) and (7.4) may affect our measure of interwovenness. However, we shall not here investigate this in more detail.

2.3. We shall devote the rest of this chapter to a brief discussion of 1) the confirmation theoretic aspects of explanation, 2) scientific reduction and 3) the indispensability of theoretical concepts within scientific explanation.

Our models of deductive explanation discussed above were only concerned with the logical aspects of explanation and hence with *potential* explanation. To make a potential explanation *actual* some requirements concerning the truth and/or the evidential (and possibly theoretical) support of the explanandum and its explanans are needed. One plausible candidate, which we shall adopt, is simply:

(7.14) If $E(L, Tc)$ then L and Tc should be accepted as true.

The term 'true' of course means something like 'true in the actual world' or 'true in intended model(s)'. The notion of acceptance is a notoriously tricky one (cf. Chapter V), and here we shall not attempt to give an analysis of it. (Furthermore, it may be the case that most actually accepted scientific theories are false and even known to be false, but this does not speak against accepting (7.14) as an ideal for good explanatory theories.)

There is, however, one familiar requirement related to how we accept our explanans as true that we want to make more explicit. This is a requirement related to condition (7.6) and prohibiting what might be called "confirmational adhockery" (cf. NAGEL (1961), p. 43). We shall adopt the following weak version of it for our DEL-model:

(7.15) If $Cn(Tc(\lambda \cup \mu)) = H(\mu) \cup O(\lambda) \cup C(\lambda \cup \mu)$ and if $E(L, Tc)$, then $H(\mu)$ is — through some set of correspondence rules $C'(\lambda \cup \mu)$ — adequately supported by evidence based on data other than the observational data upon which the acceptance of the explanandum law L is based.

(Notice that (7.15) still allows that $O(\lambda)$ contains nothing but L although this cannot hold true for the resulting $O'(\lambda)$.) Conditions (7.14) and (7.15) are necessary conditions to make the DEL-model for potential deductive explanation a model for actual (in the above sense) deductive explanation as well.

As we have seen, the DEL-model (together with conditions (7.6) and (7.7)) seems to be capable of giving an adequate account of many troublesome issues in the theory of explanation while it correctly emphasizes some features considered essential for good deductive explanations of scientific laws. Let us summarize these features below.

Based on our discussion in Section 1 we found condition (7.1) — the consistency condition — of the DEL-model acceptable. Condition (7.2) is obviously also acceptable. Condition (7.3′) was discussed above, and the indispensability of theoretical concepts will be commented upon below. Conditions (7.4) and (7.5) were arrived at from general information-theoretic considerations. (7.4) was found to take care of circular explanations of the most vicious kind. (7.5) is supposed to guarantee that an explanation provides a proper amount of relevant (information-theoretically) redundant information. It is essentially (7.5) that establishes the hierarchical tree-structure of deductive explanation. Condition (7.6) refers to the dynamics of theorizing. According to (7.6), it is essential that an explanatory theory be at least capable of growth. Condition (7.15) then actually realizes this possibility by requiring the growth of theory in the evidential sense. It can be noticed here that our condition (7.6) guarantees against *ad* hoc_1-type and condition (7.15) against *ad* hoc_2-type of the three kinds of *ad hoc*-explanations in LAKATOS (1970). In addition, our theoretical adhockery condition (7.7) seems to be a special kind of Lakatos' *ad* hoc_3-explanations.

We shall not go more deeply into the problems of confirmation here but just make one interesting remark on the relation between explanation and various notions of inductive support (cf. Chapter VIII). It seems that between such notions as explanation, generalization, confirmation, corroboration, etc., there are many connected features. Indeed, it might be required that theories of explanation and inductive support should always be developed simultaneously. One argument for this arises from an investigation by SMOKLER (1968). He pointed out that there are two essentially different notions of inductive support, one corresponding to "abductive inference" (in the sense of the early Peirce) and the other to "enumerative induction" (the latter includes eliminative induction). Within abductive inference it is true to say that evidence supports a hypothesis if the hypothesis explains the evidence. Of the familiar principles of qualitative confirmation abductive inference satisfies the conditions of consistency, nonuniversalizability, converse entailment, converse consequence and equivalence but it does not satisfy the conditions of entailment and special consequence (cf., however, the modified conditions in Chapter VIII). On the other hand, enumerative induction makes true the conditions of consistency, nonuniversalizability, entailment, special consequence, and equivalence but it does not make true converse entailment nor converse consequence condition. (See e. g. SMOKLER (1968) for an exact formulation of these conditions.) As the reader can verify, apart from some details (cf. Theorem VII.1), the notion of theoretical explanation that our DEL-model makes precise therefore belongs to abductive inference rather than to inductive enumeration. Our DEL-model then also serves to explicate a notion of corroboration characteristic of abductive inference (cf. NIINILUOTO and TUOMELA (1973) on this). Corresponding to Smokler's notion of enumerative induction we of course also get an implicit definition of a converse relation which might be dubbed inductive systematization or inductive generalization.

The picture that emerges from this is that we have a dichotomy of theorizing both within explanation (interpretive versus phenomenological theorizing) and inductive support (abductive inference versus enumerative induction). Interpretive or theoretical explanation demonstrably goes together with abductive inference (corroboration). It can also be argued that some forms of phenomenological theorizing (explanation and generalization) go together with the above wide notion of enumerative induction and with a high probability criterion of confirmation (see NIINILUOTO and TUOMELA (1973) and the next chapter).

Let us now go on to comment *scientific reduction* from the point of view of our account of deductive explanation. In the context of reduction it has to be emphasized still more strongly than in the context of ordinary deductive explanation that real examples of scientific reductions seldom if ever consist only of neat deduction. For a reducing theory usually simultaneously corrects the reduced theory, and therefore a deductive relationship will hold only between the reducing theory and a corrected and approximate version of the reduced theory. Still we want to maintain that some continuity of ideas and knowledge can often be seen also in scientific reductions. The Feyerabendian picture of scientific change as a series of successive mutually incompatible and incommensurable theories (reminiscent of isolated Leibnitzian monads) seems to us a misleading overemphasis (cf. FEYERABEND (1965)).

First consider *intertheoretic* reduction, viz. reduction in which a (corrected) core theory (axiomatized by a statement) H_2 (μ_2) is reduced to another theory H_1 (μ_1). We now say that H_1 (μ_1) (potentially) reduces H_2 (μ_2) if and only if there are (theoretical) correspondence rules or "bridge laws" C_{12} ($\mu_1 \cup \mu_2$) such that H_1 & C_{12} explains H_2 [10]. What are the conditions that the relation of explanation has to

---

10 Here C_{12} is to be understood in a broad sense so that H_1 & C_{12} corresponds to T above.

satisfy? We suggest that essentially our DE-model conjoined with conditions (7.6) and (7.7) is adequate for this purpose. However, condition (7.3) has to be slightly modified. First we require that both the explanans and the explanandum contain universal statements (or rather laws). Secondly, we do not require that $\mu_1 \cap \mu_2 = \phi$ but something else. In the case of *homogenous* reductions we require that $\mu_2 \subseteq \mu_1$ and in the more interesting case of *inhomogenous* reductions we require that *not* $\mu_2 \subseteq \mu_1$. It has been emphasized by HEMPEL (1969) that the reduction of concepts (members of μ_2) has to be distinguished from the reduction of principles (H_2). This is certainly acceptable. But still our condition (7.7) implies that there is no better way of reducing principles than by simultaneously performing a concept-reduction. For we saw that explicit definitions of the members of μ_2 in terms of those of μ_1 make (7.7) true most adequately.

Let us suppose that H_2 (μ_2) explains some law L (λ) by means of some (empirical) correspondence rules C_2 ($\lambda \cup \mu_2$). If H_1 (μ_1) reduces H_2 (μ_2) by means of C_{12} ($\mu_1 \cup \mu_2$) does it in conjunction with C_{12} explain also L (λ)? As our results concerning the formal properties of the explanatory relation E show, this need not always be the case as (7.4) may be violated. However, it may well be possible that H_1 (μ_1) explains L (λ) by means of some other correspondence rules. Incidentally, this shows that the idea of reduction originally defined by KEMENY and OPPENHEIM (1956), and critically discussed by HEMPEL (1969), is a completely different notion from the above of intertheoretic reduction (if explanation is construed in accordance with our DE-model). In Hempel's formulation of this instrumentalistic idea of reduction we say that a theory H_1 (μ_1) & C_1 ($\lambda \cup \mu_1$) reduces a theory H_2 (μ_2) & C_2 ($\lambda \cup \mu_2$) if and only if

1) not $\mu_2 \subseteq \mu_1$;
2) if H_2 (μ_2) & C_2 ($\lambda \cup \mu_2$) explains some L (λ) then also H_1 (μ_1) & C_1 ($\lambda \cup \mu_1$) explains L (λ);
3) H_1 (μ_1) & C_1 ($\lambda \cup \mu_1$) is at least as well systematized as H_2 (μ_2) & C_2 ($\lambda \cup \mu_2$).

Clearly, intertheoretic reduction in the above sense and Kemeny-Oppenheim-Hempel-reduction are noncomparable in the sense that neither implies the other. Furthermore, as the property (g) of the explanation relation E shows (see Theorem VII.1), a theory may be reduced to a theory which is incompatible with it if reduction is understood in the Kemeny-Oppenheim-Hempel sense. This gives one sense in which science may proceed by means of a sequence $T_1, \ldots, T_n, T_{n+1}, \ldots$ of incompatible theories such that T_{n+1} (at least approximately) reduces the previous theory T_n. It should be emphasized, however, that this kind of reduction is not theoretically very interesting as it has nothing to say about the core of science, i. e. about general theoretical principles.

The final topic of this chapter is the problem of the indispensability of theoretical concepts within deductive explanation. We have in fact already presented some philosophical reasons for this. It still remains to be seen whether there are logical reasons. By this we mean simply the question whether our above logical conditions for explanation — excepting (7.3′) of course — allow for the elimination of theoretical concepts. More explicitly, we have to investigate whether theoretical concepts are logically indispensable in the sense of the following definition (cf. Section 1 of Chapter II). The theoretical terms (members of μ) of a theory $T(\lambda \cup \mu)$ are *logically indispensable for deductive explanation* if and only if

1) $E(L, Tc)$ for some L in $\mathscr{L}(\lambda)$; Tc is a set of ultimate sentential components of $T(\lambda \cup \mu)$;
2) there is no (recursively axiomatizable) subtheory $T'(\lambda)$ in $\mathscr{L}(\lambda)$ such that $E(L, Tc')$, where Tc' is a set of ultimate sentential components of $T'(\lambda)$.

In 1) E can be assumed to satisfy the conditions of the DEL-model whereas in 2) E is assumed to satisfy the DE-model for explanation.

Consider now the example by Sellars described at the beginning of this section. We shall discuss it in a simplified form (compare the more complex probabilistic formulation in CORNMAN (1972), for which our conclusions hold as well). Let us have $\lambda = \{O_1, O_2, O_3\}$ and $\mu = \{P\}$ such that '$O_1(x)$' stands for 'x is a piece of gold', '$O_2(x)$' for 'x dissolves in *aqua regia* at rate r_1', '$O_3(x)$' for 'x dissolves in *aqua regia* at rate r_2', and '$P(x)$' for 'x has microstructure m'. Let then the discovered empirical law about gold be

$$(L) \quad (x)(O_1(x) \supset O_2(x) \vee O_3(x)).$$

The law L is DEL-explained by the theory

$$(T) \quad (x)(O_1(x) \,\&\, P(x) \supset O_2(x)) \,\&\, (x)(O_1(x) \,\&\, -P(x) \supset O_3(x))$$

That is, $E(L, Tc)$ where

$$Tc = \{(x)\,(O_1(x) \,\&\, P(x) \supset O_2(x)),\ (x)\,(O_1(x) \,\&\, -P(x) \supset O_3(x))\}.$$

This explanation by means of an underlying theoretical feature clearly reduces, if not the randomness at least the unorderliness of the world as exhibited by L. Notice also that T can indeed be said to explain *why* observational aspects of gold-samples satisfy L.

Can we now find a subtheory $T'(\lambda)$ (or a $Tc'(\lambda)$) of $T(\lambda \cup \mu)$ such that $E(L, Tc')$? Craig's transcription method gives as a maximal subtheory $T'(\lambda)$ of $T(\lambda \cup \mu)$ the statement L conjoined with itself a certain number of times. Does this subtheory explain L in the sense of the DE-model? It is easily seen that it does not, because condition (7.4) is violated. This will in general be the case for Craigian transcriptions of theories, as the explanans would always contain the explanandum conjoined with itself a certain number of times. Hence we have gained strong support for the claim that theoretical terms are logically indispensable for the deductive explanation of laws. We showed earlier that theoretical terms are indeed logically dispensable for deductive systematization in general, but this does not seem to be true for deductive explanation which is an important strengthened form of deductive systematization. If an instrumentalist still insists that our argument is not conclusive it is his task to provide us with another effective method of transcribing theories such that the transcribed theory preserves explanatory power.

In the case of *singular* deductive explanations we can say at least this. Suppose that $O_2(a)$. Then, given that $O_1(a) \,\&\, P(a)$, T deductively explains that $O_2(a)$. But there is no way of explaining $O_2(a)$, given $O_1(a) \,\&\, P(a)$, on the basis of the Craigian transcription of T. This is because in the Craigian transcription corresponding to the enlarged theory $T^* = T \,\&\, O_1(a) \,\&\, P(a)$ there is no general statement which would entail $O_2(a)$ in conjunction with $O_1(a)$. Furthermore, notice that one must here be able to "measure" the values of P (directly or indirectly) both when one tries to explain by means of the original theory and when one tries to do it by means of the Craigian transcription. Thus even if an instrumentalist had succeeded in making the explanation by means of the Craigian transcription, he must first have been able to employ the theoretical terms. But then the instrumentalist must defeat himself and admit that theoretical statements are capable of factual truth in the fullest sense (=the evidential sense) (cf. SELLARS (1965), p. 369). (This of course is an argument which goes beyond our definition of the logical indispensability of theoretical terms for deductive explanation.)

In any case, we have shown the logical indispensability of P in T against the Craigian transcription of T^* within singular deductive explanation, too.

Our instrumentalist thus seems forced to accept our result that in general the Craigian transcription of a theory is inferior in its explanatory power in comparison with the original theory. He may still argue that the Ramsey sentence of a theory preserves its explanatory power and that hence theoretical terms are dispensable for the deductive explanation of observational statements. In this case our definition of the logical indispensability of theoretical terms for deductive explanation has to be slightly modified. In condition 2) the subtheory $T'(\lambda)$ must be allowed to be in second-order logic so that the Ramsey sentence becomes one of such possible subtheories. We argued in Chapter III that the Ramsey sentence method, especially Bohnert's version, is not really an elimination device for theoretical terms when it is made to work properly. But let us still briefly examine the explanatory power of the Ramsey sentence.

Consider the Ramsey-sentence T^R of our example theory T. It is $(E\,\Pi)\,((x)\,(O_1(x)\ \&\ \Pi(x) \supset O_2(x))\ \&\ (x)\,(O_1(x)\ \&\ -\Pi(x) \supset O_3(x)))$. Now T^R explains L in the sense of the DE-model. Thus the members of μ are dispensable for deductive explanation in the sense of our new definition. However, as T entails T^R, we claim in the spirit of general information theoretic principle (I) that T explains L *better* than T^R. (Notice here that it is not necessary to claim that logically stronger theories always and without qualifications are better explainers, even if a theory always supersedes its Ramsey sentence.) We might then in an obvious way redefine the notion of logical indispensability of theoretical terms by using a comparative notion of explanation rather than merely a qualitative one. The result would be that theoretical terms, here P, are not logically dispensable for deductive explanation. The same argument can be made in the case of corresponding singular explanations. We conclude that even if the Ramsey sentence of a theory preserves the explanatory power of the original theory in one sense, it does not do so in another, perhaps more crucial, sense, contrary to e. g. CARNAP (1966), p. 252. Hence theoretical terms are technically dispensable for deductive explanation in the first but not in the second sense. This result together with our conclusion in Chapter III, according to which the Ramsey method is not really an elimination method, not at least in spirit, gives support to the indispensability rather than to the dispensability of theoretical concepts within deductive explanation[11].

"Explanation of the world" is certainly one of the main goals of science (cf. thesis (GS) in Chapter II). If science employs theoretical terms, surely their purpose must be to help in explanation. Let us now try to reconstrue the original theoretician's dilemma argument from this point of view (see Section I.1. for the original formulation):

(1) Theoretical terms either serve their purpose or they do not serve it.

(2″) If they do not serve it, then they are logically dispensable for scientific explanation.

(3″) If they serve their purpose, then they establish explanations of observable phenomena.

(4‴) If they establish such explanatory relationships, then the same explanatory relationships can be established without theoretical terms.

(5⁗) If these same explanatory relationships are so established, then theoretical terms are logically dispensable for scientific explanation.

(6″) Theoretical terms are logically dispensable for scientific explanation.

Which of the steps of this argument are acceptable and which are not? The first step is of course acceptable as it is a tautology. Thesis (2″) is also acceptable as such. Thesis (3″) can be considered acceptable (at least for deductive explanation) on methodological grounds. The same qualifications that were made in the case of (3′) are to be imposed here, too.

On the other hand, we have found strong reasons against accepting (4‴). This is because Craigian transcriptions clearly fail to preserve explanatory power and because of our above arguments against

11 It seems that the only way an instrumentalist could try to defend himself here would be this. Suppose (against the assumption in the above example) that we can find an *observational* predicate P to substitute for Π in T^R. Then we could get a logically equally strong DE-explanation (both in the case of law-explanation and singular explanation) as when P is theoretical. However, there is no guarantee that such an observational predicate P can be found.

Ramsey sentences. Thesis (5′′′′) as well as the earlier (5″) (Chapter II) and (5‴) (Chapter III) are trivially acceptable as they stand. But our arguments concerning the gains due to theoretical concepts in Chapter VI as well as our philosophical and methodological comments related especially to the explanatory condition (7.3′) of the DEL-model and to the additional desiderata (7.6) and (7.7) for explanation strongly indicate this: (5″), (5‴), and (5′′′′) cannot be strengthened to comprise other kinds of dispensability than logical for the purpose of deductive systematization in general and especially not for the purpose of explaining (observable) events or patterns. Thus (5) (Chapter I) and (5′) (Chapter II) are not acceptable.

So far we have shown that *at least* the original general form ⟨(1), (2), (3), (4), (5), (6)⟩ and the above important special form ⟨(1), (2″), (3″), (4‴), (5′′′′), (6″)⟩ are clearly not acceptable. Our final judgment concerning the other versions considered cannot be given before discussing inductive systematization.

Chapter VIII

Theoretical Concepts within Inductive Systematization

1. Problems of Inductive Inference

1.1. The importance of inductive systematization (broadly understood) has grown considerably since the adoption of probabilistic techniques within such sciences as biology, meteorology, and the social sciences. Only in recent years have philosophers become interested in the details of the problems of inductive explanation and systematization. However, the role of theories and theoretical concepts within the inductive tasks of science has hardly been discussed at all.

We shall in this chapter take up some central philosophical problems arising within inductive systematization. Especially we shall discuss the questions of the methodological desirability and the logical indispensability of theoretical concepts within certain simple situations of inductive systematization.

In Chapter II we cited Hempel's claim, according to which theoretical concepts can be indispensable for inductive systematization. Let us start by discussing one of Hempel's classical examples of inductive systematization (HEMPEL (1958), p. 214 f.). Consider a simple theory T formalized within monadic predicate logic. As our observational predicates we have 'soluble in ether' (E), 'bursts into flame' (F), 'has a garlic-like odor' (G), 'produces skin burns' (S), 'soluble in turpentine' (T), 'soluble in vegetable oils' (V). As our theoretical predicates we have 'white phosphorus' (P) and 'has an ignition temperature of 30⁰ C' (I). As axioms of T we have first the following statement which gives observational necessary conditions for P:

(8.1) $(x)\ (P\ (x) \supset (E\ (x)\ \&\ G\ (x)\ \&\ S\ (x)\ \&\ T\ (x)\ \&\ V\ (x)))$.

Next we have the following theoretical statement:

(8.2) $(x)\ (P\ (x) \supset I\ (x))$.

Finally we have the correspondence rule

(8.3) $(x)\ (I\ (x) \supset F\ (x))$.

Hempel's argument now goes as follows. Consider an individual a showing the symptoms of P, that is, $F\ (a)\ \&\ G\ (a)\ \&\ S\ (a)\ \&\ T\ (a)\ \&\ V\ (a)$. This evidence is supposed to be an inductive sign of $P\ (a)$, or give inductive support to $P\ (a)$. Thus we can inductively infer or induce $P\ (a)$ on the basis of (8.1) and our evidence. Next we deductively infer $I\ (a)$ on the basis of (8.2) and $P\ (a)$. Finally, we deduce the new observational consequence $F\ (a)$ from $I\ (a)$ and (8.3). The important thing here is of course that the conclusion $F\ (a)$ is not obtainable deductively from the theory T and the evidence but that an inductive leap is needed in the inference. As this inductive leap cannot (seemingly) be made by using observational statements only, the argument takes this to show the indispensability of theoretical concepts for the inductive systematization of observational statements.

It can be and it has been argued that the above example as well as other similar examples of Hempel, Scheffler, and Lehrer (see e. g. Hempel (1963), Scheffler (1963), and Lehrer (1969)) do not show what they purport to show. There are two main types of reasons given in the counterarguments (cf. the critical survey in Niiniluoto (1972b)). First, it has been argued that in examples of the above kind theoretical concepts do not after all establish inductive systematization (see Chapter II and below for this notion). Secondly, it can be argued that, even if they did achieve inductive systematization, the same inductive systematization can be achieved by means of an observational subtheory or transcription of the original theory. The Craigian and Ramseyan transcriptions are examples of such subtheories.

In order to discuss the first kind of reasons we consider some factually interpreted scientific language $\mathscr{L}$. Let us in our metalanguage write $I\ (H, K)$ for 'the statement H is inducible from the statement

K'. In general, the following two main types of confirmation theoretic interpretations for the qualitative relation I have been offered:

(A) $I(H, K)$ if and only if K confirms (inductively supports) H.

(B) $I(H, K)$ if and only if H may rationally be accepted on the basis of K.

The most usual technical explicates for $I(H, K)$ have been:

(A′) $I(H, K)$ if and only if $p(H/K) > p(H)$ (positive relevance criterion).

(B′) $I(H, K)$ if and only if $p(H/K) \geqq 1 - \varepsilon$, for some $\varepsilon < .50$ (high probability criterion).

It is a well known fact that (B′) as a rule of acceptance leads to the lottery paradox unless it is suitably qualified. Notice also that in fact all proposed inductive acceptance rules serve to explicate (B) and that (A′) may also be regarded as an explicate of (B). We shall later have more to say about the interpretation of the relation I.

Some crucial and debated conditions that the relation I has been assumed to satisfy are the following:

(C1) For all H there is a K such that not $I(K, H)$. (Nonuniversalizability)

(C2) If $H \vdash K$ then $I(K, H)$. (Entailment)

(C3) If $H \vdash K$ then $I(H, K)$. (Converse entailment)

(C4) If $I(K, H)$ and $F \vdash K$ then $I(F, H)$. (Converse consequence)

(C5) If $I(K, H)$ and $K \vdash F$ then $I(F, H)$. (Special consequence)

(C6) If $H \vdash K$ and $I(F, K)$ then $I(F, H)$. (Partial transitivity)

In these conditions K, F, and H are arbitrary contingent statements of $\mathscr{L}$. Conditions (C4), (C5), and (C6) are weak transitivity principles. It is well known that a qualitative notion of confirmation is not fully transitive (cf. SALMON (1965)), and the question is whether it satisfies any weakened forms of transitivity.

It is an equally well known fact that one and the same notion of qualitative confirmation cannot jointly satisfy the above conditions. More specifically, arguments by HEMPEL (1945) and SKYRMS (1966) show that all the sets {(C1), (C3), (C5)}, {(C1), (C4), (C5)}, and {(C1), (C2), (C4)} are internally inconsistent. That (C6) is unacceptable is shown in SALMON (1965).

Suffice it here to show as an example that the first of the above sets is inconsistent. Consider any given statement H. We show that H confirms any other statement K, i. e. $I(K, H)$. For by propositional logic we have $H \,\&\, K \vdash H$, and $H \,\&\, K \vdash K$. By (C3) we have $I(H \& K, H)$. But now (C5) gives us $I(K,H)$, which contradicts (C1). The inconsistency proofs for the other sets of conditions are equally trivial. (C6) is shown to be unacceptable as follows. Let x be an even prime number. This entails that x is a prime number. The latter fact confirms the statement which says that x is an odd number. But this statement contradicts the premise that x is an even prime number, and hence it cannot be confirmed by the latter.

Let us now consider Hempelian inductive systematization. We replace the theory T (axiomatized by (8.1)—(8.3)) by a simpler but inductively equally problematic theory T_1 axiomatized by

(8.4) $(x)\,(P(x) \supset O_1(x))$, and

(8.5) $(x)\,(P(x) \supset O_2(x))$

where P is a theoretical predicate, i. e. $\mu = \{P\}$, and O_1 and O_2 are observational predicates ($\lambda = \{O_1, O_2\}$). It is now claimed that $I(O_2(a), T_1 \,\&\, O_1(a))$. Given $O_1(a)$ we are supposed first to induce $P(a)$ from it, and then to deduce $O_2(a)$ from $P(a)$. Assuming that inductive inference is indeed connected to the logical form of statements, we are in this inference tacitly relying on two principles of induction. These are converse entailment (C3) (in the first step) and special consequence (C5) (in the second step, to get an inductive link between $O_1(a)$ and $O_2(a)$). But these principles were just shown to be mutually inconsistent.

To illustrate another "transitivity" paradox, consider a theory T_2 axiomatized by the conjunction of the following two statements:

(8.6) $(x)\,(O_1(x) \supset P(x))$

(8.7) $(x)\,(O_2(x) \supset P(x))$.

In T_2 we are assumed to be able to induce $O_2(a)$ from $O_1(a)$ via $P(a)$. That is, we first deduce $P(a)$ from $O_1(a)$, and then induce $O_2(a)$ from $P(a)$. In connection with the first step we have to use (C3), and then, to get an inductive link between $O_1(a)$ and $O_2(a)$, we have to rely on (C6). But (C6) was just argued to be unacceptable.

Can the above kind of transitivity paradoxes be avoided? Unless they can, theoretical terms and theories have not been shown to establish inductive systematization between observational statements. We shall below consider four possible solutions.

First, one may argue that inductive inference in the above examples is not connected with the logical form of statements in the manner assumed above. For instance, one may claim that the inductive inference from the consequent of an implication-statement to its antecedent is not generally plausible even if in some special pragmatic contexts (such as in Hempel's example above) it can be done.

Secondly, one may argue that conditions (C1)—(C6) have been formulated incorrectly. Consider for instance the above inconsistency proof for the set $\{C_1, C_3, C_5\}$. If K and H are completely irrelevant to each other, H does not confirm $H \,\&\, K$ but only the conjunct H, one may argue against the proof. H confirms $H \,\&\, K$ only if H and K are somehow intimately relevant to each other. We now suggest that two statements are in a confirming relationship when one *explains* the other, but that this is not always the case when only a relation of mere deducibility holds between them. If this general idea is accepted then (C2)—(C6) are to be rejected. Instead of them we get new conditions (C2*), (C3*), (C4*), (C5*), and (C6*) in which $\vdash$ has all over been replaced by a relation of explanation E. Now if this relation E is taken to satisfy the conditions of the DE-model (or DEL-model) of Chapter VII then the proofs by HEMPEL (1945) and SKYRMS (1966) for transitivity paradoxes do not go through. For these proofs rely on trivial deductions of the kind $H \,\&\, K \vdash K$ and $H \vdash H \vee K$, or the like, which do not qualify as DE-explanations. (For example, in deriving the paradox within the Hempelian theory T_1 we seem to need the premise $T_1 \,\&\, P(a) \vdash O_1(a) \,\&\, T_1$ and the premise $T_1 \,\&\, P(a) \vdash O_2(a)$, and within the DEL-model these deductions are not explanations.)

Our suggestion to connect confirmation with explanation rather than with mere deducibility thus clearly removes at least some spurious difficulties within the theory of confirmation. We conjecture, furthermore, that the positive relevance criterion satisfies *all* of the crucial conditions (C2*)—(C5*), whereas the high probability criterion satisfies (C2*) and (C5*) but fails to satisfy (C3*) and (C4*). Our conjecture seems to hold true at least within some systems of inductive logic, but no general proof will be attempted here. If our conjecture is true it shows that positive relevance and explanation are indeed closely connected (cf. our remarks on deductive explanation in VII.2.3. and on inductive explanation below in VIII.2. and VIII.3.).

A third way out of the paradoxes of transitivity is to claim that the inductive relations occurring in the inductive principles (C1)—(C6) represent intuitively fundamentally different notions. SMOKLER (1968) argues that there are basically two different types of inductive inference, which he calls *abductive* and *enumerative* inference. (Enumerative inference here includes eliminative inference.) In slight contrast to Smokler, we suggest that the positive relevance criterion can be regarded as representing abductive inference (cf. SMOKLER (1968) and Chapter VII). The high probability criterion fully represents enumerative inference. Of the criteria (C1)—(C6), the positive relevance criterion satisfies (C1), (C2) (provided $P(K) < 1$), (C3) (provided $p(K) < 1$), but it fails to satisfy (C4), (C5), and of course (C6). The high probability criterion satisfies (C1), (C2), and (C5) but does not satisfy (C3) and (C4) nor (C6).

If our conjecture about the relationship between explanation and confirmation is true, it seems better to characterize abductive and enumerative inference with respect to conditions (C2*)—(C5*) rather than (C2)—(C5) and perhaps by direct reference to positive relevance type criteria vs. high probability type criteria.

A fourth possible solution to the paradoxes of transitivity is to "reinterpret" all the observational statements within the richer language of the theory. It then follows that in our example theories T_1 and T_2 one may conceive of the inductive inference from $O_1(a)$ to $O_2(a)$ via the theory as a *one-step* argument (and not as a two-step argument as above) within the framework of the theory (or "in the light of the theory"). Mutually contradictory inductive principles are then not used jointly any more.

We shall in Section 3 of this chapter discuss the last two types of solutions within Hintikka's inductive logic.

2. Theoretical Concepts within Inductive Systematization

2.1. We still have to sharpen our conceptual tools in order to be able to discuss seriously whether theories can establish inductive systematization between observational statements and whether theoretical terms are indispensable or desirable within inductive systematization. In accordance with our definition of deductive systematization (Chapter II) we now define (assuming the scientific theory in question to be axiomatized by a statement $T(\lambda \cup \mu)$ in $\mathscr{L}(\lambda \cup \mu)$):

A theory $T(\lambda \cup \mu)$ establishes *inductive systematization* with respect to $\mathscr{L}(\lambda)$ and to an inductive relation I if and only if for some non-tautological statements H and K of $\mathscr{L}(\lambda)$

(a) $I(H, T \,\&\, K)$

(b) not $I(H, K)$

(c) not $T \,\&\, K \vdash H$[1].

Here the statement K can be or contain a statement describing all the available evidence. For some purposes, however, it is better to explicitly relativize the above definition to the evidential situation described by E. Then we get:

A theory $T(\lambda \cup \mu)$ establishes *inductive systematization* with respect to $\mathscr{L}(\lambda)$ and to an inductive relation I, given the evidence E, if and only if for some statements H and K of $\mathscr{L}(\lambda)$

(a′) $I(H, T \,\&\, K \,\&\, E)$

(b′) not $I(H, K \,\&\, E)$

(c′) not $T \,\&\, K \,\&\, E \vdash H$.

Now we are in the position to define what can be meant by the logical indispensability of theoretical concepts (members of μ) for inductive systematization. Corresponding to our unqualified notion of inductive systematization we get:

The theoretical concepts of a theory $T(\lambda \cup \mu)$ are *logically indispensable for induction systematization* with respect to $\mathscr{L}(\lambda)$ and I if and only if whenever $T(\lambda \cup \mu)$ establishes some inductive systematization with respect to $\mathscr{L}(\lambda)$ and I there is no subtheory of $T(\lambda \cup \mu)$ in $\mathscr{L}(\lambda)$ which establishes the same inductive systematization[2].

An evidence-dependent notion of indispensability corresponding to our second notion of inductive systematization is obtained by relativizing both sides of this definition to E. A further absolute notion

1 Condition (a) can be explicated in various ways to yield different senses of 'inductive systematization'; see NIINILUOTO (1972b). However, our main results are not affected by this general ambiguity, as we shall below use only explicates deriving from the positive relevance criterion.

2 Notice that even if a theoretical concept P were shown to be logically indispensable in this sense, there might still be observational theories (either in $\mathscr{L}(\lambda)$ or in some enriched observational language) which are not subtheories of $T(\lambda \cup \mu)$ and which establish the same inductive systematization as $T(\lambda \cup \mu)$ with respect to $\mathscr{L}(\lambda)$.

of indispensability is again obtained from this relativized notion by stating that it suffices that the right hand side holds for some E. The obvious candidate for the subtheory of $T(\lambda \cup \mu)$ in these definitions is of course the Craigian transcription of $T(\lambda \cup \mu)$. Another candidate is the Ramsey sentence of $T(\lambda \cup \mu)$. ($\mathscr{L}$ is then to be considered a second-order language.)

As the present investigation focuses on the logical aspects of scientific systematization we shall have to classify cases of systematization by means of logical criteria only — although in the hope of being able to capture something of philosophical interest. Let us now recall some logical distinctions made in Chapter II. First, the statements in a systematization can be singular or (essentially) general. If the premises contain essentially general statements (e. g. scientific laws) we call the systematization nomological, otherwise anomological. (We shall below discuss only nomological systematization.) Secondly, if the premises contain general probabilistic statements we call the systematization probabilistic, otherwise nonprobabilistic. We shall here mainly deal with nonprobabilistic systematizations in this sense of the word. (However, we shall assume that the statements in the systematizations can meaningfully be assigned inductive probabilities in the metalanguage.) The third and most important logical aspect about scientific systematizations is the nature of the relationship holding between the premises and the conclusion of a systematization. If this relation is that of logical deduction we speak of deductive systematization, otherwise of nondeductive systematization. The important subcase of nondeductive systematization we shall below be concerned with is just inductive systematization, viz. a systematization where the premises of the argument stand in an inductive relationship to the conclusion.

2.2. Until this we have been discussing scientific systematization as an argument of inference. This idea is obviously acceptable in the case of deductive systematization. But it does not seem very plausible in the case of inductive systematization. Consider, for instance, a typical example of Hempelian inductive-probabilistic explanation (cf. HEMPEL (1965), p. 390):

$$\begin{array}{ll} p(G(x)/F(x)) = r & \\ F(a) & [r] \\ \hline G(a) & \end{array}$$

Here the conclusion $G(a)$ is supposed to be inferrable from the law $p(G/F) = r$ and the initial condition $F(a)$ with the inductive strength r (given in brackets). Now, if the probability r in the law is very high we are in a fairly good position to "detach" $G(a)$ inductively from the premises. But if r is small, say $< .50$, we obviously cannot rationally expect $G(a)$ to occur on the basis of the premises. However, in some cases of this kind the initial probability of $G(a)$ may be very small in comparison with its probability relative to the premises. Then the premises are probabilistically very relevant to $G(a)$, and they may be regarded as having explanatory power with respect to $G(a)$. In information-theoretic terminology we may then say that the premises convey a substantial amount of information concerning $G(a)$, and thereby considerably reduce the initial uncertainty associated with it.

Our viewpoint in this book is that inductive explanation, and indeed a major part of inductive systematization, is best conceived of as information-providing argumentation, but it is argumentation that does not lead to detaching a conclusion from some premises. Thus, for instance, to explain something inductively is to give a proper amount of information relevant to the explanandum (cf. our condition (I) in Chapter VII). As we shall in this chapter generally measure information in terms of probabilities (for instance, by positive relevance), we can alternatively say that within inductive systematization explaining something is stating some propositions inductively (or probabilistically) relevant to the explanandum (cf. e.g. SALMON (1970), GREENO (1970), JEFFREY (1969)).

It is then most natural to adopt the positive relevance interpretation for the inductive relation I (see condition (A') in VIII.1.1.). Notice that this explication says nothing about the *strength* of the inductive relationship holding between K and H. We shall, however, tentatively proceed as if its strength were proportional to, if not identical with, $p(H/K) - p(H)$, which (or some of its normed versions) has widely been accepted as a measure of either explanatory power or inductive support (cf. HINTIKKA (1968)).

Let us now apply our explication of the relation I as positive relevance to the above definition of inductive systematization. The defining conditions (a) and (b) containing I in the first definition now become:

(α) $\quad p(H/T \,\&\, K) > p(H)$

(β) $\quad p(H/K) \leqq p(H)$.

Our second notion of inductive systematization can be interpreted in several ways by using the notion of positive relevance. Corresponding to (*a*′) we have the following possibilities:

(α_1') $\quad p\,(H/T \,\&\, K \,\&\, E) > p\,(H/E)$

(α_2') $\quad p\,(H/T \,\&\, K \,\&\, E) > p\,(H/K \,\&\, E)$

(α_3') $\quad p\,(H/T \,\&\, K \,\&\, E) > p\,(H/T \,\&\, E)$.

Corresponding to (b′) we get

(β') $\quad p\,(H/K \,\&\, E) \leqq p\,(H/E)$.

Of the above explicates of (*a*′) (α_1') gives us the joint effect of T and K over H, given E. (α_2') gives the impact of T over and above K. Given (β'), (α_1') implies (α_2'). Finally, (α_3') explicates the probabilistic effect of K on H "seen in the light of the theory T".

Corresponding to the above special explicates for establishing inductive systematization we can in an obvious way interpret our above definitions for the logical indispensability of theoretical terms.

2.3. As we remarked, such theoreticians as Salmon, Jeffrey, and Greeno, *inter alii*, have explicated inductive explanation by means of positive probabilistic relevance. Within our framework this implies that a theory $T\,(\lambda \cup \mu)$ has explanatory power with respect to the observational language $\mathscr{L}\,(\lambda)$ exactly when it establishes some inductive systematization (with respect to $\mathscr{L}\,(\lambda)$) in the positive relevance sense. While such a notion of inductive explanation may be somewhat too broad we shall in this chapter assume that it is basically acceptable, even if some refinements might be needed[3].

Until now, the only systematic attempt to discuss the role of theoretical concepts within inductive systematization (explanation) has been that of GREENO (1971). However, from the point of view of our discussion his (otherwise excellent) treatment partly begs the issue

3 Explanations in the social sciences have sometimes been divided into explanations giving sufficient conditions and explanations stating necessary conditions for explananda. (cf. von WRIGHT (1971)). The first answer questions of the form *Why necessary*? and the second questions of the form *How possible*? Our treatment in Chapter VII deals with explanations of the first kind while inductive explanation in terms of positive relevance accounts for some central logical aspects of the second type of explanations, too. For if a fact (statement) F is explained by citing fact G necessary for F (i. e. $\vdash F \supset G$) then obviously $p\,(F/G) > p\,(F)$.

for the following reason. Greeno makes only one basic (probabilistic) assumption about the theory $T(\lambda \cup \mu)$ containing theoretical concepts. He assumes that the theoretical concepts *screen off* the observational concepts. Within our framework this entails that $T(\lambda \cup \mu)$ has explanatory power with respect to $\mathscr{L}(\lambda)$. Notice that this assumption does not follow from our characterization of theoreticity in Chapter I. However, in Chapter VII we (provisionally) accepted thesis (3″) of theoretician's dilemma. This thesis requires theoretical concepts to have deductive explanatory power. With the same methodological qualifications as earlier, we are willing to accept (3″) for inductive explanation as well. We think, however, that it is quite legitimate and plausible to inquire under which conditions and how theoretical concepts come to get their inductive explanatory power.

If theoretical concepts are found to have inductive explanatory power (or to establish inductive systematization)we may call them inductively desirable (independently of whether they are logically indispensable for inductive systematization). But as positive relevance is in fact a metrical measure we may also consider the following stronger sense of desirability:

The theoretical terms of a theory $T(\lambda \cup \mu)$ are *desirable for inductive systematization* with respect to a set L of statements of $\mathscr{L}(\lambda)$ if and only if the explanatory power of $T(\lambda \cup \mu)$ with respect to L is never smaller than the explanatory power of any subtheory $T'(\lambda)$ of $T(\lambda \cup \mu)$. Here L is a set of mutually exclusive and jointly exhaustive statements of $\mathscr{L}(\lambda)$, e. g. the set of its constituents. The theoretical terms of $T(\lambda \cup \mu)$ may be said to be *strongly desirable* with respect to L if the explanatory power of $T(\lambda \cup \mu)$ with respect to L is in addition strictly greater than that of any subtheory $T'(\lambda)$. This notion of strong desirability is our metrical counterpart to our earlier qualitative notion of logical indispensability. (The notions of desirability may be relativized to the evidence similarly as in the case of the notion of indispensability earlier.)

We may here measure explanatory power simply by positive relevance (as above), but we may also consider various well-known information theoretic measures proposed in the literature which rely on the explicates of *transmitted information* (cf. HINTIKKA (1968)). Below we propose three entropy-measures of explanatory power. The first two of them respect the positive relevance criterion but the third one does not (see Theorem VIII.1. and NIINILUOTO and TUOMELA (1973), Ch. 7).

For simplicity, let us assume that the language $\mathscr{L}(\lambda)$ has a finite set $L=\{L_1,\ldots, L_i,\ldots, L_n\}$ of basic or constituent statements which are mutually incompatible and jointly, exhaustive. Then we propose the following normed measures for explanatory power (*expl*) of a theory T with respect to L[4]:

$$(8.8) \qquad expl_1 (T, L) = \frac{inf(T//L)}{inf(L)}$$

$$(8.9) \qquad expl_2 (T, L) = \frac{cont(T//L)}{cont(L)}$$

$$(8.10) \qquad expl_3 (T, L) = \frac{cont(T///L)}{cont(L)}$$

In the equations (8.8)—(8.10) the symbols on the right hand sides can be concisely defined as follows (cf. HINTIKKA (1968)):

$$(8.11) \qquad inf (L) = \sum_{i=1}^{n} p (L_i)\, inf (L_i)$$

$$(8.12) \qquad cont (L) = \sum_{i=1}^{n} p (L_i)\, cont (L_i)$$

In (8.11) and (8.12) the *inf*- and *cont*-measures are the usual ones:

$$inf (L_i) = -\log_2 p (L_i)$$
$$cont (L_i) = 1 - p (L_i).$$

Next we have

$$(8.13) \qquad inf (T//L) = inf (L) - inf (L/T).$$

In (8.13)

$$inf (L/T) = -\sum_{i=1}^{n} p (L_i/T) \log_2 p (L_i/T).$$

$$(8.14) \qquad cont (T//L) = cont (L) - cont (L/T).$$

---

4 We do not explicitly write out our observational evidence here. If needed, it may be understood that $T=T' \,\&\, E$ where T' is the proper explanatory theory and E the evidence. Somewhat different measures of explanatory power are obtained if one relativizes to E all the probabilities employed in the following measures of explanatory power. The resulting measures explicate the explanatory power of T with respect to L *relative to* E (see NIINILUOTO and TUOMELA (1973)).

In this equation

$$cont\ (L/T) = \sum_{i=1}^{n} p\ (L_i/T)\ cont\ (L_i/T)$$
$$= \sum_{i=1}^{n} p\ (L_i/T)\ (1 - p\ (L_i/T)).$$

Finally we have

(8.15) $$cont\ (T///L) = cont\ (L) - cont\ (L, T)$$

Here

$$cont\ (L, T) = \sum_{i=1}^{n} p\ (L_i/T)\ cont\ (L_i, T),$$

in which

$$cont\ (L_i, T) = cont\ (L_i\ \&\ T) - cont\ (T) = cont\ (T \supset L_i).$$

What we have in the nominator of the measures (8.8)—(8.10) is different measures of the information (entropy) transmitted by the theory T concerning L. The denominator normalizes this information to make $expl_j\ (T, L)$ have the maximum value of one (for all $j=1, 2, 3$). If $p\ (L_i/T)$ is zero or one for all L_i in L, then $expl_j\ (T, L) = 1$ for all $j=1, 2, 3$. Furthermore, we immediately get for our measures $expl_j$ in the case of two theories T_1 and T_2 the following results relating explanatory power and positive relevance:

Theorem VIII.1:

(a) $expl_1\ (T_1, L) > expl_1\ (T_2, L)$ if and only if
$$\sum_{i=1}^{n} p\ (L_i/T_1) \log_2 p\ (L_i/T_1) > \sum_{i=1}^{n} p\ (L_i/T_2) \log_2 p\ (L_i/T_1)$$

(b) $expl_2\ (T_1, L) > expl_2\ (T_2, L)$ if and only if
$$p\ (T_1)\ [1 - \sum_{i=1}^{n} p\ (L_i/T_1)^2] < p\ (T_2)\ [1 - \sum_{i=1}^{n} p\ (L_i/T_2)^2]$$

(c) $expl_3\ (T_1, L) > expl_3\ (T_2, L)$ if and only if
$$\sum_{i=1}^{n} p\ (L_i/T_1)^2 > \sum_{i=1}^{n} p\ (L_i/T_2)^2.$$

Obviously, if $expl_j\ (T\ (\lambda \cup \mu), L) \geqq expl_j\ (T\ (\lambda), L)$, $j=1, 2, 3$, for all subtheories $T\ (\lambda)$ of $T\ (\lambda \cup \mu)$ then the predicates in μ are desirable in the sense of our definition.

Our measures of explanatory power and our notion of desirability of theoretical terms can in an obvious way be applied also to single statements, although we preferred here to give explicitly only the general formulation (see PIETARINEN and TUOMELA (1969) and NIINILUOTO and TUOMELA (1973)). In this case the relationship between the measures $expl_j$, $j=1, 2$, and positive relevance becomes still more direct, for then these measures are positive if and only if the explanans is positively relevant to the explanandum.

The above measures of explanatory power are relative to a set L of observational statements. More absolute notions of explanatory power are obtained by taking into account such evidence-independent features of theories as their simplicity, absolute content, etc..

We shall in Section 3 return to these measures of explanatory power in a more specific framework, in which some results concerning the logical indispensability and desirability can indeed be obtained.

2.4. So far we have presented no conclusive arguments to show that theories containing theoretical terms are even capable of establishing inductive systematization between observational statements. Still less have we shown that theoretical terms can be logically indispensable for inductive systematization.

In discussing the inductive capacity and performance of a theory the following two points are relevant. First, it has been assumed in the literature that the logical structure of the theory reflects its inductive capacity or that the inductive capacity of the theory is wholly based on its structure. Secondly, the inductive systematization capacity of the theory is demonstrated by a two- or many-step argument leading to the desired inductive conclusion. We demonstrated above the difficulties in regarding inductive systematization as this kind of argument. The claims of HEMPEL (1958) and SCHEFFLER (1963) do not even show that theoretical terms serve to establish inductive connections, primarily because the inductive relation I lacks the required kind of transitivity property. The same holds true for Lehrer's recent attempt to argue for the logical indispensability of theoretical terms, as he relies on an unacceptable transitivity principle in his rules of inductive acceptance (see LEHRER (1969) and the criticism by NIINILUOTO (1971) and (1972b)).

Let us now go to our first point and to the difficult problem of assigning probabilities to statements. Consider the theory T_2 axiomatized by (8.6) and (8.7). Suppose that we have observed that $O_1(a)$. Then we deduce $P(a)$ by (8.6). Whereas $O_2(a)$ cannot be obtained deductively from T_2, $O_1(a)$ and $P(a)$, we may still consider its inductive probability and likelihoods in this situation.

Assume for the sake of argument that

(8.16) $p(O_2(a)/O_1(a) \,\&\, P(a)) > p(O_2(a))$

(8.17) $p(O_2(a)/O_1(a)) = p(O_2(a))$

These assumptions can be made without contradicting the theory T_2 and the usual Kolmogorov's axioms of the calculus of probability. But now it might seem not only that T_2 establishes inductive systematization but even that P is logically indispensable for inductive systematization (in the sense of our definition) in the theory T_2.

Let us examine what is wrong with this argument. One trouble may be taken to be this: the probability statements in (8.16) and (8.17) are not logically implied by T_2 and the calculus of probability. Therefore they may seem arbitrary, and our argument would not be acceptable to some theoreticians (especially not to objectivists). However, for a subjectivist the above probability assignments can be quite nonarbitrary and acceptable. What the argument then may seem to show under a subjectivistic probability interpretation (probability as degree of belief) is something like the *believed* indispensability of P in T_2. Furthermore, a subjectivistic instrumentalist might as well (instead of (8.17)) claim in the opposite way that $O_1(a)$ is positively relevant to $O_2(a)$ whenever $O_1(a) \,\&\, P(a)$ is. What an objectivist (and a scientific realist) needs is a more objective justification for the probabilities of statements. Preferably this should be by direct reference to the external world (or then by reference to the logical structure of statements hopefully reflecting the structure of the world).

Let us next consider the following trivial probabilistic theory T_3 which avoids the above difficulty. T_3 is taken to be axiomatized by the following two statements (assumed to hold for any x):

(8.18) $po(O_2(x)/P(x) \,\&\, O_1(x)) > po(O_2(x))$

(8.19) $po(O_2(x)/O_1(x)) = po(O_2(x))$.

Here the probability measure po is assumed to represent an objective (statistical) probability *in re*. Then objective probabilities (po) and inductive probabilities (p) can be directly connected by the identification of their values in the manner proposed e. g. by HEMPEL (1965), p. 389: "If e is the statement '$(p\ (G, F) = r)$ & Fb', and h is 'Gb', then $c\ (h, e) = r$". Here 'p' and 'c' correspond, respectively, to our 'p_o' and 'p'. Applying the axioms of T_3 to an individual a we get from (8.18) and (8.19)

(8.16) $p\ (O_2\ (a)/P\ (a)\ \&\ O_1\ (a)) > p\ (O_2\ (a))$ and

(8.17) $p\ (O_2\ (a)/O_1\ (a)) = p\ (O_2\ (a))$.

We then have, given T_3,

(i) $I\ (O_2\ (a),\ O_1\ (a)\ \&\ P\ (a))$

(ii) not $I\ (O_2\ (a),\ O_1\ (a))$

Does this prove that the theoretical concept P is logically indispensable in T_3? It does not (in the sense of our definition), for instead of (i) we need the stronger statement

(i*) $I\ (O_2\ (a),\ O_1\ (a)\ \&\ T)$.

In other words, it must be the case that

(8.16*) $p\ (O_2\ (a)/O_1\ (a)\ \&\ T) > p\ (O_2\ (a))$.

However, as (i) and (ii) hold given the truth of T_3, we have found a new sense of inductive systematization (and indispensability). In this new sense and in view of (8.16) P is indeed logically indispensable within the probabilistic theory T_3. It should be noticed that we have to assume that our evidence is $O_1\ (a)\ \&\ P\ (a)$ to be able to make use of (i). This means that P must here have an evidential use. Recall that we have assumed in this book that good theoretical predicates will have at least some evidential uses, which, among other things, guarantees them a full existential status. Our present assumption and hence our argument for the indispensability of P in T_3 need not of course be accepted by an instrumentalist.

Can P be logically indispensable for inductive systematization within T_3 in any stronger sense? It does not seem possible to prove that P is indispensable in the sense derived from (i*) and (ii). But we do have an intermediate case. For Hempel's above principle for identifying objective and inductive probabilities entails for the present case the truth of

$$p\ (O_2\ (a)/(O_1\ (a)\ \&\ P\ (a)\ \&\ T)) > p\ (O_2\ (a)).$$

Thus we have instead of (i*)

$$\text{(i**)} \qquad I\,(O_2\,(a),\, O_1\,(a)\ \&\ P\,(a)\ \&\ T).$$

In view of (8.17) P is then seen to be logically indispensable (in the sense of our (α) and (β)) in the "applied" theory T & $P(a)$, i. e. relative to T *and* the initial condition $P(a)$. Thus we have found one interesting sense in which a theoretical concept having some (however indirect) evidential uses can be logically indispensable.

We shall in the next section consider the issue of establishing inductive systematization for nonprobabilistic theories from a different angle viz. within Hintikka's system of inductive logic. But to comment on the indispensability of theoretical terms let us now assume — at least for the sake of argument — that (both probabilistic and) nonprobabilistic theories (with theoretical terms) can establish inductive systematization between observational statements. A scientific instrumentalist would now mostly likely argue that either the Craigian transcription or the Ramsey sentence of the theory $T(\lambda \cup \mu)$ in question will preserve its inductive capacity (i. e. either thesis (4′) or (4″) of the theoretician's dilemma is considered valid).

Let us first consider Craigian elimination. An interesting feature of many example theories claimed to establish inductive systematization is that they have no nontautological observational consequences. For instance, Hempel's theory axiomatized by (8.1)—(8.3) (or the simplified form (8.4)—(8.5)) is a case in point. Thus, if such a theory establishes inductive systematization, its Craigian transcription — being a logical tautology — clearly cannot preserve it.

An instrumentalist can now make the counterargument that this in fact shows that the original theory does not after all establish inductive systematization. (Cf. Bohnert (1968), Stegmüller (1970), Cornman (1972).) However, as Niiniluoto (1972a) has convincingly argued, this counterargument is fallacious. He shows that a theory's having deductive observational content is not necessary for its establishing inductive systematization between observational statements (in the sense of our definition). Moreover, the fact that

$$I_T = \{F \text{ in } \mathscr{L}(\lambda) \,|\, I(F, T), \text{ not } T \vdash F, \text{ not } I(F, T \vee -T)\} \neq \phi$$

is neither necessary nor sufficient for T to have observational consequences. This result relies on the lack of reasonable transitivity properties of the relation I.

We can thus accept the result that a Craigian transcription does not at least always preserve the inductive capacity of the original theory provided it establishes any inductive systematization. (For additional arguments to this effect see SCHEFFLER (1963) and CORNMAN (1972).) *Thus thesis (4′) of the theoretician's dilemma argument is generally false.*

SCHEFFLER (1963) suggests that Craig's replacement method should be extended by specifying *recursively* which statements confirm which in a theory. However, there does not seem to be much hope for finding such an extended recursive replacement method for the following reason (given in NIINILUOTO (1972b)). Consider the set

$$G_T = \{F \supset H \mid F, H \text{ in } \mathscr{L}(\lambda), I(H, F \,\&\, T), \text{ not } I(H, F), \text{ and not } T \vdash F \supset H\}.$$

It can be proved that the theory T establishes inductive systematization with respect to $\mathscr{L}(\lambda)$ if and only if $G_T \neq \phi$. However, Niiniluoto shows that G_T is not a deductively closed set. Hence G_T cannot be recursively axiomatized[5].

Let us next consider the inductive performance of the Ramsey sentence T^R of a theory T. The situation here is closely analogous to the Craigian case. Consider the simplified Hempelian theory T_1 axiomatized by (8.4) and (8.5). Let us again accept for the sake of argument Hempel's and Scheffler's claim that this theory establishes inductive systematization. Can a Ramseyan eliminationist show that P is still logically dispensable here? Consider the Ramsey sentence

$$T_1^R = (E\, \Pi)\, [(x)\, (\Pi(x) \supset O_1(x)) \,\&\, (x)\, (\Pi(x) \supset O_2(x))].$$

Now, T_1^R is tautological, and it remains tautological if we substitute $-P$ for P in it. Thus, while T establishes a confirmatory link between $O_2(a)$ and $P(a)$ but not between $O_2(a)$ and $-P(a)$, T_1^R is totally insensitive to this difference (cf., however, Section III.2.).

Instrumentalists like Bohnert have argued as follows. As the original theory T_1 has no nontautological observational consequences, there can be no empirical reasons to believe in the truth of T_1 rather

5 CORNMAN (1972) also tries to extend Craig's replacement method but he does *not* prove (for any inductive relation I) that his extended method is *recursive*, which of course is to miss the main point of the problem. In addition, it has been shown by NIINILUOTO (1972b) that even if the method were recursive it could not capture exactly those inductive relationships which hold between the observational statements of a theory. This result is again due to the lacking transitivity properties of inducibility.

than in the truth of a theory T_1' obtained from T by substituting '$-P$' for 'P' (BOHNERT (1968)). Bohnert takes this to imply that the argument for the alleged confirmatory link cannot exist between $O_2(a)$ and $P(a)$. If there are hidden reasons for preferring T over T' they have to be made explicit and conjoined to T, but then, says Bohnert, they have to show up in the resulting new Ramsey sentence, too.

However, as we saw, a theory's having no nontautological deductive observational content is not a sufficient condition for its not establishing inductive systematization between observational statements. Therefore a Ramseyan eliminationist is wrong in the above claim. Furthermore, it is up to him to show that the implicit background knowledge accounted for by the use of meaningful theoretical predicates in T_1 can *recursively* and in a *general* fashion be incorporated into the Ramsey sentence of T_1.

We now seem justified to conclude that the Ramsey sentence is inductively inferior to the original theory, provided the latter is capable of establishing any inductive systematization between observational statements. *Hence thesis (4″) of the theoretician's dilemma argument ban be rejected.*

3. Theoretical Concepts and Inductive Logic

3.1. The purpose of this section is to illustrate the problems of inductive systematization within Hintikka's system of inductive logic and to seek answers to some open questions within this framework. As this system of inductive logic contains more inbuilt assumptions than the mere Kolmogorovian axioms, new results may be expected merely for this reason.

The general idea in our approach is this. In accordance with the general outlook of this book we shall be concerned with *general* rather than with singular knowledge and hence with the inductive systematization of generalizations rather than singular statements. We shall discuss the inductive probabilities of empirical (observational) statements (mainly generalizations) by reinterpreting or redescribing them by means of a richer conceptual system. Thus a generalization G originally stated within $\mathscr{L}(\lambda)$ is now described by means of a richer language $\mathscr{L}$ $(=\mathscr{L}(\lambda \cup \mu))$. Moreover, we can then better express our background assumptions T (conceptual or factual) within the richer system and compare the conditional probabilities $p\,(G/E)$ (E describes the empirical evidence) and $p\,(G/E\ \&\ T)$ within with varying evidence and different background information.

Another way of interpreting the situation is this. We will be in a good position to discuss the *inductive explanation* of G by means of a theory T, given the evidence E, and the logical indispensability within inductive systematization of the theoretical or nonempirical concepts of T (if it contains any). Still another, and more general, way to characterize the situation is to say that we are applying a *hypothetico-inductive method* to scientific inference. A scientific theory T is first invented or postulated. T is then tested observationally, primarily by means of its *inductive* consequences (cf. theories with *no deductive* observational content). Furthermore, T is used for *inductive* explanation and prediction, etc., analogously with the classical *hypothetico-deductive* method.

We shall employ Hintikka's two-dimensional system of inductive logic for monadic predicate logic (see HINTIKKA (1964), (1965), and (1966c)). Due to limitations of space, a familiarity with this system will have to be assumed. Furthermore, we shall omit most of the (straightforward) proofs of the formulas below to be able to concentrate on conceptually central issues[6].

To start our technical discussion let $\mathscr{L}\,(\lambda)$ be a monadic language (without identity) with k primitive predicates O_i ($i=1,\ldots,k$) and N individual constants a_j ($j=1,\ldots,N$). The *attributive constituents* or *Ct-predicates* ($K=2^k$ of them) are of the form

$$(8.20)\qquad Ct_j\,(x) = (\pm)\,O_1\,(x)\ \&\ (\pm)\,O_2\,(x)\ \&\ldots\&\ (\pm)\,O_k\,(x),$$

where $(\pm)$ is replaced with a negation sign or nothing[7]. The *Ct*-predicates describe all the different *kinds* of individuals that can be specified by means of the resources of $\mathscr{L}\,(\lambda)$. Our *constituents* (2^K of them), or the maximally strong descriptions of the world, here take the form

$$(8.21)\qquad C_w = (Ex)\,Ct_{i_1}\,(x)\ \&\ (Ex)\,Ct_{i_2}\,(x)\ \&\ldots\&\ (Ex)\,Ct_{i_w}\,(x)\ \&\ \&\ (x)\,(Ct_{i_1}\,(x) \vee Ct_{i_2}\,(x) \vee\ldots\vee Ct_{i_w}\,(x)).$$

6 The reader is referred to NIINILUOTO and TUOMELA (1973) for the proofs and a detailed and more extensive technical treatment. Their results substantially generalize those arrived at in TUOMELA (1969).

7 Cf. our general description of the attributive constituents, constituents and distributive normal forms in II.3. (and elsewhere).

Constituent C_w says that there are *exactly* w specified kinds of individuals exemplified in the world. Every general sentence G of $\mathcal{L}(\lambda)$ can be expressed as a disjunction of such constituents. Thus $G = G^{(1)} = C_1 \vee \ldots \vee C_n$ is the *distributive normal form* G (at depth 1). If this disjunction contains only one member we call G a *strong* generalization, otherwise it is called *weak*.

Suppose that we have completely observed n of the N individuals of our universe. Complete observation means that we know which Ct-predicate each individual in this sample exemplifies. Let the exemplified Ct-predicates be $Ct_{i_1}, Ct_{i_2}, \ldots, Ct_{i_c}$ (c kinds of individuals exemplified). Let E be a singular *evidence* statement in $\mathcal{L}(\lambda)$ describing our sample.

Constituent C_w is compatible with the evidence E if $c \leqq w \leqq K$. Hence we get its posterior probability by Bayes' formula

$$p(C_w/E) = \frac{p(C_w)\, p(E/C_w)}{\sum_{i=1}^{K-c} \binom{K-c}{i} p(C_{c+i})\, p(E/C_{c+i})} \tag{8.22}$$

(Here the denominator is equal to $p(E)$.)

In Hintikka's two-dimensional continuum of inductive methods there are two extralogical parameters α and λ ($0 \leqq \alpha, \lambda \leqq \infty$) which can be objectivistically interpreted to represent the degree of "uniformity" or "regularity" of the world[8]. The parameter α does this in the case of generalizations and λ in the case of singular statements. Small values of α and λ represent great uniformity while great values express irregularity or disorder. In the case of an infinite universe (i. e. $N \to \infty$) formula (11) of HINTIKKA (1966c) gives a general expression for $p(C_w/E)$ as a function of the size of the evidence sample and its distribution into the c exemplified kinds of individuals, and as a function of α, λ, and K. We shall below restrict ourselves to the case of an infinite universe and to the case $\lambda(w) = w$ (see formula (27) of HINTIKKA (1966c)).

The basic result which holds for Hintikka's two-dimensional continuum when $N \to \infty$, $\lambda > 0$, and $\alpha \neq \infty$, is that $p(C_c/E)$ approaches 1 with growing evidence, i. e.

8 The parameter λ is not to be confused with our set λ of observational predicates.

(8.23) $\lim_{e\to\infty} p\,(C_c/E) = 1$

$\lim_{e\to\infty} p\,(C_w/E) = 0$, if $w > c$.

It follows that $\lim_{e\to\infty} p\,(G/E) = 1$ if and only if C_c occurs in G.

3.2. Let us now consider in more detail the probability of a weak generalization G (in $\mathscr{L}(\lambda)$) specifying that there are certain b ($b > 0$) kinds of individuals *not* exemplifiable in our universe. We assume that

$$E \vdash G \equiv C_{j_1} \vee C_{j_2} \vee \ldots \vee C_{j_G}.$$

The evidence E says that exactly c kinds of individuals are exemplified and the generalization G specifies that b Ct-predicates are empty. Clearly, we must have $c \leqq w_i \leqq K - b$ for all $i = j_1, j_2, \ldots, j_G$. Furthermore, for all $m = 0, 1, \ldots, K - b - c$ there are $\binom{K-b-c}{m}$ constituents C_{j_i} such that $w_i = c + m$. Then we immediately get — in the case $\lambda(w) = w$ — from formula (27) of HINTIKKA (1966c):

$$(8.24)\qquad p\,(G/E) = \frac{\sum_{i=0}^{K-b-c} \binom{K-b-c}{i} \frac{(\alpha+c+i-1)!}{(n+c+i-1)!}}{\sum_{i=0}^{K-c} \binom{K-c}{i} \frac{(\alpha+c+i-1)!}{(n+c+i-1)!}}$$

Putting $n = 0$ and $c = 0$ in (8.24) gives the prior probability $p\,(G)$ in $\mathscr{L}(\lambda)$.

Let us next consider a richer language $\mathscr{L}(\lambda \cup \{P\}) = \mathscr{L}$ with the $k+1$ primitive predicates $O_1, O_2, \ldots, O_k, P$. We denote the Ct-predicates of $\mathscr{L}$ by $Ct_1^r, Ct_2^r, \ldots, Ct_{K'}^r$, where $K' = 2^{k+1} = 2K$. Now each Ct-predicate Ct_i of $\mathscr{L}(\lambda)$ can be expressed as a disjunction

$$Ct_i = Ct_{i1}^r \vee Ct_{i2}^r$$

where $Ct_{i1}^r = Ct_i \,\&\, P$ and $Ct_{i2}^r = Ct_i \,\&\, -P$ (cf. IV.1.). Instead of the observational partition with K "cells" we now have $2K$ cells and the resulting richer "carving up" of our world. Let T now be a finitely axiomatized theory in $\mathscr{L}$. T expresses our factual and/or conceptual knowledge or assumptions concerning the world. The effect of T is normally that some Ct^r-cells are specified empty by it. Let there be r ($r > 0$) such cells. We do not assume that T necessarily specifies any observational cells (Ct_i-predicates) to be empty.

Consider now the reinterpretation of the evidence E in the light of $\mathscr{L}$ and T. For each $Ct_i = Ct^r_{i1} \vee Ct^r_{i2}$ exemplified in E we have in general the following three possible cases:

(1) (a) Ct^r_{i1} or (b) Ct^r_{i2} is empty by T (both cannot be empty). If neither (1) (a) nor (1) (b) obtains we have the following possibilities left:

(2) P is "evidential" in the sense that it can (at least in principle) be applied to the individuals of the evidence sample to yield *complete* descriptions within $\mathscr{L}$ (cf. our discussion of theoretical concepts in Chapter I). Then we have the cases:

(a) Ct^r_{i1} is empty, Ct^r_{i2} is not empty;

(b) Ct^r_{i1} is not empty, Ct^r_{i2} is empty;

(c) Ct^r_{i1} and Ct^r_{i2} are both exemplified.

(3) P is "nonevidential" in the sense that it is not possible to determine whether an individual satisfying Ct_i belongs to Ct^r_{i1} or Ct^r_{i2}.

Because of limitations of space we shall below discuss only cases (1) and (2). Furthermore, the technical results for (3) are fairly similar to cases (1) and (2) (see NIINILUOTO and TUOMELA (1973)).

To illustrate various factors involved in the present situation we consider the following diagram:

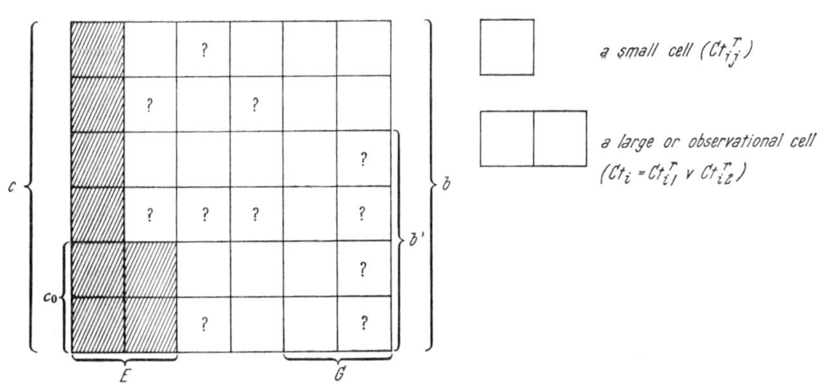

Diagram VIII.1

In this diagram the smallest cells represent the Ct^r-predicates of $\mathscr{L}$. Any pair of two adjacent small cells (starting from the first or last column) of each row represents a Ct-predicate of $\mathscr{L}(\lambda)$. As before, c is the number of such observational Ct-predicates (cells) exemplified in the evidence E (the shaded area). c_0 is the number of Ct-predicates of $\mathscr{L}(\lambda)$ corresponding to case (2) (c) above, that is, the number of genuinely splitted observational cells ($0 \leqq c_0 \leqq c$). $c' = c + c_0$ is the number of Ct^r-predicates or smallest cells exemplified in the evidence. As above, b is the number of Ct-predicates of $\mathscr{L}(\lambda)$ which are empty due to the generalization G. b' is the number of Ct^r-predicates of $\mathscr{L}$ which are empty by G but not by T. The blank smallest cells (r of them) are those empty by the theory T. Finally, the smallest cells with a question mark ($2K - r - c'$ of them) are those neither exemplified in E nor empty by T.

To get the probability $p(G/E \& T)$, we assume that

$$E \& T \vdash G \equiv C^r_{j_1} \vee C^r_{j_2} \vee \ldots \vee C^r_{j_G},$$

$$E \vdash T \equiv C^r_{j_1} \vee \ldots \vee C^r_{j_G} \vee C^r_{j_{G+1}} \vee \ldots \vee C^r_{j_T}.$$

Then let w^r_i be the number of Ct^r-predicates of $\mathscr{L}$ instantiated by a constituent C^r_i (in G or T). Clearly, in T we have $c' \leqq w^r_i \leqq 2K - r$ for all $i = j_1, \ldots, j_T, \ldots, j_G$. For G we have correspondingly $c' \leqq w^r_i \leqq$ $\leqq 2K - b' - r$, for all $i = j_1, \ldots, j_G$. Among the constituents C_r of T there are $\binom{2K-r-c'}{m}$ such that $w^r_i = c' + m$ $(m = 0, 1, \ldots, 2K - r - c')$, and within the constituents C^r_i of G there are $\binom{2K-r-b'-c'}{m}$ such that $w^r = c' + m$ $(m = 0, 1, \ldots, 2K - r - b' - c')$. Analogously with the probability $p(G/E)$ in $\mathscr{L}(\lambda)$ we now get, for $\lambda(w) = w$, in Hintikka's system:

$$(8.25) \qquad p(G/E \& T) = \frac{\sum\limits_{i=0}^{2K-r-b'-c'} \binom{2K-r-b'-c'}{i} \dfrac{(\alpha+c'+i-1)!}{(n+c'+i-1)!}}{\sum\limits_{i=0}^{2K-r-c'} \binom{2K-r-c'}{i} \dfrac{(\alpha+c'+i-1)!}{(n+c'+i-1)!}}$$

If we put $r = 0$ and $2b = b'$ in (8.25) we get the probability of G on E in the richer language $\mathscr{L}$ *without* any background assumptions or knowledge.

In the case $b' = 0$ we have $T \& E \vdash G$ and $p(G/E \& T) = 1$. This limiting case represents deductive systematization.

Formulas (8.24) and (8.25) are difficult to examine in their general form. The following theorem describes their behavior in some interesting special cases:

Theorem VIII.2. Formulas (8.24) and (8.25) for $p(G/E)$ and $p(G/E \,\&\, T)$ have the following properties:

(1) If $n \to \infty$ and $\alpha \neq \infty$ then $p(G/E) \to 1$ and $p(G/E \,\&\, T) \to 1$.

(2) If $\alpha \to \infty$, then $p(G/E) \to 0$ and $p(G/E \,\&\, T) \to 0$.

(3) If $r = K$, $c' = c$, and $b' = b$, then $p(G/E) = p(G/E \,\&\, T)$.

(4) If $\alpha = n$, then $p(G/E) = \frac{1}{2^b}$ and $p(G/E \,\&\, T) = \frac{1}{2^{b'}}$ and $p(G/E) < p(G/E \,\&\, T)$ if and only if $b > b'$.

(5) If n and α are sufficiently great in relation to $(K-1)^2$ and $(2K-r-1)^2$, then $p(G/E) < p(G/E \,\&\, T)$ if and only if $b > b'$ (and only if T has observational consequences).

(6) If $b + c = K$, $b' + c' + r = 2K$, and $b = b'$, then $p(G/E) < p(G/E \,\&\, T)$ if and only if $\alpha > n$ and $c_0 > 0$.

Let us now make some comments on these results. (1) represents the basic property of Hintikka's system (mentioned earlier) and (2) represents the reduction of this system into Carnap's λ-continuum. As to (3), its conditions are satisfied when P is *explicitly defined* in terms of the observational predicates by T. Then no observational cells are genuinely splitted, and T has no explanatory power with respect to G in the positive relevance sense.

Case (4) illustrates that a theory T introducing a theoretical concept P can be of inductive help preasymptotically ($n \ll \infty$) in a fairly regular universe if it is observationally strong (T makes b' small). Case (5) again illustrates that also asymptotically theoretical concepts may do useful work in irregular universes provided they are observationally powerful and hence strongly involved with the observational concepts. However, they are not allowed to be explicitly defined in terms of the latter. Here we have again an argument for a moderate degree of openness of theoretical concepts (cf. Chapter IV).

Cases (4) and (5) are rather interesting as they show that a theory T may establish inductive systematization only if T has observational consequences (i. e. T specifies empty some Ct-predicates of $\mathscr{L}(\lambda)$ making $b' < b$). If now $b > b'$, then all the conditions (α_i'), $i = 1, 2, 3$, (see subsection VIII.2.2.) in our definition of inductive systematization can be satisfied by taking K to be a statement to the effect that a new individual satisfies a Ct-predicate of $\mathscr{L}(\lambda)$ containing a small cell specified empty by G but not by T. This guarantees that (β') is also satisfied, and T *establishes inductive systematization* with respect to $\mathscr{L}$ (λ).

But even if T may thus establish inductive systematization the same effect is in such cases obtainable by means of its subtheory T' (λ) which specifies that exactly those Ct-predicates of $\mathscr{L}$ (λ) are empty that are empty by T, i. e. this $T'(\lambda)$ has the same observational consequences as T. Hence in cases (4) and (5) P cannot be logically indispensable for inductive systematization. Still it is in such cases *desirable* for inductive systematization (with respect to G) in the sense of our definition (Section VIII.2.).

In case (6) the condition $b+c=K$ means that in our universe exactly those Ct-predicates of $\mathscr{L}$ (λ) are exemplified which are already exemplified in the evidence E. The condition $b'+c'+r=2K$ means that the theory T leaves no question marks outside those cells of $\mathscr{L}$ (λ) which are empty by G. What result (6) says is that a theory T introducing P can help inductively in relatively irregular universes in preasymptotic situations (i. e. $\alpha > n$), provided the evidence shows some richness with respect to $\mathscr{L}$ (i. e. $c_0 > 0$).

An interesting additional fact which follows from (8.24) and (8.25) for case (6) is that $p\,(G/E)$ and $p\,(G/E\ \&\ T)$ cannot here exceed 1/2.

In order to discuss the desirability and logical indispensability of P in case (6) we shall consider Hempelian inductive systematization within our framework. Let T be the theory T_1 axiomatized by (8.4) and (8.5). As the (final) inductive link is supposed to be between O_1 and O_2 we may ask whether the generalization G_1, i. e.,

$$(x)\,(O_1\,(x) \supset O_2\,(x)), \tag{8.26}$$

would do the inductive work as well as T_1[9]. Here the observational language $\mathscr{L}$ ($\{O_1, O_2\}$) contains the following four Ct-predicates

$$Ct_1 = O_1\ \&\ O_2$$
$$Ct_2 = O_1\ \&\ -O_2$$
$$Ct_3 = -O_1\ \&\ O_2$$
$$Ct_4 = -O_1\ \&\ -O_2.$$

9 We consider here only inductive systematization of generalizations on the basis of theories, which is theoretically the most important case of inductive systematization. The probabilities of singular statements representing instances of generalizations are closely connected with the probabilities of generalizations within Hintikka's inductive logic (see Hintikka (1966c)).

Let us suppose that Ct_1, Ct_3, and Ct_4 are exemplified in the evidence, i. e. $c=3$. G_1 implies that Ct_2 is empty, i. e. $b=1$. The language $\mathscr{L}(\{O_1, O_2\} \cup \{P\})$ has the following Ct^r-predicates:

$$Ct_1{}^r = O_1 \,\&\, O_2 \,\&\, P$$
$$Ct_2{}^r = O_1 \,\&\, O_2 \,\&\, -P$$
$$Ct_3{}^r = O_1 \,\&\, -O_2 \,\&\, P$$
$$Ct_4{}^r = O_1 \,\&\, -O_2 \,\&\, -P$$
$$Ct_5{}^r = -O_1 \,\&\, O_2 \,\&\, P$$
$$Ct_6{}^r = -O_1 \,\&\, O_2 \,\&\, -P$$
$$Ct_7{}^r = -O_1 \,\&\, -O_2 \,\&\, P$$
$$Ct_8{}^r = -O_1 \,\&\, -O_2 \,\&\, -P$$

G_1 specifies that exactly $Ct_3{}^r$ and $Ct_4{}^r$ are empty, whereas exactly $Ct_3{}^r$, $Ct_5{}^r$, and $Ct_7{}^r$ are empty by T_1. Notice that thus T_1 has no observational consequences. Supposing in addition that the cell Ct_1 genuinely splits into $Ct_1{}^r$ and $Ct_2{}^r$ we get the following diagram:

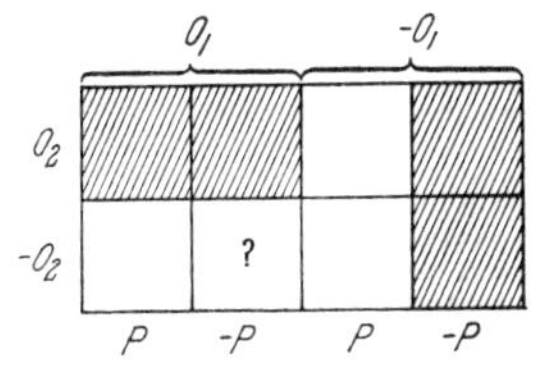

Diagram VIII.2

The four shaded small cells are thus cells exemplified in the evidence, i. e. $c'=4$. The three blank small cells are empty by T_1, i. e. $r=3$. The only small cell with a question mark means here that $b'=1$.

Formulas (8.24) and (8.25) simplify in this case to

$$\text{(8.24*)} \qquad p\,(G_1/E) = \frac{1}{1+\dfrac{\alpha+3}{n+3}}$$

$$\text{(8.25*)} \qquad p\,(G_1/E \,\&\, T_1) = \frac{1}{1+\dfrac{\alpha+4}{n+4}}$$

Hence $p\,(G_1/E) < p\,(G_1/E \,\&\, T_1)$ if and only if $\alpha > n$. The same result holds for other evidential situations and assumptions about splitting the evidence as long as the initial conditions of case (6) are respected.

Does T_1 establish inductive systematization with respect to $\mathscr{L}(\lambda)$? Assume that $n<\alpha-1$. As we now have $p\,(G_1/E \,\&\, T_1) > p\,(G_1/E)$, T_1 clearly has some explanatory power with respect to G, given E, and condition (α) for inductive systematization is satisfied. More interestingly, conditions ($\alpha_i{}'$), $i=1,2,3$, can be satisfied by taking K to be e. g. the statement which says that the next ($n+1$st) individual to be observed belongs to Ct_1. The n changes to $n+1$ in (8.24*) and (8.25*) and we have

$$p\,(G_1/E\ \&\ K\ \&\ T_1) > p\,(G_1/E\ \&\ K) > p\,(G_1/E\ \&\ T_1) > p\,(G_1/E) > 0.$$

Thus all the conditions (α_i') are satisfied. Still (β') is not true. Furthermore, there is no way of selecting K and/or changing the evidential situation so that (β') becomes satisfied. This shows that Hempel's example does not after all show that theoretical concepts are logically indispensable because the theory T_1 does not even establish inductive systematization in this case. (Could (β') have been satisfied here, the logical indispensability of the theoretical concept P would have immediately followed, as T has no nontautological subtheory in $\mathscr{L}\,(\lambda)$.) Notice, however, that as K and T_1 considered jointly increase the probability of G_1 more under E than K alone, P is *strongly desirable* (with respect to G) in T. This result might be taken as a partial vindication of Hempel when the inductive relation I is explicated as positive relevance.

3.3. Monadic theories clearly do not in all respects present representative examples of the behavior of theoretical concepts in scientific theories (cf. our results elsewhere, especially in Chapter IV). Perhaps one should look for more complicated situations in order to find examples of inductively indispensable (in our sense) theoretical concepts. However, this is not necessary as the following Hempelian monadic example shows.

For technical simplicity we now consider a monadic language $\mathscr{L}\,(\lambda)$ where $\lambda = \{O_1, O_2, O_3\}$. Thus $K=8$. Assume that our evidence statement E_n says that there are n individuals in the observational cell $Ct_1 = O_1\ \&\ O_2\ \& O_3$. Then $c=1$. Let C_w be the constituent according to which the Ct-predicates Ct_1 and $Ct_2 = O_1\ \&\ O_2\ \&\ -O_3$ are exemplified in our universe. Hence $w=2$. Let $E' = Ct_1\,(a_{n+1})$, where a_{n+1} is an unobserved individual. We shall use Hintikka's inductive logic as applied for constituents in the special simple situation $\alpha=0$, $\lambda\to\infty$ (Hintikka's "Jerusalem system"). In this system we have (see HINTIKKA (1966), p. 126):

(8.27) $$p\,(C_w/E_n) = \frac{1}{\sum\limits_{i=0}^{K-c} \binom{K-c}{i} \left(\dfrac{c+i}{w}\right)^n}$$

Applying (8.27) to our present example gives

(8.28) $$p\,(C_w/E_n\ \&\ E') < p\,(C_w/E_n) \text{ if and only if } n \geqq 4$$

Let now $\mu = \{P\}$. As our theory we choose $T_1^* = (x)\,[(P\,(x) \supset O_1\,(x))\ \&\ (P\,(x) \supset O_2\,(x))\ \&\ (P\,(x) \supset O_3\,(x))]$, which is the exact analogue of the Hempelian theory T_1 within the present framework. T_1^* has no nontautological observational consequences. In cases like this the theory does not allow the observational *Ct*-predicates to split freely in the sense that a *Ct*-predicate might be associated with P or $-P$ or both without contradicting the theory. In other words, in our diagram VIII.1. there are no larger (observational) cells outside E and G with two question marks. As shown in NIINILUOTO and TUOMELA (1973) Hintikka's Jerusalem system gives for this situation

$$(8.29) \qquad p\,(C_w/E_n\ \&\ T) = \frac{1}{(2K-r-b')^n \sum\limits_{i=0}^{2K-c'-r} \binom{2K-c'-r}{i} \left(\frac{1}{c'+i}\right)^n}$$

In the case of our theory T_1^*, $2K=16$, $r=7$, and $b'=6$. We assume that $c'=2$. Then (8.29) implies for the present situation:

$$(8.30) \qquad p\,(C_w/E_n\ \&\ T) > p\,(C_w/E_n\ \&\ E'\ \&\ T) \text{ if and only if } n \geqq 3$$

Therefore $p\,(C_w/E_3 \& E') > p\,(C_w/E_3)$ and $p\,(C_w/E_3 \& E' \& T) < p\,(C_w/E_3 \& T)$. But now consider the observational generalization $-C_w$. Corresponding to our conditions (α_3') and (β') for inductive systematization (with $H = -C_w$, $T = T_1^*$, $E = E_n$, and $K = E'$) we now have

$$p\,(-C_w/E_3\ \&\ E'\ \&\ T) > p\,(-C_w/E_3\ \&\ T)$$
$$p\,(-C_w/E_3\ \&\ E') < p\,(-C_w/E_3).$$

Therefore T_1^* *establishes inductive systematization* with respect to $\mathscr{L}(\lambda)$. Furthermore, P is *logically indispensable* as T_1^* has no nontautological observational consequences. By the same token P is *desirable* and even *strongly desirable* (with respect to G) in T.

Our example thus vindicates Hempel's claim and shows that *theoretical concepts can be logically indispensable for inductive tasks* (in our strong sense).

In our above examples we have assumed that P can be used for reporting (however indirectly it is done) at least in some central cases. Without this assumption it is hard (though not impossible) to find examples of logical inductive indispensability. All this of course fits perfectly well with what we have claimed about the nature and usefulness of theoretical concepts earlier in this book.

Other cases where a theoretical concept P can be logically indispensable are, somewhat surprisingly, some contexts where it is piecewise definable in terms of λ and T such that its definienses are neither equivalent nor logically incompatible. This supports well our claims concerning the importance of piecewise definitions (cf. Chapter IV).

Our measures *expl* of explanatory power can be applied to the different cases of Theorem VIII.2., for instance, by taking $L = \{G\}$.

Then two different rivalling explanantia T and T^* (with or without μ-predicates) may be compared with respect to their explanatory power. As can easily be verified, in general T^* explains G better than T if and only if T^* is observationally stronger (cases (4) and (5)) or exhibits more observational variety (case (6)) than T[10].

It should be noticed that our above results concerning the role of the theoretical concept P within inductive systematization are relative to the positive relevancy interpretation of I. For instance, our results do not hold for the high probability criterion ((B′) in Section VIII.1.), which partially explicates inductive acceptance. This suggests that (open) theoretical concepts are central for abductive inference but not always for enumerative induction (in the sense of SMOKLER (1968)). This observation accords well with our previous results in this book (cf. especially Chapters V, VI, and VII). It shows, for instance, that phenomenological theorizing (theorizing without theoretical concepts) may go together with enumerative induction (represented by the high probability criterion) whereas interpretative theorizing and abductive inference (represented by positive relevance) dovetail neatly.

In Section VIII.2. we arrived at the result that thesis (4) and its variants (4′), (4″) (and, in effect (4‴)) of the theoretician's dilemma argument are false for the inductive case. What we have established in this section is that theoretical terms can indeed serve their purpose within inductive systematization, viz. they can establish inductive relationships between empirical statements. In summary, all special versions of the theoretician's dilemma argument considered in this book are unacceptable (see Chapters II, III, VI, and VII). Furthermore, the original version of the dilemma (Chapter I) has been strongly disconfirmed. Hence we may conclude by saying that in general theoretical terms are indispensable in science.

---

10 Another interesting situation is the one where the explanatory power of two theories with respect to two different generalizations is compared. For instance, within the present framework we may have for a $T'(\lambda)$ and a $T(\lambda \cup \mu)$, $expl_i(T'(\lambda) \,\&\, E, G_1) \leq expl_i(T'(\lambda) \,\&\, E, G_2)$ but $expl_i(T(\lambda \cup \mu) \,\&\, E, G_1) > expl_i(T(\lambda \cup \mu) \,\&\, E, G_2)$, $i = 1,2$.

References

ACHINSTEIN, P. (1965), The Problem of Theoretical Terms, American Philosophical Quarterly *2*, 193—203.

ACHINSTEIN, P. (1968), Concepts of Science: A Philosophical Analysis, The Johns Hopkins Press, Baltimore.

ACKERMANN, R. (1965), Deductive Scientific Explanation, Philosophy of Science *32*, 155—167.

ACKERMANN, R., and A. STENNER (1966), A Corrected Model of Explanation, Philosophy of Science *33*, 168—171.

ANSCOMBE, G. E. M. (1957), Intention, Blackwell, Oxford.

BARKER, S. F. (1957), Induction and Hypothesis, Cornell University Press, Ithaca, N. Y.

BERGMANN, G. (1961), Physics and Ontology, Philosophy of Science *28*, 1—14.

BLACK, M. (1966), Craig's Theorem, in: EDWARDS, P. (ed.), The Encyclopedia of Philosophy, vol. II, The MacMillan Co & Free Press, New York, pp. 249—251.

BLALOCK, H. (1969), Theory Construction, Prentice-Hall, Englewood Cliffs.

BOHNERT, H. (1967), Communication by Ramsey-Sentence Clause, Philosophy of Science *34*, 341—347.

BOHNERT, H. (1968), In Defense of Ramsey's Elimination Method, The Journal of Philosophy *65*, 275—281.

BRAITHWAITE, R. B. (1953), Scientific Explanation, Cambridge University Press, Cambridge, England.

BRAITHWAITE, R. B. (1959), Axiomatizing a Scientific System by Axioms in the Form of Identifications, in: HENKIN, L., P. SUPPES, and A. TARSKI (eds.), The Axiomatic Method, North-Holland, Amsterdam, pp. 429—442.

BUNGE, M. (1967a), Scientific Research I-II, Springer-Verlag, Berlin—Heidelberg—New York.

BUNGE, M. (1967b), Physical Axiomatics, Review of Modern Physics *39*, 463—474.

BUNGE, M. (1968), The Maturation of Science, in: LAKATOS, I., and A. MUSGRAVE (eds.), Problems in the Philosophy of Science, North Holland, Amsterdam, pp. 120—137.

BUNGE, M. (1969), What are Physical Theories About?, American Philosophical Quarterly, Monograph Series, no. 3, pp. 61—91.

BUNGE, M. (1972), Semantics of Science, forthcoming.

CAMPBELL, N. (1920), Physics: The Elements. Reprinted as Foundations of Science, Dover, New York.

CAMPBELL, N. (1921), What is Science? Dover, New York.

CARNAP, R. (1937), Testability and Meaning, Philosophy of Science *4*, 1—30. Excerpts reprinted in FEIGL, H., and M. BRODBECK (eds.), Readings in the Philosophy of Science, Appleton-Century-Crofts, New York, 1953.

CARNAP, R. (1950a), Empiricism, Semantics, and Ontology, Revue Internationale de Philosophie *11*, 20—40.

CARNAP, R. (1950b), The Logical Foundations of Probability, The University of Chicago Press, Chicago.

CARNAP, R. (1956), The Methodological Character of Theoretical Concepts, in: FEIGL, H., and M. SCRIVEN (eds.), Minnesota Studies in the Philosophy of Science *I*, University of Minnesota Press, Minneapolis, pp. 38—76.

CARNAP, R. (1966), Philosophical Foundations of Physics. Edited by GARDNER, M., Basic Books, New York.

CHISHOLM, R. (1957), Perceiving: A Philosophical Study, Cornell University Press, Ithaca.

CORNMAN, J. W. (1968), Mental Terms, Theoretical Terms, and Materialism, Philosophy of Science *35*, *45—63*.

CORNMAN, J. W. (1971), Materialism and Sensations, Yale University Press, New Haven and London.

CORNMAN, J. W. (1972), Craig's Theorem, Ramsey-Sentences, and Scientific Instrumentalism, Synthese *25*, 82—128.

CRAIG, W. (1953), On Axiomatizability Within a System, The Journal of Symbolic Logic *18*, 30—32.

CRAIG, W. (1956), Replacement of Auxiliary Expressions, Philosophical Review *65*, 38—55.

CRAIG, W. (1957), Linear Reasoning. A New Form of the Herbrand-Gentzen Theorem, The Journal of Symbolic Logic *22*, 250—268.

CRAIG, W. (1960), Bases for First-Order Theories and Subtheories, The Journal of Symbolic Logic *25*, 97—142.

CRAIG, W., and R. L. VAUGHT (1958), Finite Axiomatizability Using Additional Predicates, The Journal of Symbolic Logic *23*, 289—308.

DUHEM, P. (1914), The Aim and Structure of Physical Theory. Reprinted by Atheneum, New York, 1962.

ESSLER, W. K. (1970), Wissenschaftstheorie I: Definition und Reduction, Karl Alber, Freiburg and Munich.

FEIGL, H. (1950), Existential Hypotheses, Philosophy of Science *17*, 35—62.

FEYERABEND, P. (1965), Problems of Empiricism, in: GOLODNY, R. G. (ed.), Beyond the Edge of Certainty, Prentice-Hall, Englewood Cliffs, pp. 145—260.

FISHER, J. (1966), The Identification Problem in Econometrics, McGraw-Hill, New York.

FREGE, G. (1884), Die Grundlagen der Arithmetik, Wilhelm Koebner, Breslau.

FODOR, J. (1968), Psychological Explanation: An Introduction to the Philosophy of Psychology, Random House, New York.

GIEDYMIN, J. (1970), The Paradox of Meaning Variance, The British Journal for the Philosophy of Science *21*, 257—268.

GLYMOUR, C. (1971), Theoretical Realism and Theoretical Equivalence, in: BUCK, R. G., and R. S. COHEN (eds.), Boston Studies in the Philosophy of Science *VIII*, D. Reidel, Dordrecht, pp. 275—288.

GOODMAN, N. (1957), Review of: Craig, W. (1956), The Journal of Symbolic Logic 22, 317—318.

GREENO, J. G. (1970), Evaluation of Statistical Hypotheses Using Information Transmitted, Philosophy of Science *37*, 279—293.

GREENO, J. G. (1971), Theoretical Entities in Statistical Explanation, in: BUCK, R. G., and R. S. COHEN (eds.), Boston Studies in the Philosophy of Science *VIII*, D. Reidel, Dordrecht, pp. 3—26.

HANSON, N. R. (1957), Patterns of Discovery, Cambridge University Press, Cambridge.

HEMPEL, C. G. (1945), Studies in the Logic of Confirmation, Mind *54*, 1—26, 97—121.

HEMPEL, C. G. (1952), Fundamentals of Concept Formation, The University of Chicago Press, Chicago.

HEMPEL, C. G. (1958), The Theoreticians Dilemma, in: FEIGL, H., M. SCRIVEN, and G. MAXWELL (eds.), Minnesota Studies in the Philosophy of Science *II*, University of Minnesota Press, Minneapolis, 1958. Reprinted in: HEMPEL, C. G. (1965), Aspects of Scientific Explanation, Free Press, New York, pp. 173—226.

HEMPEL, C. G. (1963), Implications of Carnap's Work for the Philosophy of Science, in: SCHILPP, P. A. (ed.), The Philosophy of Rudolf Carnap, Open Court, La Salle, Ill., pp. 685—709.

HEMPEL, C. G. (1965), Aspects of Scientific Explanation, Free Press, New York.

HEMPEL, C. G. (1969), Reduction: Ontological and Linguistic Facets, in: MORGENBESSER, S., P. SUPPES, and M. WHITE (eds.), Philosophy, Science, and Method, St. Martin's, New York, pp. 179—199.

HEMPEL, C. G. (1970), On the "Standard Conception" of Scientific Theories, in: RADNER, M., and S. WINOKUR (eds.), Minnesota Studies in the Philosophy of Science *IV*, University of Minnesota Press, Minneapolis, pp. 142—163.

HEMPEL, C. G., and P. OPPENHEIM (1948), Studies in the Logic of Explanation, Philosophy of Science *15*, 135—175. Reprinted in: HEMPEL, C. (1965), Aspects of Scientific Explanation, The Free Press, New York, pp. 245—290.

HERMES, H. (1950), Zum Begriff der Axiomatisierbarkeit, Math. Nachrichten *4*, 343—347.

HILPINEN, R. (1966), On Inductive Generalization in Monadic First-Order Logic With Identity, in: HINTIKKA, J., and P. SUPPES (eds.), Aspects of Inductive Logic, North-Holland, Amsterdam, pp. 133—154.

HINTIKKA, K. J. (1964), Distributive Normal Forms and Deductive Interpolation, Zeitschr. f. math. Logik und Grundlagen d. Math. *10*, 185—191.

HINTIKKA, K. J. (1965a), Distributive Normal Forms in First-Order Logic, in: CROSSLEY, J., and M. DUMMETT (eds.), Formal Systems and Recursive Functions, North-Holland, Amsterdam, pp. 47—90.

HINTIKKA, K. J. (1965b), Are Logical Truths Analytic? Philosophical Review *74*, 178—203.

HINTIKKA, K. J. (1966a), An Analysis of Analyticity, in: WEINGARTNER, P. (ed.), Deskription, Analytizität und Existenz *3-4*, Forschungsgespräch des Internationalen Forschungszentrums für Grundfragen der Wissenschaften, Pustet, Salzburg and Munich, pp. 193—214.

HINTIKKA, K. J. (1966b), Kant Vindicated, in: WEINGARTNER, P. (ed.), Deskription, Analytizität und Existenz *3-4*, Forschungsgespräch des Internationalen Forschungszentrums für Grundfragen der Wissenschaften, Pustet, Salzburg and Munich, pp. 234—253.

HINTIKKA, K. J. (1966c), A Two-Dimensional Continuum of Inductive Methods, in: HINTIKKA, J., and P. SUPPES (eds.), Aspects of Inductive Logic, North-Holland, Amsterdam, pp. 113—132.

HINTIKKA, K. J. (1968), The Varieties of Information and Scientific Explanation, in: ROOTSELAAR, B., and J. F. STAAL (eds.), Logic, Methodology, and Philosophy of Science *III*, North-Holland, Amsterdam.

HINTIKKA, K. J. (1970a), Information, Deduction, and the A Priori, Noûs *4*, 135—152.

HINTIKKA, K. J. (1970b), Surface Information and Depth Information, in: HINTIKKA, J., and P. SUPPES (eds.), Information and Inference, D. Reidel, Dordrecht, pp. 27—61.

HINTIKKA, K. J. (1971), On the Model Theory of Partial Definability, Mimeographed paper, 10 p.

HINTIKKA, K. J. (1972a), Constituents and Finite Identifiability, Journal of Philosophical Logic *1*, pp. 45—52.

HINTIKKA, K. J. (1972b), On the Different Ingredients of an Empirical Theory. Forthcoming in the proceedings of the IVth International Congress for Logic, Methodology, and Philosophy of Science.

HINTIKKA, K. J., and I. NIINILUOTO (1973), On Theoretical Terms and Their Ramsey-Elimination: An Essay in the Logic of Science (in Russian), Filosofskiye Nauki *1*, 49—61. Forthcoming in English.

HINTIKKA, K. J., and R. TUOMELA (1970), Towards a General Theory of Auxiliary Concepts and Definability in First-Order Theories, in: HINTIKKA, K. J., and P. SUPPES (eds.), Information and Inference, D. Reidel, Dordrecht, pp. 298—330.

HULL, C. L. (1943), The Problem of Intervening Variables in Molar Behavior Theory, Psychological Review *50*, 273—291.

HURWICZ, L. (1950), Generalization of the Concept of Identification, in: KOOPMANS, T. (ed.), Statistical Inference in Dynamic Economic Models, Wiley, New York.

HURWICZ, L. (1962), On the Structural Form of Interdependent Systems, in: NAGEL, E., P. SUPPES, and A. TARSKI (eds.), Logic, Methodology, and Philosophy of Science, Stanford University Press, Stanford, pp. 232—239.

JEFFREY, R. C. (1969), Statistical Explanation vs. Statistical Inference, in: RESCHER, N. (ed.), Essays in Honor of Carl G. Hempel, D. Reidel, Dordrecht, pp. 104—113.

KAKKURI-KETONEN, M.-L. (1972), On Explicit Definitions. Manuscript.

KEMENY, J. G., and P. OPPENHEIM (1956), On Reduction, Philosophical Studies *7*, 6—19.

KENNY, A. (1963), Action, Emotion and Will, Routledge and Kegan Paul, London.

KOOPMANS, T. (1953), Identification Problems in Economic Model Construction, in: HOOD, W., and T. KOOPMANS (eds.), Studies in Econometric Method, Wiley, New York, pp. 27—48.

KUEKER, D. W. (1970), Generalized Interpolation and Definability, Annals of Mathematical Logic *1*, 423—468.

KUHN, T. S. (1962), The Structure of Scientific Revolutions, University of Chicago Press, Chicago (2nd edition 1969).

LAKATOS, I. (1970), Falsificationism and the Methodology of Scientific Research Programmes, in: LAKATOS, I., and A. MUSGRAVE (eds.), Criticism and the Growth of Knowledge, Cambridge University Press, Cambridge, pp. 91—195.

LEHRER, K. (1969), Theoretical Terms and Inductive Inference, American Philosophical Quarterly, Monograph Series, no. 3, Oxford.

MACCORQUODALE, K., and P. MEEHL (1948), On a Distinction between Hypothetical Constructs and Intervening Variables, Psychological Review *55*, 97—107.

MACH, E. (1893), The Science of Mechanics. Translation of the second German Edition. Open Court, La Salle, Ill.

MANDELBAUM, M. (1964), Philosophy, Science and Sense Perception: Historical and Critical Studies, The Johns Hopkins Press, Baltimore.

MAXWELL, G. (1963), The Ontological Status of Theoretical Entities, in: FEIGL, H., and G. MAXWELL (eds.), Minnesota Studies in the Philosophy of Science *III*, University of Minnesota Press, Minneapolis, pp. 3—27.

MAXWELL, G. (1970), Structural Realism and the Meaning of Theoretical Terms, in: RADNER, M., and S. WINOKUR (eds.), Minnesota Studies in the Philosophy of Science *IV*, University of Minnesota Press, Minneapolis, pp. 181—192.

MONTAGUE, R. (1961), Deterministic Theories, in: WASHBURNE, R. (ed.), Decisions, Values and Groups *II*, Pergamon Press, Oxford, pp. 325—370.

NAGEL, E. (1957), A Budget of Problems in the Philosophy of Science, Philosophical Review *66*, 205—225.

NAGEL, E. (1961), The Structure of Science, Harcourt, Brace and World, London.

NIINILUOTO, I. (1971), Can We Accept Lehrer's Inductive Rule? Ajatus *33*, 254—265.

NIINILUOTO, I. (1972a), Empirically Trivial Theories and Inductive Systematization. Forthcoming in: BOGDAN, R., and I. NIINILUOTO, Logic, Probability, and Language, D. Reidel, Dordrecht.

NIINILUOTO, I. (1972b), Inductive Systematization: Definition and a Critical Survey, Synthese *25*, 25—81.

NIINILUOTO, I., and R. TUOMELA (1973), Theoretical Concepts and Hypothetico-Inductive Inference, D. Reidel, Dordrecht.

OMER, I. (1970), On the D-N Model of Scientific Explanation, Philosophy of Science *37*, 417—433.

PAP, A. (1958), Semantics and Necessary Truth, Yale University Press, New Haven.

PAP, A. (1962), An Introduction to the Philosophy of Science, Free Press, New York.

POPPER, K. R. (1959), The Logic of Scientific Discovery. First English edition, Hutchinson, London.

PRZELECKI, M. (1969), The Logic of Empirical Theories, Routledge and Kegan Paul, London.

PRZELECKI, M., and R. WOJCICKI (1969), The Problem of Analyticity, Synthese *19*, 374—399.

PRZELECKI, M., and R. WOJCICKI (1971), Inessential Parts of Extensions of First-Order Theories, Studia Logica *28*, 83—99.

PUTNAM, H. (1962), What Theories Are Not, in: NAGEL, E., P. SUPPES, and A. TARSKI (eds.), Logic, Methodology and Philosophy of Science, Stanford University Press, Stanford, pp. 240—251.

PUTNAM, H. (1965), Craig's Theorem, The Journal of Philosophy *62*, 251—260.

PIETARINEN, J., and R. TUOMELA (1969), On Measures of the Explanatory Power of Scientific Theories, in: Akten des XIV. Kongresses für Philosophie, vol. II, Verlag Herder, Wien, pp. 241—247.

RAMSEY, F. (1931), Theories, in: The Foundations of Mathematics and Other Logical Essays, Littlefield, Adams and Company, Paterson, N. J., pp. 212—236.

ROBINSON, A. (1963), Introduction to Model Theory. North Holland, Amsterdam.

ROZEBOOM, W. (1960), Studies in the Empiricist Theory of Scientific Meaning I-II, Philosophy of Science *27*, 359—373.

ROZEBOOM, W. (1963), The Factual Content of Theoretical Concepts, in: FEIGL, H., and G. MAXWELL (eds.), Minnesota Studies in the Philosophy of Science *III*, University of Minnesota Press, Minneapolis, pp. 273—357.

ROZEBOOM, W. (1970), The Crisis in Philosophical Semantics, in: RADNER, M., and S. WINOKUR (eds.), Minnesota Studies in the Philosophy of Science *IV*, University of Minnesota Press, Minneapolis, pp. 196—219.

RUSSELL, B. (1917), Mysticism and Logic, Doubleday Anchor Book, New York, 1957. Originally published by Barnes & Noble.

RYLE, G. (1956), Dilemmas, Cambridge University Press, Cambridge.

SALMON, W. C. (1965), Consistency, Transitivity, and Inductive Support, Ratio *7*, 164—169.

SALMON, W. C. (1970), Statistical Explanation, in: COLODNY, R. G. (ed.), The Nature and Function of Scientific Theories, University of Pittsburgh Press, Pittsburgh pp. 173—231.

SCHEFFLER, I. (1963), The Anatomy of Inquiry, Alfred A. Knopf, New York.

SCHEFFLER, I. (1968), Reflections on the Ramsey Method, The Journal of Philosophy *65*, 270—274.

SELLARS, W. (1961), The Language of Theories, in: FEIGL, H., and G. MAXWELL (eds.), Current Issues in the Philosophy of Sciences, Holt, Rinehart and Winston, New York.

SELLARS, W. (1963), Science, Perception, and Reality, Routledge and Kegan Paul, London.

SELLARS, W. (1965), Scientific Realism or Irenic Instrumentalism, in: COHEN, R. S., and M. W. WARTOFSKY (eds.), Boston Studies in the Philosophy of Science, II, Humanities Press, New York. Reprinted in: SELLARS, W. (1967), Philosophical Perspectives, Charles C. Thomas, Springfield, Ill., pp. 337—369.

SHERIF, M., and C. SHERIF (1953), Harmony and Tension in Groups, Harcourt, Brace and World, New York.

SHOENFIELD, J. (1967), Mathematical Logic, Addison-Wesley, Reading, Mass.

SIMON, H. A. (1947), The Axioms of Newtonian Mechanics, Philosophical Magazine, ser. 7, *33,* 888—905.

SIMON, H. A. (1959), Definable Terms and Primitives in Axiom Systems, in: HENKIN, L., P. SUPPES, and A. TARSKI (eds.), The Axiomatic Method, North Holland, Amsterdam, pp. 443—453.

SIMON, H. A. (1970), The Axiomatization of Physical Theories, Philosophy of Science *37,* 16—26.

SIMON, H. A., and G. GROEN (1972), Ramsey-Eliminability and the Testability of Scientific Theories. Unpublished manuscript.

SKINNER, B. F. (1953), Science and Human Behavior, Macmillan, New York.

SKINNER, B. F. (1969), Contingencies of Reinforcement, Appleton Century Crofts, New York.

SKYRMS, B. (1966), Nomological Necessity and the Paradoxes of Confirmation, Philosophy of Science *33,* 230—249.

SMART, J. J. C. (1968), Between Science and Philosophy, Random House, New York.

SMOKLER, H. (1968), Conflicting Concepts of Confirmation, The Journal of Philosophy *65,* 300—312.

SNEED, J. D. (1971), The Logical Structure of Mathematical Physics, D. Reidel, Dordrecht.

SPECTOR, M. (1966), Theory and Observation I-II, The British Journal for the Philosophy of Science *7,* 1—20, 89—104.

STEGMÜLLER, W. (1969), Wissenschaftliche Erklärung und Begründung, Springer-Verlag, Berlin—Heidelberg—New York.

STEGMÜLLER, W. (1970), Theorie und Erfahrung, Springer-Verlag, Berlin—Heidelberg—New York.

STOPES-ROE, H. V. (1958), Some Considerations Concerning "Interpretative Systems", Philosophy of Science *25,* 143—156.

SVENONIUS, L. (1959), A Theorem on Permutations in Models, Theoria *25,* 173—178.

SUPPES, P. (1957), Introduction to Logic, Van Nostrand, Princeton.

TUOMELA, R. (1968a), The Application Process of a Theory, Annales Academiae Scientiarum Fennicae, ser. B, 154—3, Helsinki.

TUOMELA, R. (1968b), Identifiability and Definability of Theoretical Concepts, Ajatus *30,* 195—220.

TUOMELA, R. (1969), Auxiliary Concepts Within First-Order Scientific Theories, Doctoral Dissertation, Department of Philosophy, Stanford University.

TUOMELA, R. (1970a), On Construct Validity of Tests, Ajatus *32*, 47—66.

TUOMELA, R. (1970b), Meaning and Behavior, Ajatus *32*, 67—95.

TUOMELA, R. (1971), The Role of Theoretical Concepts in Neobehavioristic Theories, Reports from the Institute of Philosophy, no. 1, University of Helsinki, Helsinki.

TUOMELA, R. (1972), Deductive Explanation of Scientific Laws, Journal of Philosophical Logic *1*, 369—392.

TUOMELA, R. (1972), Model Theory and Empirical Interpretation of Scientific Theories, Synthese *25*, pp. 165—175.

WINNIE, J. A. (1967), The Implicit Definition of Theoretical Terms, British Journal for the Philosophy of Science *18*, 223—229.

WINNIE, J. A. (1971), Theoretical Analyticity, in: BUCK, R. G., and R. S. COHEN (eds.), Boston Studies in the Philosophy of Science, vol. VIII, D. Reidel, Dordrecht, pp. 289—305.

WRIGHT, G. H. VON (1971), Explanation and Understanding, Cornell University Press, Ithaca.

ZADEH, L. A., and E. POLAK (1969), System Theory, McGraw Hill, New York.

Index of Names

Subject Index